The Tryal of
Capt. William Kidd
for Murther & Piracy

CAPTAIN KIDD
from an old magazine clipping

The Tryal of
Capt. William Kidd
for Murther & Piracy

Edited by
Don C. Seitz

DOVER PUBLICATIONS, INC.
Mineola, New York

Library of Congress Cataloging-in-Publication Data

The tryal of Capt. William Kidd for murther & piracy / edited by Don C. Seitz.
    p. cm.
    Originally published: New York : R.R. Wilson, 1936.
    ISBN 0-486-41730-1 (pbk.)
    1. Kidd, William, d. 1701—Trials, litigation, etc. 2. Trials (Murder)—England—London. 3. Trials (Piracy)—England—London. I. Seitz, Don Carlos, 1862–1935.

KD372.K53 T79 2001
345.42'02523—dc21

2001017202

Manufactured in the United States of America
Dover Publications, Inc., 31 East 2nd Street, Mineola, N.Y. 11501

List of Illustrations

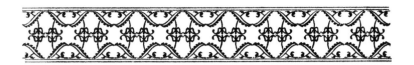

WILLIAM KIDD

THE eminent New Yorker, born a Scotsman, in Greenock, whose career terminated at a rope's end, was hardly used by Fate, but what he suffered at her hands has been well atoned for by that sister Goddess — FAME — who oft in the course of history has righted many wrongs, posthumously, of course, but none the less creditably.

Our stout captain lives in the minds of men as a pirate of almost incredible repute, whose missing treasures have kept men digging for more than two centuries on sandy bars by secluded bays or inlets from Maine to Madagascar. In plain recording it may be said that William Kidd was a bold and capable navigator of high standing among the mercantile community in both Boston and New York. In 1691 Governor Bradstreet of Massachusetts and council, commissioned Kidd to ward the coast against the forays of a French privateer, for which the New York Legislature voted him £150, May 14th, and later he did such good service in this same line for the inhabitants of Antigua, that they gave him a ship named after their island home.

The mercantile gentlemen in both cities were, however, none too nice in their undertakings. Those of New York were especially questionable, being not in the least careful with whom they dealt, or whence came the wares in which they trafficked, so long as the profits were large. The Madagascar trade was the most flourishing

of the time from 1690 to 1700. Not that Madagascar
furnished either market or goods, but because it had
become a refuge for pirates who maintained ports and
garrisons, sallying out to prey not only upon the commerce of the Great Mogul with the Red Sea and the
Persian Gulf, but attacking the ships of Europe that
traded with India, China and the Spice Islands. Ships
sailed regularly out of the harbor for the Indian Ocean,
returning in due season with handsome cargoes of spoil
gained by trade with pirates. The richest merchants
of the city were their friends and patrons, some were
even commissioned by the Governor to prey upon the
French, with whom his gracious Majesty William III
was at war, but really that it might not be unseemly to
welcome them to port with their ill-gained cargoes.

The Governor in 1696 was Colonel Benjamin Fletcher, who had succeeded Henry Slaughter in 1692, after
Captain Jacob Leisler's rebellion. Leisler, who really
sought to bring about a decent rule in the Province, had
been hanged for treason at the corner of Park Row and
Frankfort Street, where the Pulitzer Building now
stands, and Fletcher, coming from England to quiet the
conditions, found his hands full with the unrepentant
rebels. The King had been pleased to express a willing-
ness to pardon all such as would petition, but this offer
met with no response from men like Gerardus Beekman
and others of the Holland breed, who felt they had done
no wrong for which they should humble themselves to
another Dutchman, as was William of Orange.

Moreover, Fletcher, an ever loyal soldier, had lost
much of his estate in Ireland during the rebellious conditions that followed the accession of William III to

the English throne, and sought to fill his empty purse by selling land grants and privileges, which included the "commissions" noted. Charges were laid against him at Whitehall by Peter De La Noy, who had been Mayor of New York, and who, writing on June 13, 1695, after accusing Fletcher of swindling the Indians out of land and goods, favoring certain traders in return for fat slices of the profits, added in writing to the Lords of Trade: "I had almost forgot another useful piece of policy he has to get money. We have a parcell of pirates in these parts which (people) call the Red Sea men, who often get great bootys of Arabian Gold. His Excellency gives all due encouragement to these men, because they make all due acknowledgement to him; one Coats, a captain of this honble order, p'sented his Excellency with his ship, which his Excellency sold for £800, and every one of the crew made him a suitable p'sent of Arabian gold for his protection; one Capt. Twoo (Tew) who is gone to the Red Sea upon the same errand was before his departure highly caressed by his Excellency in his coach and six horses and presented with a gold watch to engage him to make New York his port at his return. Twoo retaliated the kindness with a present of jewells, but I can't learn how much further the bargain proceeded; time must show that."

It was also alleged that Fletcher tried to prevent the election to the Colonial Assembly of certain citizens who had been obnoxious to him, and it is in connection with this allegation that Captain Kidd first appears in the town's history. The Lords of Trade, before whom the accusations were laid, appointed a commission to look into the facts, which body in a report made August 28,

1695, quotes Kidd to this purport: "William Kidd, master of Yᵉ Brigantine *Antegoa* being sworn says at the Election of Assemblymen for the town of New York about three months since he saw soldiers and seamen with clubbs &cᵃ in the field. Many went out to the field lest they should be prest and he heard there were pardons given to severll persons over night before the election and the deponent and other masters of ships were spoke to by the Sheriff to bring their seamen in shoar to vote."

Continuing the examination on September 14th: "The Deponent further says That Mr. John Tutall, the Sheriff of New York, spoke to him to get his people from on board his vessell, they being Inhabitants of New York, to vote at the Election about three months since for such persons as the Governr desired should be elected but the deponent cannot say it was by order from the Governr. The Deponent further says the soldiers came, into the field a great many together without their soldiers cloaths or their arms, with sticks in their hands but they did not vote."

Besides the charge of interfering in the election, Philip French accused the Governor of taking graft in in the form of plate and two snuff boxes. Fletcher acknowledged that he had received the snuff boxes from two gentlemen whom he "had the opportunity to oblige," but denied that he had named any one whom he wished elected to the assembly as charged by Kidd. He begged that Leislerites be either pardoned or executed to save him further perplexities as to their status. They were therefore pardoned without humbling themselves to the King. Fletcher next found a troublesome opponent in the person of Robert Livingston, first of the famous family, who had some time before come out of Scotland and contrived to make himself Secretary for Indian Affairs in the colony. Fletcher saw no reason for such an officer and stopped his pay. He also refused to pass on sundry claims for expenditures made by Livingston, who went over his head to the Lords of Trade and got the better of the Governor. The latter drifted into a hot paper controversy with Sir William Phipps, the Lieutenant-Governor of Massachusetts Bay, and was unable to make head against him more than against Livingston. Phipps and Livingston enlisted strong support at Court through Richard Coote, Earl of Bellomont, late Governor of Barbadoes, and by this relationship, with the powerful Earl of Orford. And here is to be found the beginning of the Kidd legend.

The Lords of Trade for the moment did nothing with the charges. Communication was slow, and months drifted by. Livingston, whose perquisites in the Indian trade were interfered with by Fletcher's practices, sought to get even with him on the sea. Observing the prosperous condition of the Madagascar traffic it occurred to him that money might be made by spoiling the despoilers and selecting Kidd as a likely person for the task, went with him to London to secure a King's commission against the Red Sea and Mozambique pirates, as well as the French, after the manner of Fletcher's letters of Marque, which would be denied him at home. He had the support in his idea of Sir William Phipps with whom, as stated, Fletcher had fallen out. This was no light backing, for Phipps had won his way to title and great repute by successfully salvaging several millions in silver ingots from a lost Spanish galleon in Bahama waters, and was an accepted authority on treasure-hunting. Kidd procured his commissions, and a vessel, *The Adventure Galley*, newly built at Deptford, where she was launched at Castle's shipyard, December 4, 1695. She came to the Nore late in February and prepared for sea. By royal mandate about sixty sailors were pressed for service on board. This enforced crew sailed around the 10th of April, stopping at Plymouth, which port was left on the 23d, making for New York, to gather a more adequate force of men better fitted for the service than those provided by His Majesty. Bellomont afterwards made this a point against him.

The arrangements included a tenth interest for the King. The co-partners represented by Bellomont included the Earl of Orford, the Earl of Romney, John Somers, the Lord Chancellor; the Duke of Shrewsbury and Sir Edmund Harrison. Four Nobodies: Samuel Newton, George Watson, Thomas Reynolds and John Rowley, whose names appear in the King's grant, were apparently put in as dummies to guard the noble gentlemen against the chance of scandal. Bellomont issued an instruction to the captain, of which this is a copy:

LONDON, 25th *February*, 1695/6.

CAPTAIN WILLIAM KIDD,

You being now ready to sail, I do hereby desire and direct you, that you and your Men do serve God in the best Manner you can: That you keep good Order, and good Government, in your Ship: That you make the best of your Way to the Place and Station where you are to put the Powers you have in Execution: And, having effected the same, You are, according to Agreement, to sail directly to Boston in New England, there to deliver unto me the Whole of what Prizes, Treasure, Merchandize, and other Things, you shall have taken by virtue of the Powers and Authorities granted you: But if, after the Success of your Design, you shall fall in with any English Fleet bound for England, having good convoy, you are, in such case to keep them Company, and bring all Your Prizes to London notwithstanding any Covenant to the contrary in our Articles of Agreement. Pray fail not to give Advice, by all Opportunities, how the Galley proves; how your Men stand, what Progress you make; and, in general, of all remarkable Passages in your Voyage, to the time of your Writing. Direct your Letters to Mr. Edmund Harrison. I pray God grant you good Success, and send us a good Meeting again.

BELLOMONT.

Kidd and Livingston invested about $3,000 apiece in the venture, the others added enough to bring the total capital involved up to $50,000. Kidd's commission came direct from the hands of King William III, and gave him authority to proceed against the French, as well as to capture pirates. He had a distinct agreement with Bellomont and Livingston, guaranteed by bond, both of which documents follow:

Articles of Agreement made this Tenth day of October in the year of our Lord 1695, between the Right Honble Richard Earle of Bellomont of the one part, and Robert Livingston Esq. and Capt William Kidd of the other part:

WHEREAS the said Capt. Kidd is desirious to obtain a commission as Captain of a private man-of-war in order to take prizes from the Kings ennemies and otherwise to annoy them, and whereas also certain persons did some time since depart from New England, Rhode Island, New York and other parts in America and elsewhere wth an intention to pyrates and to comit spoyles and depredations against the laws of Nations in the Red Sea or elsewhere, and to return wth such goods & riches as they should get, to certain places by them agreed upon, of which said persons and places the said Capt. Kidd hath notice and is desirious to fight with & subdue the pyrates and also other pyrates with whom the said Capt. Kidd shall meet at sea, in case he is impowered so to do. And whereas it is agreed between the said parties that for the purposes aforesaid a good and sufficient ship to the likeing of the sd Capt Kidd shall be forthwith bought, whereof the said Capt. Kidd is to have the command. Now these presents witness and it is agreed between the said parties:—

1. The said Earle of Bellomont doth covenant and agree at his proper charge to procure from the Kings Majesty or from the Lords Comrs of the Admiralty (as the case shall require) one or more commissions impowering him the said Capt. Kidd to act against the Kings enemies and to take prizes from them, as a private man of warr, in the usuall manner and also to fight with conquer and subdue pyrates and to take them and their goods; with such large and beneficial powers and clauses in such commissions as may be most proper and effectuall in such cases.

2. The said Earle doth covenant and agree that within three months after the said Capt. Kidds departure from England for the purposes in these presents mentioned, he will procure at his proper charge a grant from the King to be made to some indifferent & trusty person, of all such merchandizes goods treasure and other things as shall be taken from the said pyrates or any other pyrates whatsoever by the said Capt. Kidd, or by the said ship or any other ship or ships under his command.

3. The said Earle doth agree to pay four fifth parts (the whole in five parts to be divided) of all moneys which shall be laid out for the buying such good and sufficient ship, for the purposes aforesaid, together rigging and other apparell and furniture thereof, & providing the same with competent victualling; the said ship to be approv'd of by the said parties; and the said other fifth part of the charges of the

said ship to be paid for by the said Robert Livingston and William Kidd.

4. The said Earle doth agree that in order to the speedy buying the said ship and in part of the said four parts of five of the said charges, he will pay down the sum of sixteen hundred pounds by way of advance, on or before the sixth day of November next ensuing.

5. The said Robert Livingston and Capt. William Kidd do joyntly and severally covenant and agree that on or before the said sixth day of November when the said Earle of Bellomont is to pay the said sum of sixteen hundred pounds in as aforesaid, they will advance and pay down four hundred pounds in part of the share and proportion which they are to have in the said ship.

6. The said Earle doth agree to pay such further sum of money as shall compleat and make up the said four parts of five of the charges of the said ships apparell furniture and victualling, unto the sd Robert Livingston and William Kidd, within seven weeks after the date of these presents; and in like manner the sd Robert Livingston and William Kidd do agree to pay such further sum as shall amount to a fifth part of the whole charge of the said ship within seven weeks after the date of these presents.

7. The said Capt. Kidd doth covenant and agree to procure and take with him on board of the said ship one hundred mariners or seamen or thereabout, and to make what reasonable and convenient speed he can, to sett out to sea with the said ship, and to saile to such parts and places where he may meet with the said pyrates, and to use his utmost indeavour to meet with subdue and conquer the said pyrates, or any other pyrates and to take from them their goods merchandizes and treasure, also to take what prizes he can from the King enemies and forthwith to make the best of his way to Boston in New England & that without touching at any other port or harbour whatsoever or without breaking bulk or deminishing any part of what he shall so

take or obtain, on any pretence whatsoever, of which he shall make oath in case the same be desired by the said Earle of Bellomont, and there to deliver the same into the hands or possession of the said Earle.

8. The said Capt. doth agree that the contrct and bargain which he will make with his said ship crew shall be no purchase no pay, and not otherwise, and that the share and proportion which his said Crew shall by such contract have of such prizes goods merchandizes and treasure as he shall take as prize or from any pyrates, shall not at the most exceed a fourth part of the same, and shall be less than a fourth part in case the same may reasonably and conveniently be agreed upon.

9. The said Robert Livingston and Capt. William Kidd do joyntly and severally agree with the said Earle of Bellomont that in case the said Capt. Kidd do not meet with the sayd Pyrates which went from New England Rhode Island New York and elsewhere as aforesaid, or do not take from any other pyrates or from any of the Kings enemies such goods merchandizes and other things of value as being divided as herein after is mentioned shall fully recompence the said Earle for the moneys by him expended in buying the said four fifth parts of the said ship and premisses, that then they shall refund and repay to the said Earle of Bellomont the whole money by him to be advanced in sterling mony or mony equivalent thereunto on or before the twenty fifth day of March which shall be in the year of our Lord one thousand six hundred ninty and seven, the danger of the seas and of the enemie and mortality of the said Capt. Kidd allways excepted, upon paymt whereof the said Robert Livingston and William Kidd are to have the sole property in the said ship and furniture, and this indenture to be delivered up to them, with all other Covenants and obligacons thereunto belonging.

10. It is agreed between the said parties that as well the goods merchandizes treasure and other things which shall be taken from the said pyrates or any pyrates by the said

William Kidd, as also all such prizes as shall be by him taken from any of the Kings enemies, shall be divided in manner following, that is to say such part as shall be for that purpose agreed upon by the said Capt. Kidd so as the same do not on the whole exceed a fourth part) shall be paid or delivered to the ships crew for their use, and the other three parts to be divided into five equall parts whereof the said Earle is to have to his own use four full parts and the other fifth part to be equally divided between the said Robert Livingston and the said William Kidd, and is to be paid and delivered them by the said Earle of Bellomont without deduction or abatement on any pretence whatsoever; but it is always to be understood that such prizes as shall be taken from the Kings enemies are to be lawfully adjudged prizes in the usuall manner, before any division or otherwise intermedling therewith them according to the true intent of the said commission to be granted in that behalfe.

Lastly it is convenanted and agreed between the parties to these presents, that in case the said Capt. William Kidd do bring to Boston aforesaid and there deliver to the Earle of Bellomont goods merchandize treasure or prizes to the value of one hundred thousand pounds or upwards wch he will have taken from the said pyrates or other pyrates or from the Kings enemies that then the ship, which is now speedely to be bought by the said parties, shall be and remain to the sole use and behoofe of him the said Capt. William Kidd as a reward and gratificacon for his good services therein.

ROBERT LIVINGSTON (seal)

WILLIAM KIDD (seal)

MEMORANDUM. Before the signing sealing and delivery of these presents it was covenanted and agreed by the said Earle of Bellomont with the said Robert Livingston Esqr and the said Capt. William Kidd that the person to whom the grant above mentioned in these articles shall be made by his Maty shall within eight days at the most after such grant has passed the Great Seal of England assign and transfer unto each of them the said Robert Livingston Esq. and the said Capt. William Kidd respectively their heires or assignes one full tenth part (the ship's crew's share and proportion being first deducted) of all such goods treasure or other things as shall be taken by the said Capt. Kidd by vertue of such Commission as aforesaid, and the said grantee shall make such assignment as aforesaid in such manner as by the said Robert Livingston Esqr and the sd Capt. William Kidd or their council learned in the law shall be reasonably devised and required, and then these presents were sealed and delivered, (the sixpenny stamp being first affixed) in the presence of us.

MARTHA BREHEN.

JOHN MADDOCKS.

JOHN MOULDER.

Whereas the necessary fitting equipping and setting the *Adventure Galley* bought by the above mentioned William Kidd in pursuance of these present Articles, could not be compleatly finished & perfected within the time thereby limited and consequently that all the severall sums of mony therein covenanted to be paid were not actually paid by all or any of the parties to the above written covenants and agreements within the time thereby expressly limitted and directed; but that nevertheless all the said sums have since been paid, and the said ships bought for the voyage and design expressed in these articles is now compleatly fitted and provided with all things necessary and lyes ready to depart, and that also the severall Commissions have been obtained by the Earle of Bellomont; it is hereby further mutually declared covenanted and agreed by and between the abovesaid Right Honourable the Earle of Bellomont and Robert Livingston and William Kidd on behalfe of themselves and all others concerned therein, that notwithstanding the delay in the dispatch of the sd ship or galley and of any of the paymts of the monys expressed in the above written agreements, that yet nevertheless all and singular the severall agreements articles and clauses therein mentioned and intended are hereby declared to be and are and shall remain in as full force and vertue, as if the said ship had been dispatched and all the sums of mony had been actually paid within the time limitted and directed by the said Articles; any thing herein to the contrary notwithstanding. Dated in London the 20th day of Feb. 1695/6.

WILLIAM KIDD.

Signed sealed and delivered
in the presence of
JOHN FOCHE Junr WILLIAM THOMPSON.
A true Copy
(signed) BELLOMONT.

BOND OF ROBERT LIVINGSTON TO THE EARL OF BELLOMONT.

Noverint universi per presentes me Robertum Livingston de London Armigerum teneri et firmiter obligari pr honorabile Richardo Comiti de Bellomont in regno Hiberniae in decem mille libris bone et legalis monetoe Angliae solvênd eidem Comiti de Bellomont out suo certo Attornat. Executor. vel Administratôr. suis ad quam quidem solucônem bene et fideliter faciênd. obligo me heredes executores et administratores meos firmiter per presentes Sigillo meo sigillât. Dât. decimo die Octobris anno regin Domi. nostri Willielmi terij Dei Gratia Angliae Scotiae Franciae et Hiberniae Regis, Fidei Defensoris Septimo, anno Dôm. 1695

The Condicôn of this obligacon is such that if the above bounden Robert Livingston his executors and Administrators do well and truely observe perform fullfill accomplish pay and keep all and singular the Covenants grants articles clauses provisoes payments conditions and agreements whatsoever which on the part and behalfe of the said Robert Livingston his executors & Administrators are or ought to be observed perform'd fullfill'd accomplished paid and kept, comprized or mentioned in certain Articles of Agreement bearing date with these presents made or expressed to be made between the sd Earle of Bellomont of the one part and the said Robert Livingston and Capt. William Kidd of the other part, in all things according to the true intent and meaning of the same, then this present obligacôn to be void and of none effect, or else to be and remain in full force power and vertue.

ROBERT LIVINGSTON.

Sealed and Delivered (the sixpenny
  Stamp being affixed) in the prsence of us
        MARTHA BREHEN
        JOHN MADDOCK
        JOHN MOULDER

Beside these there was a detailed arrangement with the Earl of Bellomont and Robert Livingston of which this is a copy:

ARTICLES OF AGREEMENT,

Made the 10th Day of October, in the Year of our Lord 1695. Between the Right Honourable RICHARD EARL OF BELLO-MONT of the one part, and ROBERT LEVINGSTON Esq. and CAPTAIN WILLIAM KIDD, Of the other part.

Whereas the said Capt. William Kidd is desirous of obtaining a Commission as Captain of a Private Man of War in order to take Prizes from the King's Enemies, and otherways to annoy them; and whereas certain Persons did some time since depart from New England, Rode-Island, New-York, and others parts in America and elsewhere, with an intention to become Pirates, and to commit Spoils and Depredations, against the Laws of Nations, in the Red-Sea or elsewhere, and to return with such Goods and Riches as they should get, to certain places by them agreed upon; of which said Persons and Places, the said Capt. Kidd hath notice, and is desirous to fight with and subdue the said Pirates, as also other Pi-rates with whom the said Capt. Kidd shall meet at Sea, in cafe he be impowered fo to do; and whereas it is agreed between the faid Pirates, That for the purpofe aforefaid a good and fufficient Ship, to the liking of the faid Capt. Kidd, fhall be forthwith bought, whereof the faid Capt. Kidd is to have the Command. Now thefe Prefents do witnefs, and it is agreed between the faid Parties,

I. That the Earl of Bellomont doth convenant and agree, at his proper Charge, to procure from the King's Majefty, or from the Lords Commiffioners of the Admiralty (as the Cafe fhall require) one or more Commiffions, impowering him the faid Capt Kidd to act againft the King's Enemies, and to take Prizes from them, as a private Man of War in the ufual manner; and alfo to fight with, conquer and fubdue Pirates, and to take them and their Goods; with other large and beneficial Powers and Claufes in fuch Commiffions as may be moft proper and effectual in fuch Cafes.

II. The faid Earl of Bellomont doth covenant and agree, That within three Months after the faid Capt Kidd's departure from England, for the purpofes in thefe Prefents mentioned, he will procure, at his proper charge, a Grant from the King, to be made to fome indifferent and trufty Perfons, of all fuch Merchandizes, Goods, Treafure and other things as fhall be taken from the faid Pirates, or any other Pirate whatfoever, by the faid Capt. Kidd, or by the faid Ship, or any other Ship or Ships under his Command.

III. The faid Earl doth agree to pay four Fifth parts, the whole in Five parts to be divided, of all Moneys which fhall be laid out for the buying fuch good and fufficient Ship for the purpofes aforefaid, together with Rigging and other Apparel and Furniture thereof, and providing the fame with competent victualling the faid Ship, to be approved of by the faid Parties; and the faid other one Fifth part of the said Charges of the faid Ship to be paid for by the faid Robert Levingfton and William Kidd.

IV. The faid Earl doth agree, That in order to the fpeedy buying the faid Ship, in part of the faid four parts of Five of the faid Charges, he will pay down the fum of fixteen hundred Pounds, by way of Advance, on or before the fixth day of November next enfuing.

V. The faid Robert Levingfton and William Kidd do jointly and feverally covenant and agree, That on and before the fixth day of November, when the faid Earl of Bellomont is to pay the faid Sum of fixteen hundred pounds as aforefaid, they will advance and pay down four hundred pounds in part of the Share and Proportion which they are to have in the faid Ship.

VI. The faid Earl doth agree, to pay fuch further Sums of Money as fhall compleat and make up the faid four parts of Five of the Charges of the faid Ship's Arrival, Furniture and Victualling, unto the faid Robert Levingfton and William Kidd within feven Weeks after the date of thefe Prefents; and in like manner the faid Robert Levingfton and William Kidd do agree to pay fuch further Sums as fhall amount to a fifth part of the whole Charge of the faid Ship within feven Weeks after the date of thefe Prefents.

VII. The said Capt. Kidd doth covenant and agree to procure and take with him on board of the faid Ship one hundred Mariners or Seamen, or thereabouts, to make what reasonable and convenient fpeed he can, to let out to Sea with the faid Ship, and to fail to such parts or places where he may meet with the faid Pirates, and to ufe his utmoft endeavours to meet with, fubdue and conquer the faid Pirates, or any other Pirates, and to take from them their Goods, Merchandizes and Treafure, alfo to take what Prizes he can from the King's Enemies, and forthwith to make the beft of his way to Boston in New England, and that without touching at any other port or harbour whatfoever, or without breaking Bulk, or diminifhing any part of what he fhall fo take or obtain, on any pretence whatfoever, of which he shall make Oath, in cafe the fame be defired by the faid Earl of Bellomont, and there to deliver the fame into the hands and poffeffion of the faid Earl.

VIII. The faid Capt. Kidd doth agree, That the Con-

tract and Bargain which he will make with his faid Ships-
Crew fhall be No Purchafe no Pay, and not otherwife; and
that the fhare and proportion with his faid Ships-Crew fhall
by fuch Contract have of fuch Prizes, Goods, Merchandizes
Treafures as he fhall take as prize, or from any Pirates, fhall
not at the moft exceed a fourth part of the fame, and fhall
be lefs than a fourth, in cafe the fame may reafonably and
conveniently be agreed upon.

IX. The faid Robert Levingftone and Capt. William
Kidd, do jointly and feverally agree with the faid Earl of
Bellomont, That in cafe the faid Capt. Kidd do not meet
with the faid Pirates which went from New-England, Rode-
Ifland, New-York, and elfewhere as aforefaid, or do not take
from any other Pirates, or from any of the King's Enemies,
fuch Goods, Merchandize, or other things of Value, as being
divided, as herein after is mentioned, fhall fully recompence
the faid Earl for the Moneys by him expended, in buying the
faid four fifth parts of the faid Ship and Premifes, that then
they fhall refund and pay to the faid Earl of Bellomont the
whole Money by him to be advanced in Sterling Money or
Moneys equivalent thereunto, on or before the five and twentieth day of Murch, which fhall be in the year of our Lord
1697. (the Danger of the Seas, and of the Enemies, and
Mortality of the faid Capt. Kidd always excepted) upon pay-
ment whereof the faid Robert Levingftone and William Kidd
are to have the fole property in the faid Ship and Furniture,
and this Indenture to be delivered up to them with all other
Covenants and Obligations thereunto belonging.

X. It is agreed between the faid parties, That as well the
Goods, Merchandizes, Treafure and other things which fhall
be taken from the faid Pirates, or any Pirates, by the faid
William Kidd, as alfo all fuch Prizes as fhall be by him taken
from any of the King's Enemies, fhall be divided in manner
following, that is to fay, Such part as fhall be for that purpofe, agreed upon by the faid Capt. Kidd (fo as the fame do
not in the whole exceed a fourth part) fhall be paid or delivered to the Ships-Crew for their ufe, and the other three

parts to be divided into five equal parts, whereof the said
Earl is to have his own use four full parts, and the other
Fift his to be equally divided between the said Robert Levingstone and William Kidd, and is to be delivered them by
the said Earl of Bellomont, without Deduction or Abatement
on any pretence whatsoever; but it is always to be under
stood, that such Prizes as shall be taken from the King's
Enemies, are to be lawfully adjudged Prizes in the usual manner, before any Division or otherwise intermedling therewith,
than according to the true Intent of the said Commission to
be granted in that behalf.

XI.   Lastly, it is covenanted and agreed between the said
parties to these presents, That in case Capt. William Kidd
do bring to Boston aforesaid, and there deliver to the Earl
of Bellomont Goods, Merchandize, Treasure or Prizes to the
value of one hundred thousand Pounds or upwards, which he
shall have taken from the said Pirates, or from other Pirates,
or from the King's Enemies; that then the Ship, which is
now speedily to be brought by the said Pirates, shall be and
remain to the sole use and behalf of him, the said Capt. William Kidd, as a Reward and Gratification for his good Service therein.

Memorandum, Before the Sealing and Delivery of these
Presents it was covenanted and agreed by the said Earl of
Bellomont, with the said Robert Levingstone Esq; and Captain William Kidd, that the person to whom the Grant above-
mentioned in these Articles, shall be made by His Majesty,
shall, within eight Days at the most after such Grant has
passed the Great Seal of England, assign and transfer to each
of them, the said Robert Levingstone Esq; and Captain William Kidd, their Heirs and Assigns one full tenth part (the
Ship-Crew's share and proportion being first deducted) of all
such Goods, Treasure, or other thing as shall be taken by the
said Captain Kidd by virtue of such Commissions as aforesaid; and the said Grantee shall make such Assignment as
aforesaid, in such manner as by the said Robert Levingstone
Esq; and Capt. William Kidd, or their Councel Learned in

the Law fhall be reasonably advifed and required. And then thefe Prefents were fealed and delivered (the Six-penny Stamp being firft afixed) in the prefence of us

Verf. Copid. Exam.22   Martha Breken
Jany 1695. per Geo.   John Maddock
Fisher, near Hick's-Hall,   John Moulder.
London.

                                            Bellomont.

That Kidd presumed much upon the importance of his noble backers is shown in an undated memorandum, presumed to have been written by Edmund Dummer of the Admiralty office, found among the papers preserved by the Duke of Portland in Welbeck Abbey, published by the Royal Manuscripts Commission. It reads:

(1699, winter.) — When Kidd set forth on his intended voyage to Madagascar, his pretences, owners, and admiralty power were as public as his rodomantades thereof were vain; his authority was as ample as any King's commander, and therefore he should pay no respect to the King's colours wheree'er he met them.

A captain of a yacht taking notice of his carriage, gave particulars to his people (in case he should not be on board himself) to fire shot into him if he did not strike as he passed him at Greenwich. It happened he was not aboard when Kidd passed him, and he having a front wind as he said, showed no respect. But being shot, believing the yacht out of danger of call, Kidd's men in the tops turned up, and clap their backsides in derison. The captain on this contempt acquaints the Admiralty (by testimony of the hands of his men) the whole story. That Board trifled away time about it, taking the testimony to be insufficient without it was sworn to; that he got done presently. But by this time Kidd was gotten away from Gravesend, and going by the Nore, the ship there took notice of him upon the same account and sent him into Sheerness, and rendered an account thereof to the Admiralty; and here the thing slept, and inquiry was made into the character of this captain; and a while after he and two more captains of the yachts were suspended under pretence of countenancing the bringing over a parcel of alamodes. But, that being examined, and no ground found for it, they were restored; where this proceeding interfered in this time I cannot tell, however.

Without any further notice, or inquiry, or judgment given upon the conduct and arrogance of this fellow, he was let loose from Sheerness, and from under the guard at the Nore, by a mysterious passiveness from all sides, and we hear no more of this person till he showed the King's authority for robbing, which, I take it, was to Captain Warren near the Cape of Good Hope, saying he had as good a commission for his proceeding as the said Warren had for his conduct. If this be true, and that partnership hath been owned by some in high state, it is a case of the highest immorality that ever was attempted in this nation by any one, much less by such as hath had the ministry of the most important affairs thereof; and for which there is hardly any punishment or censure universal enough to reach unto the proportion and extent of so national a villainy and a mischief so universal to all corners in the world.

Kidd reached New York about the Fourth of July, but lingered through the summer picking up his crew and information about the trade. He sailed for Mozambique, it would appear, on the 5th of September, reckoning from the date of a letter sent by Governor Fletcher to the Lords of Trade on the 17th, containing this terse reference:

Capt. Wm. Kidd Commander of the *Adventure Gally* did sail from hence 12 dayes agoe having 150 men on board, on on his way hither he took a French Banker which was condemned here and appraised at 350£. I have the King's tenths and shall account to the Lords of the Admiralty direct. He also extracted one fifteenth for himself, but does not mention the last. There is a receipt for that amount extinct in the Royal Archives.

Fletcher, himself, did not hurry about answering the the charges made against him. In a letter following the one with its reference to Kidd's sailing he offered a lame defense in this fashion:

I brought over with me from the Plantations office by their Majesties commands, the draft of a bill against Piracy, which was enacted here to be of force for some time, which act did give pardon and liberty to all such as should come into the Province within the limitation of that time, and enter into bond for their good behaviour and not to depart from the province without Lycence; in which time a ship commanded by one Coats which bad been in the time that Capt. Leisler took upon him the Govemt taken from the enemy condemned, and sold to the use of the Captors and hearing that Captn Leisler was dead, they threw a good deal of East India goods overboard, and most of them separated and left the ship at the East end of the Island of Nassaw, when I heard of this, I called the Councill who were of the opinion to have the ship brought up to New York, which was accordingly done and these few that came in her, had the benefit of that act, and gave bond accordingly; there has never been any other since come into this Province.

Captn Tue (Tew) brought no ship into this Port, he came here as a stranger and came to my table, as other strangers do when they come into the Province. He told me he had a sloop of force well mann'd and not only promised but entered into Bond to make War upon the French, in the mouth of Cannada River, and whereupon I gave him a commission and instructions accordingly. I have given some private commissions to others of a like nature, who have done service against the King's enemies.

An Irishman, one Hoare, by a Commission from Sr Wm Beeston of Jamaica took a considerable prize from the French loaded with sugar & indigo, which he carried into Road Island and then disposed of the loading, as I am informed the prize ship being of better force and fitter for his purpose he put on board of her and applyed to me for a commission to go against the French on the banks of New Foundland and Mouth of Canada River, which I gave him and took security for his obeying my instructions. I have not heard of him since.

It may be my unhappiness, but not my crime if they turn Pyrates, I have heard of none yet that have done so."

This was begging the question. Tew was one of the most notorious sea robbers of the day. The others all vindicated DeLaNoy's charges. Writing further to the Lords of Trade from Albany under the date of December 20th, 1696, Fletcher took this shot at Livingston:

I know I shall be hard push'd upon his score, but if I suffer 'tis in a righteous cause, for he is known of all men here to have neither religion or morality, his whole thirst being at any rate to inrich himself and has said I am credibly informed by many persons, he had rather bec alled Knave Livingston that poor Livingston.

He also intimated that his accusers were unworthy of belief being merely "two Scotchmen." The commission found the charges fully sustained, and drily vindicated the two Scots, with this remark:

The proofs of the facts are Colonel Fletcher's accusers to your Lordships, and not two Scotchmen (as he suggests) altho' being Scotchmen would be no credit to their evidence.

The conclusions of the commission were accepted and almost two years after DeLaNoy made his charges, Bellomont was appointed Governor of the Colonies on the 16th of March, 1697. His commission did not issue from King William's hand until the 18th of June. Fletcher, ignorant of the change, continued his correspondence with the Lords of Trade. In a letter, late in the Spring of 1697, long after Kidd's departure from New York on his venturesome voyage, is found this invidious mention evidently thrown in as an anchor to windward:

One Captⁿ Kidd lately arrived here and produced a commission under the Great Seal of England, for suppression of Piracy, when he was here, many flockt to him from all parts, men of desperate fortunes and necessities in expectation of getting vast treasure, he sailed from hence with 150 men as I am informed a great part of them are of this Province; it is generally believed here, they will have money, pr fas aut nefas, that if he misse therof the design intended for which he has commission, 'twill not be in Kidd's power to govern such a horde of men under no pay.

Bellomont had hard luck in reaching his seat of government. His Ship was blown off the coast when near New York and compelled to make haven at Barbadoes, where he had formerly ruled, so he wrote from that island to the Lords of Trade on January 8, 1698. He left the next day but did not reach New York until the 2nd of April following, so stormy and baffling were the winds. He found plenty of trouble, well arranged for him. Fletcher's corrupt following, long since advised of his delayed coming, had been busy piling up difficulties. He discovered "constant cabals and clubbs" organized against him, and "a great trade managed between this port and Madagascar" indubitably in pirate goods. He also found ample evidence of Fletcher's complicity in the trade and of its popularity with the "best citizens," with William Nicoll, a member of the Governor's Council, "a man of much sense and knowledge in the law," as their attorney. He also found Capt. Evans of the frigate *Richmond*, supine, if not a party to all the piratical proceedings. Fletcher was shipped to England where, in

a letter written to William Blaithwaite from the Lords
of Trade on August 5, 1698, he complains bitterly of Bellomont's "persecution." There let us leave him. Bellomont was required to look into the Livingston-Fletcher
dispute and promptly vindicated the former, restoring
his salary and emoluments, finding him "'a fitt and capable" person, as one should discover a partner to be.

Bellomont soon found himself immersed in difficulties.
The business community in New York charged him
with smothering trade by his efforts to enforce strict
virtue on the waterfront, and to cap the sheaf of his
troubles, the luckless Kidd, of whose enterprise he was
a backer, was soon found to have gone astray: The
first word of this came to Bellomont on January 5, 1698
via a letter from the Lords of Trade who wrote: "In a
letter from Mr. Randolph, dated New York the 25th of
August last, he sent us a list of vessels cleared out in
the Custom House in New York from the 25th of March
to the 17th of August last for Curacoa and Madagascar.

"Upon this mention of Madagascar, which has been
a great rendezvous of pirates, it may be proper to acquaint your Lordship that preparations have somewhile
been making here for sending a squadron of ships of war
to suppress them there and at St. Maria, or wherever
else in those seas they can be met with, and that in order to the reducing of them either by offers of pardon
or otherwise, directions were given for a proclamation
proper for that service, in which (upon news of Captain
Kidd's having committed some notorious acts of piracy)
his name was ordered to be joined with Every's as persons to be exempted from pardon, which we suppose
hath been or will accordingly be done."

In the meantime Kidd had proceeded on his enterprise. Two hundred leagues east of the Cape of Good Hope he ran foul of a Royal Squadron; the *Windsor, Tyger, Vulture,* and *Advice,* en route for a pirate hunt in the Indian Ocean under Commodore Warren, and convoying some slow tubs of Indiamen. The warships brought him to, and coming on board Kidd showed his Royal Commission and was treated courteously, though his mission was not known to Warren, who had left Plymouth only a few days after the *Adventure* sailed. The Commodore had lost many men by death on his slow voyage, and asked Kidd to spare him some from his numerous company. This he refused. The *Adventure* being in need of a mainsail, Kidd begged to be supplied, but no canvas could be loaned. He drank copiously of Warren's wine and became ill-mannered and boastful, saying he would take a sail from the first ship he met, and Warren, preforce, sent him hiccoughing to his galley. He kept the squadron company for six days, and then a calm befalling, set his sweeps at work in the night and by dawn was hull down on the horizon. He did not stop at Cape Town. Warren, suspicious of him, warned his Indiamen to look out for themselves as they proceeded without guardianship. One of them, the *Sidney,* reached Johanna alone and met the *Adventure* at anchor. There Kidd ordered Captain Gifford to strike his colors, which was refused, and nothing came of the command. Two others of the convoy came in later and Kidd invited the three Captains to dine. They declined to come. The natives complained that Kidds' company were abusive, and the captains warned him to change his conduct. The men were disorderly and much out of control.

The *Adventure* proceeded to Madagascar where all the pirates were found to be absent on business connected with the profession, so Kidd sought action along the Mozambique Channel and the East coast of Africa. There is record that he made landing at Bas Mabber, on the Somali shore and helped himself to corn from a native granary. The next port made was Perin, where he dropped anchor to await the Mocha fleet, which, coming into view, he attacked a large vessel, but perceiving the *Sceptre*, an East India guardship coming up he went no further. Irresolute it would appear as to what course to take, he turned up on August 29, 1697, off Sanjan, north of Bombay and forced Thomas Parker, Captain of the *Mary*, a brigantine of Surat, to go with him as pilot, with a Portuguese seaman to act as interpreter. In a week he was at Carwar calling on the British factor, Harvey, for supplies. He was considered a pirate and refused food, while the local authorities armed their forces against a possible assault. Eight of the crew deserted saying they were being made pirates against their will. On the 4th of October he sent this letter to the factor at Calicut:

Adventure galley,
October ye 4th, 1697.

Sɪʀ,

I can't but admire yᵗ ye people is so fearfull to come near us for I have used all possible means to let them understand I am an Englishman and a friend, not yᵗ offering to molest any of their canoes, so think it convenient to write this yᵗ you may understand whome I am which (1) hope may end all Suspition. I come from England about 15 mos. agone with yᵉ King's commission to take all Pyrates in these seas, and from Carwar came abt a month agone, so do believe yᵗ (you) have heard whome I am before y^t and all I come for here is wood and water whh if you will be pleas'd to order me shall honestly satisfie for ye same or anything that they'll bring off, which is all from him who will be very ready to serve you in what gett in my power.

WILLIAM KIDD.

This appeal brought nothing so Kidd sailed for the Laccadives. It was at this time that he killed William Moore, his quartermaster, striking him with a bucket heat of an altercation. News of this got back to Bombay with later consequences. Two Portuguese coast guards chased him, one of which came up and was greeted with a braodside, which wrecked it. In April, 1698 the Indiaman *Sedgwick* reported having been pursued by the *Adventure*, but outdistanced her. There then ensued the direct act of piracy of which Kidd was finally accused, the taking of the *Quedagh Merchant*. Her Captain was an Englishman named Wright, although she was the property of some Armenian merchants who were on board. The master gunner was a Frenchman and there were several Dutch in the crew, natives making up the rest. The spoil was around £12,000 outside of the ship, Kidd getting 25% of it. This was his sole known "treasure" for all his misadventures.

Active operations of the various pirates in the Indian Ocean had about killed trade with England, while the anger of the Mogul threatened to drive the English from the land. Sir John Gayer sent powerful appeals for aid in checking the marauders and public sentiment in London was greatly stirred, as was the sense of adventure also, by the tales of lavish wealth garnered by the rovers. As a result the English, French and Dutch engaged in a compact to end piracy, thus appeasing the Mogul and making the profession unprofitable. The details of his voyage Kidd gives in his journal, which will be found further on.

English, French, Dutch and Portuguese warships were soon scouring the African coast and the Eastern seas. The rascals scattered to the four winds. Many were Americans and some of these, somehow, managed to get home. Several were seized in New York. Others were located in Philadelphia, which, tolerant of roguery even to this day, failed to prosecute. Markham, the Lieutenant-Governor, was openly charged with being in partnership with the piratical ring. Most of the gentry licensed by Fletcher made a safe home-coming, though some with empty holds, for news of the change had reached Madagascar and suspicious cargoes had been dropped by the way. Bellomont, writing on November 14, 1698, records that eight or nine vessels had reached port, which ordinarily would have "brought in a 100,000 in gold and silver," for which deprivation the merchants of the city were drinking Colonel Fletcher's health and mourning the departure of good times, which always seem to follow reform in government — Fortune having small use for virtue.

Through the hostile attitude toward Bellomont of the mercantile community in New York, the new scandal assumed wide proportions. As London first knew that Captain Kidd had turned pirate and was being sought for by the King's ships, this placed the Governor in a sorry situation at home, from which he was never able to rightly extricate himself. The story spread in England made Kidd out a pirate worthy to stand with

Morgan, the Buccaneer, or the enterprising Avery. He was reported as burning towns, torturing inhabitants and amassing incredible stores of treasure. Just as these tales reached their highest point in imaginative creation, sometime in May, Kidd came tamely into Delaware Bay in a small sloop, the *Antonio*, accompanied by James Gillam, a passenger from Madagascar where he had been a pirate. Most of his crew abandoned ship. The report sent to London by Bellomont declared that he had with him "a vast treasure, and had sent his boat on to the Horekills where he was supplied with what he wanted and from which the people frequently went on board of him." The sloop remained but two days at Horekills and then made for Gardiner's Island at the mouth of Peconic Bay, off the east end of Long Island, a neighborhood tolerant of pirates, this evidently with the hope of getting into touch with Bellomont, who was in Boston. Most of the departing members of the crew scattered safely, some were caught. Lieutenant- Governor Markham wrote the Earl that he had several of Kidd's men in custody and awaited instructions. "I have writ to him to keep them in gaol," observes Bellomont "till he receives orders from the King how to dispose of them." He adds: "I hear he has seized a good deal of money with them but says not a word of that. Mr. Basse, the Governor of the Jerseys has got some pirates with a good store of money at Burlington in West Jersey. I hear they were Kidd's men, too; the same thing I heard has happened to the Governor of Maryland. I mean his seizing pirates and their money. All these were brought from Madagascar by Shelly and were a good many of them Kidd's men that forsook him and went on board the Mocha frigate. If it be intended these men and their money shall be secured in the same manner Kidd and his men were that came hither were and their effects, then it will be proper that orders be sent accordingly. Otherwise the aforenamed governors will keep the money and the pirates escape."

One of Basse's prisoners who surrendered in East Jersey was Darby Mullins, whose later fate it was to follow his captain to his doom. All this occurred in April, 1699. Writing to the Lords of Trade apropos of these transactions on May 15, 1699, Bellomont said that piracy would continue until good judges, an honest attorney general and a man-of-war with a dutiful captain were furnished him from England. Had he a man-of-war at his command he could have taken Shelly and £50,000 that captain was reported to have with him, and would have engaged a great ship presumed to be that of one Maze that lay off the coast four or five days and then flitted away. Maze was one of the pirates whom Kidd was specifically commissioned to capture.

The Earl further asked for lawful authority to exact bonds for shipmasters to secure them sailing to ports from which they cleared, mentioning one Baldridge, who, given papers for Antigua, really went to Madagascar after contraband cargo. "Now that I have occasion to mention Baldridge," writes the Earl, "I will acquaint you with a particularity told me of him by Kidd, when I first examined him in council because you had directed in your Letter of the 25th of last October, or 5th of last January, that I should inquire after some pirates killed in St. Maries near Madagascar. I questioned Kidd about it and he told me Baldridge was the occasion of that Insurrection of the Natives and the death of the Pirates, for that having inveigled a great number of the Natives of St. Maries, men, women and children and sold them for slaves to a French Island called Mascarine or Mascaron Manritius, which treachery of Baldridge's the Natives on the island revenged on those pirates by cutting their throats."

From Gardiner's Island Kidd managed to get word to Livingston who came promptly to his aid. Livingston sent James Emott, of the brokerage firm of Emott and Weeks, who represented the leading New York interests in the Madagascar trade, to Boston, where a fellow-countryman and friend, Duncan Campbell, the postmaster, chartered a sloop and with Emott proceeded to Gardiner's Island on the 12th of June. There the pair met Kidd, with the result that Campbell, through Emott, presented a memorial to Bellomont, under date of June 19th, reading:

I, Duncan Campbell, being at Rhode Island on Saturday the 17th of June current; that Morning I went in a Sloop, in Company with Mr. James Emott of New York, and Two other Men belonging to the said Sloop, towards Block Island; and, about Three Leagues from that Island, I met a Sloop commanded by Captain Kidd, and having on boarda bout Sixteen men besides: after hailing of which Sloop, and being informed, That the said Kidd was Commander thereof, he the said Kidd desired me to come on board the same; Which I accordingly did; and, after some Discourse passed, the said Kidd desired me to do him the Favour as to make what Speed I could for Boston, and acquaint your Excellency, That the said Kidd had brought a Ship, about 5 or 600 Tons from Madagascar, which some considerable time since he met within . . . and commanded her there to bring to; and that thereupon the Pilot, being a Frenchman, came on board the said Kidd's Ship, and told him, the said Kidd, He was welcome, and that the said Ship, to which the said Pilot belonged, was a lawful Prize to him, the said Kidd, she sailing under a French pass, whereupon he, the said Kidd, and Company, took the said Ship; and afterwards, understanding that the same belonged to the Moors, he, the said Kidd, would have delivered her up again; but his Men violently fell upon him and thrust him into his Cabin, saying, The said ship was a said Prize (sic); and then carried her into Madagascar, and rifled her of what they pleased: But before they got into Madagascar, the Galley under Command of him, the said Kidd, became so leaky, that she would scarce keep above Water; whereupon the Company belonging thereto, having taken out her Guns, and some other Things, and put them on board the Prize, set the said Galley on Fire.

The said Captain Kidd further told me, That, when he and his Company were arrived at Madagascar several of his Company moved him to go and take a Ship called the *Moca Frigate*, that lay ready fitted at a Place not far distant from them, in the Possession of certain Privateers; and to go in the same for the Red Sea; but that he the said Kidd said, That if they would join with him, he would attempt the Taking of the said Ship, supposing her a lawful Prize, being formerly belonging to the King of England; but would not afterwards go with them on the said Design to the Red Sea: Whereupon Ninety of his, the said Kidd's Men, deserted him, went and took the said Ship, and sailed with the same on the on the said Design, as he, the said Kidd, was informed; obliging one Captain Culliver, the then Commander of her, to go along with them.

And the said Kidd further told me, That his Men having left him, and his Design frustrated, he thought it his best Way to preserve the said Ship then in his Possession, and the Goods on board her, for his Employers, or the proper Owners thereof; And accordingly, with the few Men he had then left, which would not join with the other Ninety in their aforesaid Design, being about Twenty in Number, and with a few other men, that he procured at Madagascar, to assist him in navigating the said Ship, he intended to have brought the same to Boston, according to his Orders; but, touching in his Way at the Island of St. Thomas, and other Places in the West Indies, he there heard, That great Complaints were preferred against him, and he proclaimed a Pirate; which occasioned him to sail to a Place called Mona, near Hispaniola; from whence he sent to Curaso, and bought there the Sloop on which he is now on board, and took into her to the Value of about 8 or 10,000£ in Goods, Gold and Plate; for which Gold and Plate he traded at Madagascar, and was produced by the Sale of sundry Goods and Stores, that he took out of the *Adventure Galley*, formerly commanded by him; and hath left the Ship taken by his Company, and carried to Madagascar, as aforesaid, at or near Mona abovesaid, in the Custody of about Six Men of his own Company, and Eighteen others that he got from Curaso; the Merchant of whom he bought the said Sloop, being intrusted therewith; unto which he had promised to return again in Three Months; the said Kidd resolving to come into Boston or New York; to deliver up unto your Excellency what Goods and Treasure he hath on board; and to pray your Excellency's Assistance, to enable him to bring the said Ship left by him at Mona aforesaid, from thence; the said Ship being disabled from coming for want of Furniture.

But the said Captain Kidd further informed me, That by reason of what his Men had heard in the West Indies, as aforesaid, of their being proclaimed Pirates, they would not consent to his coming into any Port without some Assurance from your Excellecny, That they should not be imprisoned nor molested: And the said Captain Kidd did several times protest solemnly, That he had not done anything since his going out in said Gelley contrary to his Commission or Orders, more than what he was necessitated unto, being overpowered by his Men that deserted him, as aforesaid; who evil-intreated him several times for his not conseting to, or joining with them in, their Actions: And all the men on board the Sloop now with him did, in like manner, solemnly protest their Innocence; and declared, That they had used their utmost Endeavours in preserving the aforesaid Ship and Goods for the Owners or Employers.

The said Kidd also saith, That, if your Lordship should see Cause so to direct, he would carry the said Ship for England, there to render an Account of his Proceedings.

Which beforegoing contains the Particulars of what Captain Kidd and his Men related to

Your Lordship's most humble Servant

DUNCAN CAMPBELL.

Kidd also sent by Campbell the two French passes he had taken with the two Eastern prizes, which he relied upon to clear himself of the charge of piracy. On the same day Bellomont returned the following reply:

BOSTON, 19 June, 1699.

CAPTAIN KIDD, — Mr. Emmot came to me last Tuesday night telling me he came from you: but was shy of telling where he parted with you. Nor did I press him to it. He told me you came by Oyster Bay in Nassau Island and sent forhim to New York. He proposed to me that I would grant you a pardon. I answered that I had never granted one yet, and that I had set myself a rule never to grant a pardon to anybody without the King's express leave or command. He told me you declared and protested your innocence and that if your men could be persuaded to follow your example, you would make no manner of scruple of coming into this port, or any other within His Majesty's Dominions. That you owned there were two ships taken, but that your men did it violently and against your will, and had used you barbarously, in imprisoning you and treating you ill the most part of your voyage, and often attempting to murder you. Mr. Emmot delivered to me the two French passes taken on board the two ships your men rifled, which passes I have in my custody, and I am apt to believe they will be a good article to justify you, if the late peace were not by the Treaty between England and France to operate in that part of the world at the time the hostility was committed, as I am almost confident it was not to do. Mr. Emmot told me that you showed a great sense of honour and justice in professing with many asseverations your settled and serious design all along to do honour to your Commission and never to do the least thing contrary to your duty and allegiance to the King. And this I have to say in your defence, that several persons in New York, who I can bring to evidence it, did tell me that by several advices from Madagascar and that part of the world, they were informed of your men's revolting from you in one place, and I am pretty sure they said was Madagascar, and that others compelled you much against your will to take and rifle two ships.

"I have advised with His Majesty's Council, and shewed them this letter, and they are of opinion that if you can be so clear as you (or Mr. Emmot for you) have said, that you may safely come hither, and be equipped and fitted out to go and fetch the other ship, and I make no manner of doubt but to obtain the King's pardon for you, and for those few men you have left who I understand have been faithful to you, and refused as well as you to dishonour the Commission you have from England.

I assure you on my Word and Honour I will perform nicely what I have promised, though this I declare before-hand that whatever goods and treasure you may bring hi-ther, I will not meddle with the least bit of them: but they shall be left with such persons as the Council shall advise until I receive orders from England how they shall be dis-posed of.

This letter was duly forwarded to Kidd who sent his exalted partner this response from Block Island:

24 JUNE, 1699.

MAY IT PLEASE YOUR EXCELLENCY,

I am honoured with your Lordship's letter of the 19th in-stant by Mr. Campbell, which came to my hands this day. For which I return my most hearty thanks. I cannot but blame myself for not writing to your Lordship before this time, knowing it was my duty: but the clamours and false stories that have been reported of me, made me fearful of visiting or coming into any harbour, till I could hear from your Lordship.

I note the contents of your Lordship's letter, as to what Mr. Emmot and Mr. Campbell informed your Lordship of my proceedings I do affirm to be true, and a great deal more might be said of the abuses of my men, and the hardships I have undergone to preserve the ship and what goods my men had left. Nine-five men went away from me in one day and went on board the *Moca Frigate*, Captain Robert Culliford, Commander, who went away to the Red Sea; and committed several acts of piracy, as I am informed: and am afraid (the men formerly belonging to my Galley) that the report is gone home against me to the East India Company, that I have been the actor. A sheet of paper will not contain what may be said of the care I took to preserve the owners' interest, and to come home to clear my own innocency. I do further declare and protest that I never did in the least act contrary to the King's Commission, nor to the reputation of my honourable owners, and doubt not but that I shall be able to make my innocence appear; or else I had no need to come to these parts of the world; if it were not for that and my owners' interest. There are Five or Six Passengers that came from Madagascar to assist me in bringing the ship home, and about ten of my own men, that came with me would not venture to go into Boston, till Mr. Campbell had engaged Body for Body for them that they should not be molested while I stayed at Boston, or till I return with the ship. I doubt not but your Lordship will write to England in my favour and for these few men who are left.

I wish your Lordship would persuade Mr. Campbell to go home to England with your Lordship's letters, who will be able to give account of our affairs and diligently follow the same that there may be a speedy answer from England. I desired Mr. Campbell to buy 1000 weight of Rigging for fitting of the ship to bring her to Boston, that I may not be delayed when I come there.

Upon receiving of your Lordship's letter, I am making the

best of my way to Boston. This with my humble duty to your Lordship and Countess, is what offers from, my Lord, your Excellency's most humble and dutiful servant,

WILLIAM KIDD.

Mrs. Kidd and her children joined the Captain at Gardiner's Island, where he landed the valuables brought by the *Antonio* from Hispaniola. Relying on Bellomont's letter, he sailed for Boston with thirteen men, reaching port on the 1st of July.The captain seems to have put full confidence in his eminent partner's good intention. Mrs. Kidd with her children and maid accompanied him in the sloop to Boston and all lodged at the house of his friend, Duncan Campbell. As to the next proceeding the Minutes of the Council for July 3, 1699 show the following:

Captain William Kidd, by command of his Excellency and Council this day at five o'clock, post meridiem, to give an account of his proceedings in his late voyage to Madagascar, the said Kidd accordingly appeared, and prayed his Lordship to allow him some time and he would prepare an account in writing of his proceedings, and present to his Lordship and the Board. Time was granted him to prepare and bring in his narrative until to-morrow at five o'clock, post meridiem, as also an invoice of the bill of lading on board the sloop and the ship, attested to by himself and some of his principal officers, with a list of the names of the men on board the sloop and ship, and of those who belonged to the *Adventure Galley*, who, he alleges, refused to obey his commands, and evil entreated him and deserted the said ship. And the Council adjourned unto the said day and hour, after Captain Kidd had given a summary account of the lading on board his sloop now in port and also on board the ship left at Hispaniola. His Excellency appointed Captain Hawes, Deputy-Collector, to put some waiters on board.

On July 4th, the captain again presented himself be-

fore the Council and asked for further time to prepare
the desired document. Failing to appear he was sum-
moned and gave the excuse that he had understood that
the hour set was five in the evening, but presented no
statement. After he retired from the presence of the
August body Bellomont advised the members that letters just received from England expressly commanded
him to seize Kidd and his accomplices "with their vessels and goods." The period of "stalling" was now past
and the captain's reliance on influence failed once for all.
This was seventeen days after Bellomont had issued the
safe conduct. There is no evidence of any letters other
than the general instructions sent him long before. His
heart had evidently failed him in the absence of Kidd's
evidence. He, according to the record, now "caused"
Kidd to be seized and apprehended for "having neg-
lected to give a narrative in writing of his proceedings,
etc., by the time set him." The next day he was brought
before the Council, when it was ordered that he be committed to prison. Some members of the Council held
commissions as Justices of Peace and one of these issued the mittimus. This was July 7, 1699. On the same
day Bellomont appointed Samuel Sewall, Nathaniel By-
field, Jeremiah Dummer and Andrew Belcher, four most
distinguished citizens of Boston, to proceed by a specially assigned vessel to Gardiner's Island to secure and ap-
praise Kidd's belongings. Hutchinson in his history of
Massachusetts asserts that when seized Kidd endeav-
ored to use his sword, but there is no reference to this
in Bellomont's papers. Taken at once to prison Kidd
was not put in a cell but resided in the apartments of
Ray, the jailer. On July 11th, the Council took cog-
nizance of Bellomont's desire to send a ship to Hispan-

iola and salvage the *Quedagh Merchant* by making the following minute:

Captain William Kidd and his accomplices, lately apprehended within this province for committing divers acts of piracy, on examination severally, acknowledging and agreeing thereon that they left a prize ship, of the burden of four hundred tons or upwards, which they took in the seas in India, at Hispaniola in the West Indies, safely moored in the river there, and in the care of Henry Bolton and eighteen or twenty men more, and a considerable quantity of bale goods of India, saltpetre, iron, sugar, etc., on board of the same,- - -

Advised, that his Lordship do forthwith cause to be taken up, equipped, and manned for his Majesty's service a suitable ship, with good force, to be managed and applied on the aforesaid affair. Which is, the securing and bringing away said ship and lading left there by said Kidd and his company, the charge thereof to be answered and secured by the goods and treasure imported here by said Kidd and company, now under seizure and in custody.

It will be plainly perceived that all the while Bellomont was playing false and insuring his own protection. The commission sent to Gardiner's Island duly "received" the treasure, which had been left in John Gardiner's custody and made the report at Boston, to wit:

A true account of all such gold, silver, jewels and merchandise, late in the possession of Captain William Kidd, which have been seized and secured by us pursuant to an order from his Excellency, Richard, Earl of Bellomont bearing date July 7, 1699.

Received, the 17th instant, of Mr. John Gardiner, viz:

		Ounces
No.	1. One bag of dust-gold.................	63¾
	2. One bag of corned gold..............	11
	and one of silver....................	124
	3. One bag of dust-gold.................	24¾

4. One bag of silver rings and
    sundry precious stones.............. 4⅞
5. One bag of unpolished stones......... 12½
6. One piece of crystal, cornelian
    rings, two agates, two amythists....... ...
7. One bag silver buttons and lamps...... ...

8. One bag of broken silver............. 173½
9. One bag of gold bars............... 353¼
10. One do............................ 238½
11. One bag of dust-gold............... 59½
12. One bag silver bars................ 309

      SAMUEL SEWALL,   NATHANIEL BYFIELD,
   JEREMIAH DUMMER,   ANDREW BELCHER.

                                               Commissioners.

Thompson's history of Long Island relates that while
Captain lay at the island he desired Mrs. Gardiner to
roast him a pig. "She being afraid to refuse" according
to Mrs. Wetmore, her great-granddaughter, "roasted it
very nice and he was much pleased with it." In return
the captain gave the lady a piece of cloth of gold, a
part of which was then (in the thirties) in Mrs. Wetmore's possession.

Previous to Kidd's coming to the prison, Joseph Bradish and Tee Wetherly, two recently arrested adventurers in the same line, had escaped from the jail by the
assistance of a maid employed by the jailor who was accused of favoring the pair. They had been retaken, but
the news of his easy treatment of Kidd getting about,
Ray was ordered by the Council to place the captain in a
stone cell. Mrs. Kidd's trunk had been left with Gardiner and was broken open by order of the commission.
A sum of $500 in cash found within was taken, but later
returned to her on clear proof that it was her own. John

Gardiner returned to Boston with the commission and produced the Kidd account, which was in effect what the Council had first called for. It appears in the records of the Council as below:

Boston, 17th July, 1699. Mr. John Gardner, of Gardner's Island, presented this note to His Excellency in Council, which he made oath was delivered to him by Captain Kidd, as was wrote with the said Kidd's own hand on board his sloop, and all the particulars therein mentioned were committed to his custody.

Examined by Isa Addington, Secretary.

That the Journal of the said Captain Kidd, being violently taken from him in the Port of St. Marie's in Madagascar, and his Life being many times threatened to be taken away from him by Ninety-Seven of his Men that deserted him there, he cannot give that exact Account he otherwise could have done: but as far as his Memory will serve, is as followeth, viz.

That the said *Adventure Galley* was launched in Castle's Yard at Deptford, about the Fourth of December, 1695; and about the latter end of February the said Galley came to the Buoy in the Nore: and about the 1st Day of March following, his Men were pressed for him for the Fleet; which caused him to stay there for Nineteen Days; and then sailed for the Donnes, and arrived there about the Eighth or the Tenth Day of April 1696; and sailed thence for Plymouth; and on the Twenty-third Day of the said month of April he sailed on his intended Voyage: and, some time in the month of May, met with a small French Vessel, with Salt and Fishing Tackle on board, bound for Newfoundland, which he took and made Prize of, and carried the same into New York, about the Fourth Day of July, when she was condemned as lawful Prize: The Produce whereof purchased provisions for the said Galley, and for her further intended Voyage.

That about the Sixth Day of September, 1696, the said Captain Kidd sailed for the Maderas, in company with one Joyner, Master of a Brigantine belonging to Bermudas, and arrived there about the 8th Day of October following: and thence to Bonavista, where they arrived about the nineteenth of the said month, and took in some Salt, and stayed Three or Four Days; and sailed thence to St. Jago, and arrived there the Twenty-fourth of the said Month, where he took in some Water, and stayed about Eight or Nine Days; and thence sailed for the Cape of Good Hope; and in the

Latitude of Thirty-two, on the Twelfth Day of December, 1696, met with Four English Men of War: Captain Warren was Commodore; and sailed a week in their Company; and then parted, and sailed to Telere, a Port in the Island of Madagascar, and being there about the Twenty-ninth Day of January, came in a Sloop belonging to Barbadoes, loaded with Rum, Sugar, Powder and Shot, one French Master, and Mr. Hatton and Mr. John Batt, Merchants; and the said Hatton came on board the said Galley, and was suddenly taken ill and died in the Cabin: And, about the latter end of February, sailed for the Island of Johanna, the said Sloop keeping Company, and arrived there about the Eighteenth Day of March; where he found Four East India Merchantsmen outward bound; and watered there all together, and staid about Four Days: And from thence, about the Twenty-second of March, sailed for Mehila, an Island Ten Leagues distant from Johanna, where he arrived the next Morning, and there careened the said Galley; and about Fifty men died there in a Week's Time.

That on the 25th Day of April 1697, set sail for the Coast of India, and came upon the Coast of Mallabar, the Beginning of the Ninth of September; and went into Carwarr upon that Coast about the middle of the same Month, and watered there: And the Gentlemen of the English factory gave the Narrator an account, That the Portuguese were fitting out Two Men of War to take him; and advised him to put out to Sea, and to take Care of himself from them, and immediately to set sail thereupon; . . . . . . about the 12th of the said month of September; and the next morning, about Break of Day saw the said Two Men of War standing for the said Galley; and spoke with him and asked him, Whence he was? Who replied from London; and they returned answer, From Goa; and so parted, wishing each other a good Voyage; And making still along the Coast, the Commodore of the said Man of War kept dogging the said Galley all the Night, waiting on Opportunity to board her; and in the Morning, without speaking a Word, Fired Six great Guns at the galley, some whereof went through her, and wounded Four of his Men; and thereupon he fired upon him again; and the Fight continued all Day; and the narrator had Eleven Men wounded: the other Portuguese man of War lay some Distance off, and could not come up with the Galley, being calm; else would have likewise assaulted the same; the said Fight was sharp, and the said Portuguese left the said Galley with such Satisfaction, that the Narrator believes no Portuguese will ever attack the King's Colours again, in that Part of the World especially. And afterwards continued upon the same Coast, cruising upon the coast of Cameroone, for Pirates that frequent that Coast, till the Begginning of the month of November 1697, When he met with Captain How in the *Loyal Captaine*, an English Ship belonging to Maderas, bound

LORD BELLOMONT

to Surratt, whom he examined; and finding his Pass good, designed to freely to let her pass about her Affairs; but, having Two Dutchmen on board, they told the Narrator's Men, That they had divers Greeks and Armenians on board, who had divers precious Stones and divers other rich Goods on board, which caused his Men to be very mutinous, and got up their Arms, and swore they would take the Ship: and two-thirds of his Men voted for the same: The narrator told them, the small Arms belonged to the Galley, and that he was not come to take any Englishmen, or lawful Traders; and that if they attempted any such thing, they should never come on board the Galley again, nor have the Boat, or small Arms; for he had no Commission to take any but the King's Enemies, and Pirates, and that he would attack them with the Galley, and drive them into Bombay; the other being a Merchantman, and having no Guns, might easily have done it with a few Hands; and, with all the Arguments and Menaces he could use, could scarce restrain them from their unlawful Design; but at last I prevailed, and with much ado I got him clear, and let him go about his Business. All which the said Captain How will attest, if living.

And that, about the 18th or 19th Day of the said month of November, met with a Moors Ship of about 200 Tons coming from Surratt, bound to the Coast of Mallabar, loaded with Two Horses, Sugar and Cotton, to trade there having about Forty Moors on board, with a Dutch Pilot, Boatswain, and Gunner; which said Ship the Narrator haled, and commanded on board; and with him came Eight or Nine Moors, and the said Three Dutchmen, who declared it was a Moors Ship; and demanding their pass from Surrat, which they shewed; and the same was a French Pass, which he believes was shewn by a Mistake; for the Pilot swore Sacrament she was a Prize, and staid on board the Galley; and would not return on board the Moor Ship; but went in the Galley to the Port of St. Marie.

And that, about the First Day of February following, upon the same Coast, under French Colours with a Design to decoy,met with a Bengall Merchantman belonging to Surratt, of the Burden of 4 or 500 Tons, 10 Guns; and he commanded the Master on board; and a Frenchman, Inhabitant of Surratt, and belonging to the French Factory there, and Gunner of the said Ship, came on board as Master; and when he came on board, the Narrator caused the English Colours to be hoisted; and the said Master was surprised, and said, You are all English; and asking, which was the Captain? Whom when he saw, said, Here is a good Prize, and delivered him the French Pass.

And that, with the said Two Prizes, sailed for the Port of St. Marie's in Madagascar; and, sailing thither, the said Galley was so leaky, that they feared she would have sunk every Hour, and it required Eight men every Two Glasses to keep her free; and was forced to woold her round with Cables to keep her together; and with much ado carried her into the said Port of St. Marie's, where she arrived about the First of April, 1698; And about the 6th day of May, the lesser Prize was haled into the careening Island or Key, the other not being arrived; and ransacked and sunk by the mutinous men; who threatened the Narrator, and the men that would not join with them to burn and sink the other, that they might not go home and tell the news.

And that, when he arrived in the said Port, there was a Pirate Ship, called the *Moca Frigate*, at an Anchor, Robert Culliford, Commander thereof; who with his Men, left the same at his coming in, and ran into the Woods; and the Narrator proposed to his Men to take the same, having sufficient Power and Authority so to do; but the Mutinous Crew told him, If he offered the same, they would rather fire Two Guns into him, than one into the other; and thereupon Ninety-seven deserted, and went into the *Moca Frigate*, and sent into the Woods for the said Pirates, and brought the said Culliford, and his Men, on board again; and all the time she staid in the said Port, which was the Space of Four or Five Days, the said Deserters, sometimes in great Numbers, came on board the said Galley and *Adventure* Prize, and carried away great Guns, Powder, Shot, small Arms, Sails, Anchors, Cables, Surgeon's Chests, and what else they pleased; and threatened several times to murder the Narrator, as he was informed, and advised to take care of himself; which they designed in the night to effect; but was prevented by him locking himself in his Cabin at Night, and securing himself with barricading the same with Bales of Goods; and, having about Forty small Arms, besides Pistols, ready charged, kept them out; Their Wickedness was so great, after they had plundered and ransacked sufficiently, went Four Miles off to one Edward Welche's House, where his the Narrator's Chest was lodged, and broke it open; and took out Ten Ounces of Gold, 40 Pound of Plate, 370 Pieces of Eight, the Narrator's Journal, and a great many Papers that belonged to him, and the People of New York that fitted them out.

That about the 15th June, the *Moca Frigate* went away, being manned with about 130 Men, and Forty Guns, bound out to take all Nations: Then it was that the Narrator was left with only Thirteen men; so that the Moors he had to pump and keep the *Adventure* Galley above Water, being carried away, she sunk in the Harbour; and the Narator, with the said Thirteen men, went on board the *Adventure* Prize; where he was forced to stay Five Months for a Fair Wind; In the meantime, some Passengers presented, that were bound for these Parts; which he took on board, to help to bring the said *Adventure* Prize.

That, about the beginning of April, 1699, the Narrator arrived at Anguilla in the West Indies, and sent his Boat on Shore; where his Men had the News That he and his People were proclaimed Pirates, which put them into such Consternation, That they sought all Opportunity to run the Ship on Shore upon some Reef or Shoal, fearing the Narrator should carry them into some English Port.

From Anguilla they came to St. Thomas'; where his Brother-in-law Samuel Bradley was put on shore, being sick; and Five more went away, and deserted him: Where he heard the same News That the Narrator, and his Company, were proclaimed Pirates, which incensed the People more and more.

From St. Thomas set sail for Moona, an Island between Hispaniola and Porto Rico; where they met with a Sloop called the *St. Anthony*, bound for Antega from Curaso, Mr. Wm. Boulton Merchant, and Samuel Wood, Master; The men on board then swore, they would bring the Ship no further. The Narrator then sent the said Sloop *St. Anthony* for Curaso, for Canvas to make Sails for the Prize, she not being able to proceed; and she returned in Ten Days; and after the Canvas came, he could not persuade the Men to carry her for New England; but Six of them went and carried their Chests and Things on board of Two Dutch Sloops; bound for Curaso; and would not so much as heel the Vessel, or do anything. The Remainder of the men not being able to bring the *Adventure* Prize to Boston, the Narrator secured her in a good Harbour in some Part of Hispaniola and left in the Possession of Mr. Henry Boulton of Antegua, Merchant, the Maker, Three of the old Men, and Fifteen or Sixteen of the men that belonged to the said Sloop *St. Anthony*, and a Brigantine belonging to one Mr. Burt of Curaso.

That the Narrator bought the said Sloop *St. Anthony* of Mr. Boulton, for the Owner's Account; and after, he had given Directions to the said Boulton to be careful of the said Ship and Lading, and persuaded him to stay Three Months till he returned; and then made the best of his Way to New York; where he heard the Earl of Bellomont was, who was principally concerned in the *Adventure Galley*; and hearing his Lordship was at Boston, came thither; and has now been 45 Days from the said Ship.

To this copy appended a further statement which Kidd had read on the day of his arrest, reading:

Boston — 7th July, 1699.
Further the Narrator saith, That the said Ship was left at St. Katharina, on the South East Part of Hispaniola, about Three Leagues to Leeward of the Westerly End of Savona. Whilst he lay at Hispaniola, he traded with Mr. Henry Boulton of Antegua, and Mr. Wm. Burt of Curaso, Merchants, to the Value of 11,200 Pieces

of Eight; whereof he received the Sloop *Antonio* at 3000 Pieces of Eight, and 4200 Pieces of Eight by Bills of Exchange, drawn by Boulton and Burt upon Messieurs Gabriel and Lemont, Merchants in Curaso, made payable to Mr. Burt, who went himself to Curaso; and the Value of 4,000 Pieces of Eight more in Dust and Bar Gold; which Gold, with some more traded for at Madagascar, being Fifty Pounds Weight, or upwards, in Quantity, the Narrator left in Custody of Mr. Gardner of Gardner's Island, near the Eastern End of Long Island, fearing to bring it about by Sea: It is made up in a Bag put into a little Box, locked, nailed, corded about, and sealed; Saith he took no Receipt for it of Mr. Gardner.

The Gold that was seized at Mr. Campbell's, the Narrator, traded for at Madagascar, with what came out of Galley.

Saith, That he carried in the *Adventure Galley*, from New York, 154 Men: Seventy whereof came out of England with him. Some of his Sloop's Company put Two Bales of Goods on shore at Gardner's Island, being their own proper Goods. The Narrator delivered a Chest of Goods, viz., Muslins, Latches, Romalls, and flowered Silk, unto Mr. Gardner of Gardner's Island aforesaid, to be kept there for the Narrator: Put no Goods on shore anywhere else: Several of his Company landed their Chests, and other Goods, at several Places.

Further saith, He delivered a small Bale of coarse Calicoes unto a Sloop Man of Rhode Island, that he had employed there. The Gold seized at Mr. Campbell's the Narrator intended for Presents to some, that he expected to do him Kindnesses. Some of his Company put their Chests and Bales in board a New York Sloop lying at Gardner's Island.

Wm. Kidd.

Presented and taken, die praedict before his Excellency and Council,
   Copy Examined by
      Isa Addington, Secretary.

Bellomont's account of the proceedings leading up to Kidd's surrender is gleaned from his letters found in the reports of the Lords of Trade. The Lords recite that writing from Boston July 8, 1699:

He informed us that Capt. Kidd, in a sloop, richly laden, having hovered a fortnight upon the Coast near New York, and given notice to the Friends he had there of his arrival he brought one of them, named Emot, along with him to Rhoad Island, and from thence sent the said Emot to his Lordship to treat about his admission and security.

Emot being accordingly came to Boston, told his Lordship that Kidd had left the Great Moorish ship he took in India, called the *Quedagh Merchant*, in a creek on the coast of Hispaniola, with goods to the value of thirty thousand pounds; That he had bought a sloop, in which he was come before to make his terms; That he had brought in the sloop with him several Bailes of East India goods, three score pound weight of gold in dust, and in ingots about a hundred weight of silver and several other things which he believed would sell for about ten thousand pound; He said also that Kidd was very innocent, and would make it appear that his men forced him, locking him up in the cabin of the *Adventure Galley*, whilst they robbed two or three ships, and that he could prove this by many witnesses. Hereupon the Earl of Bellomont answered that if Kidd could make his innocence appear he might safely come into that Port And accordingly he wrote a letter to Kidd inviting him to come in, and (upon conditions of his innocence) assuring him of protection. This letter his Lordship sent by one Campbell, Kidds countryman (viz– a Scotch man) and his acquaintance. And in three or four days Campbell returned with an answer from Kidd full of protestations of innocence, and expressing his designe of bringing his sloop into that Port.

Campbell after his returne presented three or four small jewells to the Countess of Bellomont, as if his Lordship should not have known it; But she immediately acquainted his Lordship therewith, and desired his directions whether to keep them or no. Whereupon he being fearful lest too great an appearance of nicety might create a Jealousy in Kidd or his friends, and so prevent what he desired at, advised her ladyship for the present to keep them All which matters he wrote were transacted with the Privity and Advice of the Council of the Massachusetts Bay.

Kidd came according to his letter and landed there the 1st of July, but by his trifling answers to his Lordship and the Council upon several examinations; By the endeavours of his friends Campbell and Livingston (who upon notice of Kidd's intention was posted thither from Albany) to imbezel the cargo that was abroad the Sloop; by instructions given his Lordship that a present of one thousand pounds value in gold-dust and ingots was designed to be made to his Countess. And by Livingston peremptory application to his Lordship for the discharge of a Bond and Articles which it seems he had entered into as security for Kidd upon the expedition, accompanied by threats that unless those securities were immediately given up Kidd would never bring in the aforementioned great ship that he had left on the coast of Hispaniola, his Lordship finding it necessary to act more openly, caused Kidd on the 6th of July to be seized and committed to prison, and then at the Council Board delivered the Commissioners appointed to take charge of the sloop's cargo, and to take inventories thereof, the aforementioned jewels that had been presented to his Countess.

His Lordship further adds that those commissioners were preparing inventories of everything accordingly; that he feared lest Kidd should yet escape, or be let escape out of that jail as one Bradish, a notorious Pirate and another had lately done, with the consent (as believe) of the jailor; That as the law stands in this Country a Pirate cannot be punished with death; and he therefore desires directions when to do with Bradish's crew and also with Kidd and those men of his that he had taken.

The Earl added that he was "manning a ship to go in quest of the *Quedagh Merchant* left by Kidd (as he said) on the Coast of Hispaniola, which by his account of the cargo was computed to be worthy seventy thousand pounds," and this much more of Kidd's maneuverings:

Concerning Kidd we have also been informed by the President and Council of Nevis, that he having applied to the Governor of St. Thomas (a Danish Island) for protection and being refused, it sailed to an Island called Moona, between Porto Rico and Hispaniola, and in the way, meeting with one Henry Bolton (in a large sloop) prevailed with said Bolton to go to Curasso (Curacoa) to buy him provisions and after Bolton's returne bought his sloop of him, which he laded with the finest of his goods and sailed with her towards New York, leaving Bolton in possession of his ship and the remaining part of his goods to act (as was said) as Attorney for him till his returne; But that he just sold 120 or 130 bales of Muslin to one William Bourke, an Irishman which having been carryed by said Bourke to St. Thomas were there seized on tho' afterwards upon his giving security for five thousand pieces of eight Bourke had them againe and sailed therewith to Barbadoes.

Connecticut, under its special charter, was a thorn in the side of Bellomont, as it often afforded safe refuge for persons upon whom he sought to lay his hands. He reports with some satisfaction to the Lords of Trade that he had "prevail'd with Governor Winthrop to seize and send Thomas Clarke of New Yorke prisoner thither; he had been on board Kidd's sloop at the East End of Long Island, and carried off to the value of about £5,000 in goods and treasure (that we know of and perhaps a great deal more) into Connecticut Colony, and thinking himself safe from under our power, writ my Lieutenant-Governor of New Yorke a very sawcy letter and bade us defiance. I have ordered him to be safely kept prisoner in the Fort, because the Gaol in New York is weak and insufficient and when orders come to me to send Kidd and his men to England (which I long for impatiently) I will also send Clarke as an associate of Kidd's."

The sailing of the ship taking this letter was delayed, and ten days later Bellomont added a postcript to the effect that the contumacious Clarke had appeared to surrender all the Kidd plunder in his possession in return for immunity.

Bellomont wrote the Lords of Trade on October 20,

1799, from Boston concerning "Gillam, a notorious pirate" who "was suffered to escape from Rhode Island to "Nassaw, alias Long Island," which incidentally had become a "a great Receptable for Pirates," and who "tis believed he is still there, notwithstanding the Lieutenant Governor of New York published by my direction a reward of £30 for his apprehension, and at the same time £10 apiece for two of Kidd's men that escaped from this town to Nassaw Island." Further in the same letter:

I have prevail'd with Governor Winthrop to seize and send Thomas Clarks of New Yorke prisoner thither; he had been on board Kidd's sloop at the East End of Long Island, and carried off to the value of about £5,000 in goods and treasure (that we know of and perhaps a great deal more) into Connecticut Colony, and thinking himself safe from under our power, writ my Lieutenant Governor of New Yorke a very sawcy letter and bade me defiance. I have ordered him to be safely kept prisoner in the Fort, because the Gaol of New Yorks is weak and insufficient, and when orders come to send Kidd and his men to England (which I long for impatiently) I will also send Clarke as an associate of Kidd's.

October 30, the ship not yet having set sail Bellomont took:

The opportunity of sending your Lordships the Lieutenant Governor of New York's proposition to me in behalf of Thomas Clarke of New Yorke, of his the said Clarke's offer of surrendering all the goods and treasure (which he received from on board Kidd's sloop) to the Government; which proposition of the Lieutenant Governor's is contained in the Extract of his letter of the 23d instant and goes (No. 13.) And I have advised the Lieutenant Governor to incourage Clarks, and to promise him if he would surrender all the goods and treasure, I would become Advocate for him, and he should not be troubled or prosecuted. Wherein I hope and perswade myself your Lordships will approve of my Conduct. But I have directed the Lieutenant Governor to take the security offer'd viz: £12,000 for Clarke's punctual performance of what he has proposed and also his oath to it.

Writing under date of January 5, 1700, after reciting that he has some 40 pirates in custody whom he heartily wishes were in Newgate, the Governor says: "Captain Kidd sent the Gaoler to me a fortnight ago to acquaint me that if I would let him go to the place where he left the ship the *Quedagh Merchant* and to St. Thomas Island and Curacoa, he would undertake to bring off fifty or three score thousand pounds which would otherwise be lost; That he would be satisfied to go a Prisoner to remove from me any jealousy of his designing to escape. But I sent him word he was the King's prisoner and I could hearken to no such proposition. But I had the Gaoler try if he could prevail with Captain Kidd to discover where his treasure was hid by him, but he said nobody could find it but himself and would not tell any further."

Plainly the Captain was dealing for his life and making large offers to save it. That he believed his partner in the first instance is shown by his coming to Boston, when he could safely have sailed away to rejoin the *Quedagh Merchant* in Hispaniola. No real effort had been made to capture him despite his great, if undeserved, reputation as a despoiler of honest trade. His French passes he deemed a sufficient defence from the charge. His contact with rascals at Madagascar, his tussle with a Portuguese fleet, and some other matters that looked irregular, were trifling incidents as the world went. True, he had taken no pirates, but then, so far as he knew, neither had Bellomont, though plenty were at liberty

in his domain and New York warehouses bulged with
bales looted from their rightful owners in distant seas.
The Governor reported several instances, indeed, where
he had sought to sequester doubtful cargoes, but was
prevented by the riotous or other perversive action of
the populace. In view of their attitude Bellomont continued to reside in Boston rather than New York. He
was decidedly unpopular for his virtues, and these were
often regarded as vices by the community. March 11,
1700, John Key filed thirty-two charges against him and
these went to London accompanied by a petition signed
by some thirty eminent citizens, requesting a restora-
tion of their "pristine peace, safety and prosperity."
Among Key's charges he alleged:

29 – He having got two of Kidd's crew in custody, viz:
One Buckmaster, an Englishman and Van Tayl, a Dutchman, he committed the Englishman to prison without bail
and admitted the Dutchman to bail.

30 – He has committed one Clark to prison without bail
upon his suspicion of his having some of Kidd's goods in his
custody, only because he had been on board of Kidd's vessel.

May 31, 1700, Bellomont wrote the Lords of the Treasury, who were concerned over the spoils:

According to your Lordship's orders to me in your letter
of the 7th of last September, I send you all the papers and
evidences that related to Capt. Kidd's effects and the rest of
the pirates, I sent with him in the *Advice* frigate. I now send
your Lordship the Inventories of all such treasures and effects
as are come to my hands from the Governors of Maryland
and Pennsylvania, from Colonel Quary, Judge of the Admiralty Court in Pennsylvania, and from the Lieutenant- Governor in New York. I have not thought it necessary to discharge myself upon oath of the said treasure and effects, because the Lieutenant-Governor of New York (from whom

they are sent immediately and directly to me) has exonerated himself upon oath before Council of New York, as appears by a minute of Council sent herewith; and the charges that have accrued here since the prisoners being brought amount to no more than £12 – 6 of his money. The pirates who are nine in number I have ordered to be delivered to Rear-Admiral Benbow, whom I have desired to deliver them to my Lord Jersey and the effects to Mr. Secretary Vernon, to whom the effects were consigned.

October 17, 1700, Bellomont informed the Lords of Trade:

I have been much troubled to find my name brought on the Stage in the House of Commons about Kidd. 'Twas hard I thought I should be push'd at so vehemently when it was known I had taken Kidd and secured him in order to his punishment; and was a sure sign the noble Lords concern'd with me, and myself, had no criminal design in setting out the ship. Another mortification I have met with is the loss of a rent charge of £1,000 a year which the King was pleased to give me upon an Irish forfeited estate, in recompense of the great losses I had sustained by the rebellion in Ireland. If I have serv'd the King and interest of England here, I am sure I have been strangely rewarded there.

The case dragged on without issue or decision. Anticipating criticism, on the 18th of October, 1700, writing to Mr. Secretary Vernon, Bellomont says:

I send you all the writing I have that in any way relates to Kidd, viz: the Original articles between Mr. Livingston, Kidd, and me; Captain Kidd's Original Bond for performance of Articles, and also Mr. Livingston's Bond of Performance. These Originals I send by the *Newport* Frigate, and copies of duplicates thereof by the Ship *Fortune*, Captn Deering, Commanr. The original articles are written with Mr. Livingston's own hand; there's no intricacy in all that matter. The design of the owners of said ship I have reason to know was very honest and ye successe had been very fortunate and servicable, had we not been persuaded by Mr. Livingston to put the ships under command of a most abandon'd Villian, for we were all of us strangers to Kidd, but employed him on Mr. Livingston's recommendations of his Bravery and honesty; but he broke articles with us at the very first dash, for instead of sailing to those seas which Pyrate ships frequent, he came hither directly to New Yorke and loytered away several months and Mr. Livingston (who was got hither from England before me) told me at my arrivall here, that there was a private contract between Col. Fletcher and Kidd, whereby Kidd obliged himself to give Fletcher £10,000 if he made a voyage; Mr. Livingston told me this was whispered about, but he could get such light into it as to be able to prove that was such a Bargain between 'em. That was so is palpable enough, because Coll. Fletcher suffered and countenanced Kidd's beating for voluntiers in this Town, and taking with him about 199 able sailors which is a loss to this country to this day. I must say in justification of the noble Lords concerned with me that I do not believe any of them ever saw Kidd: and for my own part I never saw him above thrice and Mr. Livingston came with him every time to my house in Dover Street, the whole matter of the out-sett of that ship was transacted by Mr. Livingston and me.

This does not coincide with the several slighting references by Fletcher to Kidd before quoted. Connecticut continued to be a thorn in the Earl's side. Harping on his old grievance in the course of a long communication concerning his numerous troubles, written to the Lords of Trade on November 28, 1700, Bellomont says:

There is a town called Stamford in Connecticut Coloney, on the border of this Province where one Major (Jonathan) Sellick lives, who has a warehouse close to the sound or sea, that runs between the mainland and Nassau Island. That man does great mischief with his warehouse for he receives abundance of goods from our vessels, and the merchants afterwards take their opportunity of running them into this town. Major Sellick received at least 10,000 worth of treasure and East India goods brought by one Clarke of this town from Kidd's sloop and lodged with Sellick. I can have no account of them: Clarke was a prisoner here on that account and gave security that he would make an emple discovery upon oath how all that treasure and goods were disposed of, but I have not seen him and whenever he appears he is so profligate that he will not value what he swears.

A letter from Bellomont, which he sought to send him by one Samuel Burgess, a New York Venturer to Madagascar, but which was taken and sent to London by Captain Lowth of the *Loyal Merchant*, now turned up to make trouble for him. He sought to explain it in a letter to Vernon, dated December 6, 1700. It leaves him in a rather shady light . . .

As to Kidd's pretence of urging to his owners the necessity of allowing the seamen pay, I can safely take my oath there was no such thing, but so far the contrary, as that as often as I saw him he told me he knew the pyrats haunts so well, that he could sail directly to 'em; but his articles with me which I sent you will shew his mind in that matter; for when we don't hear a man treat of a bargain, his hand and seal is the best evidence of his assent and consent to a bargain. As to my letter I writ to Kidd by Burgess, and which Captain's Lowth intercepted, I own I writ to him to come to New Yorke, and if it be rightly considered ,I did therein what became me. Upon my first coming hither I had reason to suspect he was turned rogue or pyrat, for contrary to his articles, with me he came hither to N. Yorke and here staid about 3 months, and Mr. Livingston whom I found here before me told me he had reason to suspect he would turn pyrate. Two of his reasons were, a bargain whispered about, that Fletcher had covenanted with Kidd to receive £10,000 if he made a good voyage; the other was the dissolute life Kidd had lived during the 3 months he staid here. But when I writ that letter to Kidd by Burgess, I had an account he was certainly turned pyrate, and then I could not be blamed to have a just in-

dignation against him, and to try by all means to get him
into my hands, and tis plain menacing him had not been the
way to invite him hither, but rather wheedling, and that way
I took, and after that manner got him at last into Boston
when I secured him: And a copy of that letter I then writ to
him, I sent you the first news of my seizing him. If I was
faulty in the letter I writ by Burgesse, I was no less so in that
I writ by Mr. Campbell what brought in Kidd to Boston.

Meanwhile the London authorities had heard from
Peter Smith in Nevis, of Kidd's presence in the West
Indies, and of his trading transactions with Boulton and
Bourke. Coming in the wake of the East India tidings
the news made a tremendous stir. The opposition in Parliament seized upon the incident to make a fierce on-
slaught on the Government, whose leaders were in-
volved with Kidd. His return to England for a Parlia-
mentary inquiry was eagerly demanded. The fact that
he had surrendered to Bellomont was soon known, and
the long delay in bringing the prisoner to London was
construed as part of a plan to lose the luckless adventur-
er and suppress the scandal. An echo of the clamor is
found in Edmund Dummer's memorandum as follows:

This Kidd, about April or May last, returns to the West
Indies, and I think at Nevis makes his first appearance; sends
to the Governor for his honour of treating with him safely,
offers him presents, and prays his procuring him a small vessel for himself, designing to quit that he was in as too heavy
and unfit for his then circumstances, his voyage being now
ended. To this the Governor would give no countenance, so
he sailed hence towards New England (where) he was soon
after known to ar (rive): there he walked publicly about (for)
awhile. But, murmur arising, he (at) last surrenders himself,
and news thereof is sent home, and at the same time he had
made his partitions and consigned them? to his owners. The
Rochester man-of-war, upon this advice, is despatched to

bring him home. But that captain, pretending to meet with great storms on the coast, returns back to Plymouth to tell only what the defects of his ship are under magnified terms, and, although there is order to lay her up, yet the Commissioner there seems to be of opinion she may be refitted in a fortnight. But the reason is lost, and before another ship can go and come, all inquisition proper to this nefarious practice will be checked.

This is the connection of matter that hath diversely and upon good authority come to my knowledge.

The *Rochester*, indeed, never made the voyage, but in time the frigate *Advice* responded to Bellomont's wish that his "forty pirates" be taken off his hands. In exact fact there were 32 of them, including beside Kidd, some notables, viz: James Gillam, his passenger, Edward Davis, Joseph Bradish, whose jail-breaking has been noticed, Joseph Palmer, and Wetherly. Palmer was of good family and much influence was successfully exerted on his behalf.

During the long delay there was much correspondence between Bellomont and his associates, growing out of the clamor. In a letter to the Earl of Shrewsbury, dated March 5th, the governor observes:

I am heartily vexed to understand that some angry gentleman in the house of Commons put so hard a construction upon a well-intended undertaking, however unlucky it proved; and that your Grace's name should be brought on the stage with some other of your friends: and it seems the harder to me that such a clamour should be raised about Kidd when it was known I had secured him and his effects, and sent an exact inventory home to the Ministers. This man-of-war carries every scrip that belonged to Kidd and the rest of the Pirates; and nothing but the necessary charges taken out. I hope the East India goods and treasure that's sent will amount to 20,000£, which will reimburse everybody, if the

King will consent it shall be so, for I doubt Kidd will be proved a pirate, and then the King's grant will be necessary.

Bellomont also wrote Sir Edmund Harrison, another of his associates, by the same mail, enclosing a list of the culprits on the *Advice*, and referring him to Mr. Secretary Vernon for the inventory, he being too ill with gout to write further, but keen enough to tip off Harrison and the others to look out for their interests. To Lord Somers he wrote:

I hope everything will answer your Lordship's wishes with respect to Kidd's and the other pirates now sent home under care of Captain Wynne. . . The preserving of Kidd and the rest and hindering their escape out of prison is in great measure owing to the remarks I gave the Sheriff and keeper of the prison here, and the caresses and good words they had every day from me; therefore I hope you and the rest of the Lords concerned will not think me over-liberal. . . . Mr. Livingstone, when he was here was heartily troubled and ashamed at Kidd's villanous behaviour, and to reflect that he had been the means of engaging you and the rest of us to be concerned with that monster; which truly put me in charity with Mr. Livingstone, that he had no design to hurt us but was deceived as well as we. Kidd, I am fully satisfied, might have taken the *Mocha Frigate*, with a vast deal of wealth had he been honest, but Joseph Palmer's desposition will convince you he never attempted her, but just the contrary. If Palmer by what he has disclosed and shall discover towards the conviction of Kidd, when he comes into England, shall be thought servicable, I entreat you to intercede for the King's pardon for him. The man seemed on his examination to be an honest young man in his own nature and this is to be said for him, he went not voluntarily with Kidd but was pressed from on board the Duchess by Lord Orford's order, and forced on board of Kidd's ship. I am heartily sorry to understand my name was brought on the stage in the House of Commons, and that you and the Duke of Shrewsbury met with that hard fate too. I am told Jack How broke the first ground as they call it in opening trenches at a seige. I find all his poison is not in his breath; there's some, too, in his tongue. 'Tis a little hard that after I had taken care to secure Kidd and his effects and had sent home a faithful account of the latter, that should not atone for the misfortune of a design honestly intended though roguishly executed. The words in question are thunder and lightning, let off in colours as black and terrible as if it had been treason and rebellion to procure that grant of pirates goods. By a letter I saw from Mr. Clement last summer to a person of his acquaintance I guessed there was something brewing up against us on Kidd's account.

To Vernon Bellomont wrote:

I have sent home by Captain Wynne all the pirates I had here and that were in Connecticut. You will find in my letter to the Council a particular account of them and their effects. . . . If the King is pleased to give us that fitted out the *Adventure galley* all the effects seized with Kidd in consideration of the charges we were at, yet I desire you will take notice that there was some pounds of gold and all of the jewels now sent home that belonged to James Gillam, whom I now send home a prisoner, who was not of Kidd's company, and only came home with him from Madagascar as a passenger. I am very well satisfied all the Lords concerned with me may have their share of Gillam's gold and jewels as well as I, though I am told here I am entitled to a third part of them, as I am Vice-Admiral of these seas; but then I utterly disclaim Sir Edmund Harrison's and Mr. Livingstone's having any manner of share of them, for they were to be concerned only with what treasure Kidd should lawfully take. I make a question whether I be obliged in honour to do more than pay Sir Edmund Harrison the money he laid down for me with the full interest thereof, in case the King gave us the full benefit of Kidd's effects, but for that matter I shall do as the Duke of Shrewsbury shall do by Sir Edmund; the Duke and I being on the same foot with him, excepting that Sir Edmund laid down my full proportion of the money for the outset of the galley, and but half of the Duke's; but I have reason to grudge Sir Edmund any further advantage than what is jsut because he used me not well in our bargain; for at first we had agreed upon much more reasonable terms for me than afterwards he would stand to, when he had made me depend on him for advancing the money, and saw that I could not easily raise it, he gave me a Presbyterian gripe, and fettered me in the writings between us.

I have desired Sir John Stanley to wait on you, and I depend upon your friendship and him in taking care of my interest I know not how much I am to be the better for these pirates and their effects; but I am sure they have cost me more trouble and torment than I ever met with in any business during my whole life. I have delivered myself fairly of them, and can safely say, and swear too, that I am not a brass farthing better for them, directly nor indirectly; but I am hitherto so much the worse, that I now find the want of that money I had out for taking them and know not which way to turn myself.

As the Lords of the Treasury leave me at liberty in the matter I have consigned the pirates goods and treasure to you as I know your respect for my Lord Chancellor and the Duke of Shrewsbury, and that you will take their consent in the disposition of these things. . . Sir Edmund Harrison has a mind that they should be consigned to him; but I do not think that proper; it would, for aught I know, draw a fresh clamour on our heads, that after I had the King's positive orders about sending over these effects, I should give his minister the go-by and direct them to a merchant. In directing them to a minister, I acquit myself with decency to the King and to the Lords of the Treasury, and to the satisfaction of the noble Lords concerned.

I am vexed at the attacks made against these noble Lords and me in the House of Commons, where I little expected a design so honestly meant would have been so grossly misconstrued; but God be thanked we have escaped the notice of a part of men that were so manifestly biased. 'Twas lucky, I find that I secured Kidd.

Joseph Palmer's last evidence now sent, is pretty strong against Kidd. He was one of Kidd's men and is now sent home a prisoner. His friends are said to be substantial people, and if he confesses all he knows at Kidd's trial, he may, I hope, deserve the King's pardon. In order to his making a confession, it were not amiss perhaps if you suffered his sister, Mrs. Byer, who goes over in the sloop, to solicit the King's pardon for him, to speak with you. She could easily persuade him to tell the whole truth, and a frown from you would make her endeavour it.

I now send home all the evidence we have against Kidd and the rest of the pirates, authenticated by a certificate under my hand and the seal of the province affixed to them. They are all sent to my Lord Jersey. The Council of Trade and you had all these evidences sent you before, except this new one of Joseph Palmer.

It will be noted that nowhere is found any concern over the honest folks who once owned the property taken by Kidd and Gillam. To pillage the pillagers was considered worthy, but any effort to find and reimburse owners was unsought of by any of the high gentry, including it would seem His Majesty the King. Just how they differed in their exact moral position from ths merchants who openly trafficked with the pirates for their stolen wares is hard at this distance to discern. Neither was there any squeamishness over hanging Kidd while they laid claim to his spoil.

"Fed up" as the moderns say with tales of the great richness amassed by Kidd, the excitement grew in England. He was pictured as the Prince of Pirates, whereas he was a wretched failure. His slow return added to the intensity of feeling, fanned by the enemies of Somers, Shrewsbury and Orford who were eager to besmirch them. It was flatly charged that no honest efforts to produce the "pirate" were under way. In the midst of the clamor the belated *Advice* arrived in late February, at Lundy's Isle, where it was delayed. A resolution was then introduced in Parliament calling for the removal of John Somers, Lord Chancellor, "from the King's presence and councils forever," which received the respectable support of 106 votes. The Government tried to explain that the delay was only normal on so long a voyage in winter weather, but the insistance that Kidd be produced before Parliament became so loud that a Royal yacht was despatched to Lundy's Isle to bring the Captain to London, where he and his fellows were lodged in Newgate.

From on board the *Advice* at the Downs, Kidd addressed a note to the Earl of Orford, of his noble associates, couched in the following terms and including a list of ninety-four names of members of his crew who deserted the *Adventure galley* and joined the piratical *Mocha frigate*:

1700, April 11. *Advice*, Downs. - - - The enclosed is copy of a protest drawn up at Boston in New England, the truth whereof those of my men that are prisoners with me are ready to attest upon oath; but it was not permitted to be done there. If your Lordship will be pleased to give yourself the trouble of reading it, you will find a plain and faithful narrative of my whole voyage in the *Adventure galley*, wherein there is nothing of moment omitted that was transacted in the said voyage. I know not what is generally thought of me, nor what is alleged against me, but I do assure your Lordship I have done nothing but what is punctually declared in the said protest, wherein if anything be accounted a crime, it was so far contrary to my sentiments that I should have thought myself wanting in my duty had I hot done tne same.

I am in hopes your Lordship and the rest of the honourable gentlemen, my owners, will so far vindicate me that I may have no injustice, and I fear not at all but upon an equitable and impartial trial my innocence will justify me to your Lordship and the world.

I doubt not but your Lordship is already informed of what effects were seized in the sloop *Antonio* in New England; but this I must needs declare in justice that there were several things of considerable value whereof they had given no account, so far as I can learn. Besides what was contained in the sloop, there is in the *Adventure* prize mentioned in the protest (as near as I can compute) to the value of ninety thousand pounds, which is left in very secure hands, and I doubt not when I am clear of this trouble but to bring the same for England without any diminution.

The enclosed list is the names of those men that left me at Madagascar and went on board the *Moca Frigate*.

In 1690 and 1691 I was in the King's service at the Leeward Islands, and lost a ship of my own of 18 guns, by the villainy of my men, who ran away with her whilst I was on shore. But before that misfortune I had performed so many good services that General Codrington, then Governor of those Islands, repaired my loss in some measure by giving me a ship named the *Antegoa*.

In 1695 I came to England with this ship, laden with merchandises from New York, and was prepared to return to New York in the same vessel. But one Robert Livingston, a merchant of Albany, within the province of New York, being then in England, and having insinuated into the Lord Bellomont, who was then nominated Governor of New England, that several persons were gone from New York to the Red Sea, who would bring back good plunder, and might be easily taken in their return home projected a design of fitting out a ship for the purpose, and obtaining a commission to seize those ships and any other prizes.

This project was received by the Lord Bellomont, and all matters were adjusted betwixt him and the rest of the owners; and I was without my knowledge pitched upon to be commander upon Livingston giving me the character of a bold and hardy man.

Then Livingston carried me to wait on my Lord Bellomont at his house in Dover Street, where both my Lord and Livingston urged me with many arguments to accept the command of this ship with the King's commission; which I refusing, the Lord Bellomont told me he was to be Governor of New York, as well as of New England, and would protect me from any charge or accusation to be brought against me; and that he had powerful friends in the Government, who would not let me suffer any damage or prejudice either in England, or elsewhere.

I, notwithstanding, pressed to be excused, and to pursue my voyage to New York; whereupon the Lord Bellomont added threats to his wheedles, and told me I should not carry my own ship out of the river of Thames, unless I would accept the command of the ship to be fitted out for this design with the King's commission. I, thinking myself safe with the King's commission, and the protection of so many great men, owners, and being apprehensive that the Lord Bellomont might oppress me at New York if I disobliged him here, was prevailed on to accept the commission and command of the ship, upon the terms contained in the articles, since published, which articles, as I was informed, were drawn by one of the principal owners, and writ fair by my Lord Bellomont, so cautious were they of having the design known abroad.

Then Livingston carried me to the houses of the Duke of Shrewsbury, the Lord Chancellor, Earl of Romney and Admiral Russell, for my satisfaction that those great men were concerned in the expedition, where he discoursed them, but would not suffer me to see or speak with any of them; and only assured me that their several proportions of money to purchase and fit out the ship were ready to be paid down.

Accordingly, in a short time after, Mr. Livingston collected their moneys, and paid them to me, and Mr. Harrison (now Sir Edmund Harrison) and Doctor Cox paid some money to me, which I believe was for my Lord Bellomont's share, which I now understand they bought of his Lordship.

The ship being bought, rigged, manned and named the *Adventure galley*, the Lord Bellomont encouraged me to proceed, by assuring me that the noble lords above mentioned should stifle all complaints that should be made in England, and he himself would prevent all clamours in those parts where he was Governor by condemning all the goods and treasure I should bring in, and disposing of them privately, and satisfying the owners for such part as should be due to them. The Lord Bellomont delivered private instructions to Livingston, which would either justify me or charge them with any miscarriages committed; but Livingston keeps them in his custody.

Before I went to sea I waited twice on my Lord Romney and Admiral Russell (now Lord Orford), who both hastened me to sea, and promised to stand by me in all my undertakings.

At the Buoy in the Nore Captain Steward, commander of the Duchess, took away all my ship's crew; but Admiral Russell, upon my application to him at Sittingbourne, caused my men to be restored to me.

In my way to New York I took a French prize, which I carried to New York, where she was condemned and sold; and with the proceeds of it I refitted the *Adventure galley*. I then sailed towards the East Indies, and there took two ships, and no more, both which had French passes from the Governors of the French factories there.

Upon the rumor of my being declared a pirate, I went for New England with intent to surrender myself, and carried a great part of the treasure and goods I took in those prizes. As soon as I arrived, I sent an account of my proceedings to my Lord Bellomont, who by a letter approved of what I had done, encouraged and invited me to come ashore, treated me very civilly for some days, and then seized me with my effects, commissions, instructions, accounts, French passes and his own letter that he had sent to me from Boston, all of which he promised to send over to England.

But now that I have notice of my trial, and have demanded all instructions and papers taken from me necessary

for my justification, the instructions, the French passes, my
Lord Bellomont's letter, and my accounts are detained from
me, without which it is impossible to make my defence, notwithstanding my commissions, and I must be sacrificed as a
pirate to salve the honour of some men who employed me,
and who, perhaps, if I had been one, and they could have
enjoyed the benefit of it, would not have impeached me upon
that account.

But the French passes will justify my proceedings, and for
me to plead to an indictment without having them to produce, will be to brand myself for a rogue and fool, and to
cast away my life for other men's faults and not my own.

I have no money to support myself, or to manage my
trial, the Lords of the Admiralty refusing to let me have any
of my effects for that purpose.

I do therefore most humbly pray that I may not be hurried
to trial till Livingston be brought under examination, and
the French passes and other papers taken from me be restored to me.

WILLIAM KIDD.

It was now the 6th of March, 1701, when Parliament
ordered the Admiralty to produce all the Kidd papers
the next day. This was done. A petition from Cogi Baba,
one of the owners of the *Quedagh Merchant*, was also
read, claiming a value for his ship of 40,000 rupees and
400,000 for its cargo. Kidd was examined but revealed
nothing of political value. Parliament therefore dropped
the case and left it to justice. Kidd's request that his
papers be sent him went unheeded.

It does not appear that the Captain knew his "French
passes" were in the budget; he seems to have believed
that Bellomont had held them back and his petition
being disregarded, he did his best to prove their exist-
ence by witnesses. Under the cruel conditions of English
law then prevailing he was not allowed counsel. The trial

of Kidd and nine seamen occupied but two days, May 8th and 9th. His fate was fixed in advance.

He was first convicted of killing William Moore, his mutinous quartermaster, though on evidence the verdict would have been no more than simple manslaughter had it occurred on land, and acquittal if at sea, where a captain's rights are considerable. The verdict against him for piracy followed even though there was no blood on his hands, and plainly he was a victim or a scapegoat. Worn out by the burden of the Kidd scandal and his efforts to manage "the unruly people" in his domain, the Earl of Bellomont died in New York on the 5th of May, 1701, of gout in the stomach, preceding his captain a week in the journey to the Unknown Shore.

Kidd, then in his 56th year, and Darby Mullins, alone of his company, with two unnamed wretches, were taken to Execution Dock on the 12th day of May to be there hanged by the neck until dead. Paul Lorrain, the Chaplain of Newgate, declares that Kidd was too confused by liquor to fully understand his ministerings when turned off on the gallows, but "fortunately" the rope broke dropping him to the ground, which so sobered him that he had a better inclination to hear the pious admonitions and show some signs of edification. The beam being unreliable, he was again hanged to a round in the ladder leading to the scaffold. Then the body was tied up in chains to rattle until the winds wasted all away,

From the aftermath it does not appear that Cogi Baba ever secured redress: A hint of what was "coming" to him is seen in this reference found in the Portland papers, excerpted from a letter by Richard Crawley to Erasmus Lewis:

1704, September 15th. A certain Cogi Baba and others, Armenians, pretend that the goods seized with Kidd belonged to them, and were piratically taken from the *Quedagh Merchant*. To prove his commissions were appointed to examine witnesses in Bengal, Surat, and Ispahen; several witnesses have been examined, to be heard the 23d instant.

One Corso, who also pretends that he was robbed by Kidd, appeared in court about six weeks or two months ago and presented his petition with some affidavits, but shortly after desired to have them again. Apparently he now does not now pretend to anything in point of law, but only to entitle himself to the Queen's bounty.

As to the fate of the *Quedagh Merchant*, Bellomont's expedition to retrieve her never set out. The Admiralty sent orders to Colonel Codington, Governor of the Leeward Islands to salvage ship and cargo, but the instructions came too late. Kidd left her in charge of Boulton when he slipped away in the *St. Antonio* to square matters with Bellomont, taking only such men as he needed and leaving the rest behind with the vessel. Bolton was to dispose of the baled goods on board, but while he was seeking a market during a five weeks absence, the crew stole everything portable and on Bolton's return, broke into open mutiny and out of the 18 left behind by Kidd, 15 levanted. Bolton had with him but one negro boy and was powerless against the ruffians. Kidd, not returning according to the hope held out when he departed, and learning that the Spanish of St. Domingo were sending a brigantine to seize the ship Bolton, abandoned her after a week's vain waiting for his principal, and made for Curacoa. The members of the crew also reached this port, where the Governor protected them dispite Bolton's urgings that they be seized and dealt with. He reported to the Admiralty that all his dealings produced but 380 pieces of eight, much less than his charges. The Spaniards finding cargo gone, and the *Quedagh Merchant* in bad repair, burned her as she lay in the river Higuey and so ended the great adventure. The wealth held out by Kidd as an inducement to let him go, if it existed, was never found, so there is still warrant for digging somewhere in the world!

Kidd's property in New York, amounting to six thousand, four hundred and seventy pounds and one shilling sterling, was confiscated and used later to found Greenwich Hospital for the seamen of England. There stood until a few years ago in the city a house that knew his presence, No. 126 William Street, where he resided for a few months, while his home in Hanover Square was undergoing repairs.

Mrs. Sarah Kidd had been twice a widow when she wedded the Captain. Her first husband was William Cox, a well-to-do merchant, at whose death she received considerable property, including a house on the present site of 86 Wall Street. Her second venture was John Cort. The Captain followed in third order. After his execution she married Christopher Rousby. The children mentioned in the narrative appear to have been from her earlier marriage.

Boulton, or Bolton, was a Worcestershire man who, in 1697, was appointed Collector of Customs at Antigua. Resigning a year later he became a trader among the Islands, with a sloop named the *St. Antonio*. Becalmed off the Isle of Mona in April 1699, he fell in with the returning Kidd and undertook the trip to Curacoa to market the muslins from the cargo of the *Quedagh Merchant*. Rejoining Kidd, they piloted the latter's vessel into the

river Higuey in Hispaniola, where she was secured a-
cross the stream to rocks and stumps on the shore.
Kidd then bought the *St. Antonio* and proceeded, with
the most portable and precious part of his possessions
as noted, to New England.

The TRYAL *of* CAPTAIN KIDD

The TRYAL *of*

CAPTAIN WILLIAM KIDD

for MURTHER *and* PIRACY

Upon Six Several *Indictments*

The TRYAL *of Captain* WILLIAM KIDD, *for*
Murther and Piracy, upon Six feveral Indictments.
Published by AUTHORITY.

As alfo, The TRYAL'S *of* Nicholas Churchill, James Howe,
Robert Lamley, William Jenkins, Gabriel Loff, Hugh Parrot, Richard Barlicorn, Abel Owens, *and* Darby Mullins,
at the fame Time and Place for PYRACY.

At the Admiralty Sessions held at the Old-Baily, London, *on,*
the 8th, *and* 9th *of* May, 1701.

THE *King's Commiffion for holding the Court being firft reade*
the Court proceeded to call the Gentlemen fummoned upon th-
Grand Jury, and the Perfons sworn were thefe Seventeen fol
lowing, VIZ.

William Broughton,	*Benjamin Travis,*
Thomas Hanwell,	*Stephen Thompfon*
Daniel Borwell,	*Thomas Cooper,*
Humphrey Bellamy,	*Robert Gower*
Nath. Rolfton, Senior,	*Thomas Sesson,*
Joshua Bolton,	*William Goodwin,*
Benjamin Pike,	*Robert Callow,*
Jofeph Marlow,	*Thomas Haws.*

Cl. of Arr. Gentlemen of the Grand Jury, stand together,
and hear the Charge.

THE *King's Majefty commands all Juftices of the High Court of*
Admiralty, that have any Authority to take any Inquifitions,
Recognizances, Examinations, or Informations of Offences
committed within the Jurifdiction of the Admiralty of Eng-
land, to deliver the Records of the fame into this Court, &c.
And all others are commanded to keep Silence upon Pain
of Imprifonment.

THEN Dr. Oxenden *gave the Charge to the Grand Jury, ex-*
plaining the Nature of the Commiffion, and the Crimes in-
quirable by vertue of it by the Grand Jury.

THEN *the Grand Jury withdrew, and after some time returned into Court, and found the Bill of Indictment against Captain* Kidd *for Murther, and another against him and* Nicholas Churchill, James Howe, Robert Lamley, William Jenkins, Gabriel Loff, Hugh Parrot, Richard Barlicorn, Abels Owen, Darby Mullins, *for Piracy. Then Proclamation (as usual) being made, the forefaid Prifoners were brought to the Bar, and Arraigned.*

Cl. of Arr. William Kidd, hold up thy Hand.

Kidd. May it please your Lordfhips, I defire you to permit me to have Council.

Mr. *Recorder.* What would you have Council for?

Kidd. My Lord, I have fome Matter of Law relating to the Indictment, and I defire I may have Council to fpeak to it.

Dr. *Oxenden.* What Matter of Law can you have?

Cl. of Arr. How does he know what it is he is charged with? I have not told him.

Mr. *Recorder.* You muft let the Court know what thofe Matters of Law are, before you can have Coucnil affigned you.

Kidd. They be Matters of Law, my Lord.

Mr. *Recorder.* Mr. *Kidd*, do you know what you mean by Matters of Law?

Kidd. I know what I mean, I defire to put off my Tryarl as long as I can, till I can get my Evidence ready.

Mr. *Recorder.* Mr. *Kidd*, You had beft mention the Matter of Law you would infift on.

Dr. *Oxenden.* It cannot be Matter of Law to put off you Tryal, but Matter of Fact.

Kidd, I defire your Lordfhip's Favour, I defire Dr. Oldifh and Mr. *Lemmon* may be heard as to my Cafe.

Cl. of Arr. What can we have Council for before he has pleaded?

Mr. *Recorder.* Mr. *Kidd*, The Court tells you, you fhall be heard what you have to fay when you have pleaded to your Indictment. If you plead to it, if you will, you may affign

Matter of Law, if you have any; but then you must let the Court know what you would infift on.

Kidd. I beg your Lordfhip's Patience till I can procure my Papers, I had a Couple of *French* Paffef, which I muft make ufe of in order to my Juftification.

Mr. *Recorder.* That is not Matter of Law. You have had long Notice of your Tryal, and might have prepared for it. How long have you had Notice of your Tryal?

Kidd. A matter of a Fortnight.

Dr. *Oxenden.* Can you tell the Names of any Perfons that you would make ufe of in your Defence?

Kidd. I fent for them, but I could not have them.

Dr. *Oxenden.* Where were they then?

Kidd. I brought them to my Lord *Bellamont* in *New-England.*

Mr. *Recorder.* What were their Names? You cannot tell without Book. Mr. *Kidd*, therefore you muft plead.

Cl. of Arr. W. Kidd, hold up thy Hand.

Kidd. I beg your Lordfhips I may have Council admitted, and that my Tryal may be put off, I am not really prepared for it.

Mr. *Recorder.* Nor never will if you could help it.

Dr. *Oxenden.* Mr. *Kidd*, You have had reafonable Notice, and you knew you muft be tried, and therefore you cannot plead you are not ready.

Kidd. If your Lordfhip permit thofe Papers to be read, they will juftifie me. I defire my Council may be heard.

Mr. *Coniers.* We admit of no Council for him.

Mr. *Recorder.* There is no Iffue joined, and therefore there can be no Council affigned. Mr. *Kidd*, you muft plead.

Kidd. I cannot plead till I have thofe Papers that I infifted upon.

Mr. *Lemmon.* He ought to have his Papers delivered to him, becaufe they are very material for his Defence. He has endeavoured to have them, but could not get them.

Mr. *Coniers.* You are not to appear for any one till he pleads, and that the Court affigns you for his Council.

Mr. *Recorder.* They would only put off the Tryal.

Mr. *Coniers.* He muſt plead to the Indictment.

Cl. of Arr. Make Silence.

Kidd. My Papers were all ſeized, and I cannot make my Defence without them. I deſire my Tryal may be put off till I can have them.

Mr. *Recorder.* The Court is of Opinion, they ought not to ſtay for all your Evidence, it may be never come. You muſt plead, and then if you can ſatisfie the Court, that there is Reaſon to put off your Tryal, you may.

Kidd. My Lord, I have Buſineſs in Law, and I deſire Council.

Mr. *Recorder.* Mr. *Kidd,* The Courſe of Courts is, when you have pleaded, the Matter of Tryal is next; if you can then ſhoe there is Cauſe to put off the Tryal, you may; but now the Matter is to plead.

Kidd. It is a hard Caſe, when all theſe Things ſhall be Kept from me, and I be forced to plead.

Mr. *Recorder.* If he will not plead there muſt be judgment.

Kidd. My Lord, would you have me plead, and not have my Vindication by me?

Cl. of Arr. Will you plead to the Indictment?

Kidd. I would beg that I have my Papers for my Vindication.

Cl. of Arr. Nicholas Churchill, hold up thy Hand.

Churchill. My Lord, I deſire I may have the Benefit of the Proclamation, I came in upon the King's Proclamation.

Mr. *Recorder.* If you do not plead, the Court muſt paſs Judgment upon you. You can have no Benefit in what you ſay, till you have pleaded. If you were Indicted for Felony, and you will not plead, the Law takes it in Nature of a Confeſion, and Judgment muſt paſs, as if you were proved guilty.

Cl. of Arr. Nich. Churchill, hold up thy Hand. *James How,* hold up thy Hand. *Robert Lamley,* hold up thy Hand. (which they did).

Mr. *Recorder. W. Kidd* had not held up his Hand.

Cl. of Arr. He does hold up his Hand. *William Jenkins,* hold up thy Hand. *Gabriel Loff,* hold up thy Hand. *Hugh*

Parrot, hold up thy Hand. *Richard Barlicorn*. hold up thy Hand. *Abel Owens*, hold up thy Hand.

Owens. I came in upon the King's Proclamation, and entered my felf into the King's Service.

Mr. *Recorder*. You muft plead firft, and then, if there be Occafion, you will have the Benefit of it. (*Then he held up his Hand*).

Cl. of Arr. Darby Mullins, hold up thy Hand.

Mullins. May it pleafe your Lordfhips, I came in voluntarily on the King's Proclamation.

Mr. *Recorder*. This is the fame Cafe with Owens, you muft fpeak to that afterwards.

Cl. of Arr. W. Kidd, You ftand Indicted by the Name of *William Kidd*, &c. Art thou guilty, or not guilty?

Kidd. I cannot plead to this Indictment, till my *French* Paffes are delivered to me.

Cl. of Arr. Are you guilty, or not guilty?

Kidd. My Lord, I infift upon my *French* Papers, pray le me have them.

Mr. *Recorder*. That muft not be now, till you have put your felf on your Trial.

Kidd. That muft juftifie me.

Mr. *Recorder*. You may plead it then, if the Court fee Caufe.

Kidd. My Juftification depends on them.

Mr. *Recorder*. Mr. *Kidd*, I must tell you, if you will not plead, you muft have Judgment againft you, as ftanding mute.

Kidd. I cannot plead till I have thefe Papers, and I have not my Witneffes here.

Mr. *Recorder*. You do not know your own Intereft; if you will not plead, you muft have Judgment againft you.

Kidd. If I plead, I fhall be acceffary to my own Death, till I have Perfons to plead for me.

Mr. *Recorder*. You are acceffary to your own Death, if you do not plead. We cannot enter into the Evidence, unlefs you plead.

Cl. of Arr. Are you guilty, or not guilty?

Mr. *Recorder*. He does not underſtand the Law, you muſt read the Statue to him.

Cl. of Arr. Mr. *Kidd*, are you guilty of this Piracy, or not guilty?

Kidd. If you will give me a little Time to find my Papers, I will plead.

Cl. of Arr. There is no Reaſon to give you Time; will you plead or not?

Mr. *Coniers*. Be pleaſed to acquaint him with the Danger he ſtands in by not pleading. What ever he ſays, nothing can avail him till he pleads.

Mr *Recorder*. He has been told ſo, but he does not believe us.

Mr. *Coniers*. If there be any Reaſon to put off his Tryal, it muſt be made appear after Iſſue is joined.

Mr. *Recorder*. If you ſay guilty, there is an End of it; but if you ſay, not guilty, the Court can examine into the Fact.

Officer. He ſays he will plead.

Cl. of Arr. W. *Kidd*, art thou guilty, or not guilty?

Kidd. Not guilty.

Cl. of Arr. How wilt thou be tried?

Kidd. By God and my Country.

Cl. of Arr. God ſend thee a good Deliverance. (And ſo of all the reſt).

Kidd. My Lord, I beg I may have my Tryal put off for Three or Four Days, till I have got my Papers.

Mr. *Recorder*. The Judges will be here by and by, and you may move the Court then; we are only to prepare for your Tryal. We do not deny your Motion; but when the Court is full, they will conſider of the Reaſons you have to offer.

Then William Kidd *was tried upon the Indictment for Murther.*

Cl. of Arr. W. *Kidd*, Hold up thy Hand, Thou ſtandeſt Indicted by the Name of *William Kidd*, late of *London*, Mariner, &c.

The Firſt Indictment for MURTHER.

THE *Jurors of our Sovereign Lord the King, do, upon their Oath, preſent, That* William Kidd, *late of* London, *Mariner*, *not having the Fear of God before his Eyes, but being moved and feduced by the Infligation of the Devil, the 30th Day of* October, *in the Ninth Year of the Reign of our Sovereign Lord,* William *the Third, by the Grace of God, of* England, Scotland, France, *and* Ireland, *King, Defender of the Faith,* &c *by Force and Arms,* &c. *upon the High-Sea, near the Coaft of* Malabar, *in the* Eaft-Indies, *and within the Jurifdiction of the Admiralty of* England, *in a certain Ship called the* Adventure-Galley, *(whereof the faid* William Kidd, *then was Commander;) then and there being, felonioufly, voluntarily, and of his Malice afore-thought then and there did make an affault, in and upon one* William Moore, *in the Peace of God, and of our faid Sovereign Lord the King, to wit, then and there being, and to the Ship aforefaid, call'd the* Adventure-Galley, *then and there belonging; and that the aforefaid* William Kidd, *with a certain Wooden Bucket, bound with Iron Hoops, of the Value of Eight Pence, which he the faid* William Kidd, *then and there had and held in his right Hand, did violently felonioufly, voluntarily, and of his Malice afore-thought, beat and ftrike the aforefaid* William Moore, *in and upon the right Part of the Head of him the faid* William Moore, *a little above the right Ear of the faid* William Moore, *then and there upon the High-Sea, in the Ship afore-faid, and within the Jurifdiction of the Admiralty of* England *aforefaid, giving to the faid* William Moore, *then and there with the Bucket aforefaid, in and upon the aforefaid right Part of the Head of him the faid* William Moore, *a little above the right Ear of the faid* William Moore, *one mortal Bruife, of which mortal Bruife the aforefaid* William Moore, *from the faid 30th Day of* October, *in the Ninth Year aforefaid, until the One and Thirtieth Day of the faid Month of* October, *in the Year afore-faid, upon the High-Sea aforefaid, in the Ship aforefaid, and within the Jurifdiction of the Admiralty of* England *aforefaid, did langifh, and languifhing did live; upon which One and Thirtieth Day of* October, *in the Ninth year aforefaid, the afore-faid* William Moore *upon the High-Sea aforefaid, near the a-forefaid Coaft of* Malabar, *in the* East-Indies *aforefaid, in the Ship aforefaid, called the* Adventure-Galley, *and within the Jurifdiction of the Admiralty of* England *aforefaid, did die;*

and so the Jurors aforesaid, upon their Oath aforesaid, do say, That the aforesaid William Kidd, *feloniously, voluntarily, and of his Malice afore-thought, did kill and murther the aforesaid* William Moore, *upon the High-Sea aforesaid, and within the Jurisdiction of the Admiralty of* England *aforesaid, in manner and form aforesaid, against the Peace of our said Sovereign Lord the King, his Crown and Dignity,* &c.

How say'st thou, William Kidd, art thou guilty of this Murther, whereof thou standest Indicted, or not guilty?

Kidd. Not guilty.

Cl. of Arr. How wilt thou be tried?

Kidd. By God and my Country.

Cl. of Arr. God send thee a good Deliverance. *Nicholas Churchill, James Howe, Robert Lamley, William Jenkins, Gabriel Loff, Hugh Parrot, Richard Barlicorn, Abel Owens, Darby Mullins,* hold up your Hands. You the Prisoners at the Bar, those Men that you shall hear called, and personally appear, are to pass between our Sovereign Lord the King, and you, upon Tryal of your several Lives and Deaths: If therefore you, or any of you, will challenge them, or any of them; your time is to speak to them as they come to the Book to be sworn and before they be sworn.

Kidd. My Lord, I desire Council may be assigned me.

Mr. *Recorder.* Capt. *Kidd,* I told you it would be your time, when the Jury was called, to offer what you had to offer; therefore if you have any Thing now to say to the Court, you had best say it.

Kidd. I beg I may have Council, Dr. Oldish, and Mr. *Lemmon,* that they may be heard on my behalf.

Mr. *J. Powel.* If he desires it, you may be Council for him, provided there may be any Matter of Law that he has to plead; otherwise he must be tried.

Dr. *Oldish.* My Lord, he moves that his Tryal for Piracy may be put off for several Reasons; one is, there is one *Davis,* that is a necessary Witness for him; he was taken a Passenger into the Ship, and therefore could not be concerned in any Piracy; Now this *Davis* stands Indicted, so that he is deprived of this Perſon, who is a neceſſary Witneſs for him in this Caſe.

Mr. *Coniers*. He is not Indicted yet, he may call him if he thinks fit.

Mr. *J. Powel*. If he be Indicted, yet he may be a Witneſs.

Dr. *Oldiſh*. My Lord, we deſire he may be here.

Mr. *J. Powel*. Where is he?

Cl. of Arr. He is in Newgate.

Mr. *J. Powel*. Let him be ſent for.

Dr. *Oldiſh*. My Lord, it is very fit his Tryal ſhould be delayed for ſome time, becauſe he wants ſome Papers, very neceſſary for his Defence. It's very true, he is charged with Piracies in ſeveral Ships; but they had *French* Paſſes when the ſeizure was made. Now if there were *French* Paſſes, it was a lawful Seizure.

Mr. *J. Powel*. Have you thoſe Paſſes?

Kidd. They were taken from me by my Lord *Bellamont*, and theſe Paſſes would be my Defence.

Dr. *Oxenden*. Had you any other Paſſes when you took the *Armenian* Ship?

Dr. *Oldiſh*. If thoſe Ships that he took had *French* Paſſes, there was juſt Cauſe of Seizure, and it will excuſe him from Piracy.

Kidd. The Paſſes were ſeized by my Lord *Bellamont*, that we will prove as clear as the Day.

Mr. *Lemmon*. My Lord, I deſire one Word as to this Circumſtance; he was doing his King and Country Service, inſtead of being a Pirate: For in this very Ship there was a *French* Paſs, and it was ſhown to Mr. *Davis*, and carried to my Lord *Bellamont*. and he made a Seizure of it. And there was a Letter writ to teſtifie it, which was produced before the Parliament; and that Letter has been tranſmitted from Hand to Hand, ſo that we cannot at preſent come by it. There are ſeveral other Papers and Letters that we cannot get; and therefore we deſire the Tryal may be put off till we can procure them.

L. C. B. *Ward*. Where are they?

Mr. *Lemmon.* We cannot yet tell whether they are in the Admiralty Office, or whether Mr. *Jodrell* hath them.

Mr. *J. Powel.* Let us fee on what you go. You talk of *French* Paſſes, you ſhould have been prepared to make Affidavit of it? What Ship was that which had the *French* Paſſes?

Mr. *Lemmon.* The ſame we were in, the ſame he is Indicted for.

Mr. *J. Powel.* Make out this, Mr. *Lemmon.*

Mr. *Lemmon.* My Lord, we deſire Mr. *Davis* may be ſent for, he will prove it.

L. C. B. *Ward.* Send for *Edward Davis.*

Mr. *Fell.* My Lord, will you have him brought into Court?

L. C. B. *Ward.* Yes.

Mr. *Soll. Gen.* They have had a Fortnight's Notice to prepare for the Tryal.

Dr. *Oldiſh.* We petitioned for Money, and the Court ordered fifty Pounds; But the Perſon that received it went away, and we had none till laſt Night.

Mr. *Oxenden.* I ordered that the Money might be paid into his own Hands, that he might be ſure to have it.

Mr. *Crawley.* Regiſter, declar'd, That he paid the fifty Pound into his own Hands on *Tueſday* Morning.

L. C. B. *Ward.* You ought to make it out, that there is a reaſonable Cauſe to put off the Tryal, or elſe it cannot be allowed.

Mr. *Lemmon.* My Lord, we will be ready tomorrow Morning.

L. C. B. *Ward.* They ought to have had due Notice, What Notice have they had?

Mr. *Soll. Gen.* A Fortnight's Notice, this Day Fortnight.

Dr. *Oldiſh.* My Lord, he ſhould have had his Money delivered to him.

Kidd. I had no Money nor Friends to prepare for my Tryal till laſt Night.

L. C. B. *Ward.* Why did you not ſignifie ſo much to the King's Officers?

Mr. *Soll. Gen.* My Lord, this we will do, let *Davis* be

brought into Court; and if that be a juft Excufe, we are contented. In the mean Time, let him be tryed for the Murther,
wherein there is no pretence of want of Witnefsef or Papers.

Officer. Davis is here, my Lord.

Cl. of Arr. Set all afide but Captain *Kidd. William Kidd,*
You are now to be tried on the Bill of Murther, the Jury is
going to be fworn; if you have any Caufe of Exception, you
may fpeak to them as they come to the Book.

Will. Kidd. I fhall challenge none, I know nothing to the
contrary but they are honeft Men.

The JURY Sworn, were

Nathaniel Long,	*Henry Sherbrook,*
Jo. Ewers,	*Henry Dry,*
Jo. Child,	*Richard Greenaway,*
Ed. Reeves,	*Jo. Sherbrook,*
Tho. Clark,	*Tho. Emms,*
Nath. Green,	*Rog. Mott.*

After Proclamation made, (as ufual) the Court proceeded
to the Tryal, as follows:

Cl. of Arr. W. Kidd, hold up thy Hand, (*which he did*)
You Gentlemen of the Jury, look upon the Prifoner, and
hearken to his Caufe. He ftands Indicted by the Name of
William Kidd, &c. as before in the Indictment. Upon this In-
dictment he has been arraigned, and thereunto has pleaded,
Not Guilty, and for his Tryal has put himfelf on God and his
Country, which Country you are. Your Charge is to enquire,
Whether he be guilty of the Murther whereof he ftands In-
dicted, in Manner and Form as he ftands Indicted, or Not
Guilty, &c.

Mr. *Knap.* My Lord, and you Gentlemen of the Jury. This
is an Indictment of Murther. The Indictment fets forth, That
William Kidd, *on the 30th of* October, *on the high Sea, on the
Coaft of* Malabar, *did affault one* William Moore, *on Board a
Ship called the* Adventure, *whereof* William Kidd *was Captain,
ftruck him with a wooden Bucket, hooped with Iron, on the Side
of the Head, near the right Ear, and that of this Bruife he died
the next Day, and fo that he has murdered the faid Perfon.* To

this Indictment he has pleaded not guilty; if we prove him Guilty you muſt find him ſo.

Mr. *Soll. Gen.* My Lord, and Gentlemen of the Jury, We will prove this as particularly as can be, that *William Kidd* was Captain of the Ship, and that *William Moore* was under him in the Ship, and that without any Provocation he gave him this Blow, whereof he died.

Mr. *Coniers.* My Lord, It will appear to be a moſt barbarous Fact, to murther a Man in this Manner; for the Man gave him no Manner of Provocation. This *William Moore* was a Gunner in the Ship, and this *William Kidd* abuſes him, and calls him *Louſie Dog;* and upon a civil Anſwer he takes this Bucket, and knocks him on the Head, whereof he died the next Day. Call *Joſeph Palmer,* and *Robert Bradinham,* (who *appeared and were Sworn.*) *Joſeph Palmer,* give my Lord and the Jury an Account of what you ſaw done by *William Kidd,* on the Coaſt of *Malabar,* as to *William Moore* his Gunner.

Joſeph Palmer. About a Fortnight before this Accident fell out, Captain *Kidd* met with a Ship on that Coast, that was called the *Loyal Captain.* And about a Fortnight after this, the Gunner was grinding a Chiſſel aboard the *Adventure,* on the high Sea, near the Coaſt of *Malabar,* in the Eaſt-Indies.

Mr. *Coniers.* What was the Gunner's Name?

Joſeph Palmer. William Moore: And Captain Kidd came and walked on the Deck, and walks by this *Moore;* and when he came to him, ſays, *Which way could you have put me in a way to take this Ship, and been clear;* Sir, ſays *William Moore, I never ſpoke ſuch a Word, nor ever thought ſuch a Thing.* Upon which Captain *Kidd* called him a *Louſie Dog.* And ſays *William Moore, If I am a Louſie Dog, you have made me ſo; you have brought me to Ruin, and many more.* Upon his ſaying this, ſays Captain *Kidd, Have I ruin'd you, you Dog?* and took a Bucket bound with Iron Hoops, and ſtruck him on the right Side of the Head, of which he died the next Day.

Mr. *Cowper.* What was the Gunner doing at that time, when he gave him that Blow?

Joſeph Palmer. He was grinding a Chiſſel at the Time that he ſtruck him.

Mr. *Cowper.* Did he give him the Blow immediately after he gave him that Anſwer?

Joſeph Palmer. He walked two or three Times backward and forward upon the Deck, before he ſtruck the Blow.

Mr. *J. Turton.* What did Captain *Kidd* ſay firſt?

Joſeph Palmer. Which way could you have put me in a way of taking this Ship, and been clear; Says the Gunner, *I never ſaid ſo, nor thought any ſuch Thing.*

Mr. *Cowper.* Hark you, Friend, explain that Matter.

Mr. Baron *Hatſell.* What was the Occaſion of thoſe Words?

Palmer. It was concerning this Ship.

L. C. B. *Ward.* What Ship was it? Name the Ship.

Palmer. It was the *Loyal Captain.* Captain *Kidd* ſaid to *William Moore, Which way could you have put me in the way to have taken this Ship, and been clear?* Says *William Moore, I never ſaid ſuch a Thing, nor thought it.* And upon that he called him *Louſie Dog.*

L. C. B. *Ward.* Was that Ship taken?

Palmer. No, ſhe was gone.

Mr. *Coniers.* You ſay he call'd him Louſie Dog.

Palmer. Yes.

Mr. *Coniers.* What did *William Moore* ſay to him them?

Palmer. He ſaid, *If I am a Louſie Dog, you have brought me to it; you have ruined me and many more.* Upon this, *ſays Captain* Kidd, *Have I brought you to ruin, you Dog?* Repeating it two or three times over and took a turn or two upon the Deck, and then takes up the Bucket, and ſtrikes him on the Head.

Mr. *Cowper.* You ſay he made a turn or two on the Deck, and then ſtruck him.

Palmer. Yes.

Mr. *Coniers.* Tell my Lord what paſs'd next after the Blow.

Palmer. He was let down the Gun-Room, and the Gunner ſaid, *Farewel, farewel, Captain* Kidd *has given me my laſt.* And Captain *Kidd* ſtood on the Deck, and ſaid, *You are a Villain.*

Mr. *Cowper.* How near was Captain *Kidd* to him when he ſaid he had given him his laſt?

Palmer. He was near him.

Mr. *Cowper.* Was he within hearing of what *Moore* said?

Palmer. Yes, he was within Seven or Eight Foot.

Mr. *Soll. Gen.* Did you apprehend that he died of that Blow?

Palmer. He was in perfect health before that.

Mr. *Soll. Gen.* What did the Surgeon think of it?

Palmer. The Surgeon is here.

Mr. *Soll. Gen.* Did you fee him afterwards?

Palmer. No, I did not fee him after till he was dead.

Mr. *Cowper.* How did the Wound appear when you faw him?

Palmer. After he was dead, the Surgeon was called to open his Head, and Captain *Kidd* faid, *You are damn'd busy without Orders.*

Mr. *Cowper.* Though we ask you Questions, you muft turn your Face there towards the Jury. Give the Jury an Account of what you faw.

Palmer. I felt on his Head, and I felt fomething give way, and about the Wound, there was a Bruife.

Mr. *Cowper.* You fay you faw him after he was carried off after the Blow, how did his Head appear then? Was he bloody.

Palmer. There was not much Blood came from him.

L. C. B. *Ward.* Was you by when thefe words were fpoken?

Palmer. Yes, my Lord.

L. C. B. *Ward.* Did you fee the Prifoner give the Blow with the Bucket upon thofe Words?

Palmer. Yes, my Lord.

L. C. B. *Ward.* How long was it before he went down the Deck?

Palmer. Presently.

L. C. B. *Ward.* Did he complain of the Wound?

Palmer. He faid. *Farewel, farewel, Captain* Kidd *has given me my laft.*

L. C. B. *Ward.* Was this *Moore* in a good Condition of Health before this Blow was given him?

Palmer. Yes, my Lord.

L. C. B. *Ward.* And afterwards he complained.

Palmer. Yes, my Lord.

L. C. B. *Ward.* When he was dead, what Marks were on his Head?

Palmer. On the right fide of his Head, on this Place (pointing to his own Head) it was bruifed a considerable Breadth; and in one Place I could feel the Skull give way.

Mr. *Cowper.* How long after the Blow did he die?

Palmer. The next day following.

Mr. *Cowper.* And you fay you faw him dead then.

Palmer. Yes, Sir.

L. C. B. *Ward.* Captain Kidd, if you will ask him any Queftions, you may.

Kidd. My Lord, I would ask this Man what this Moore was doing when this Thing happened.

L. C. B. *Ward.* Mr. *Palmer*, you hear what he fays; what was *Moore* doing?

Palmer. He was grinding a Chiffel.

Kidd. What was the Occafion that I ftruck him?

Palmer. The words that I told you before.

Kidd. Was there no other Ship?

Palmer. Yes.

Kidd. What was that Ship?

Palmer. A *Dutch* Ship.

Kidd. What were you doing with the Ship?

Palmer. She was becalmed.

Kidd. This Ship was a League from us, and fome of the Men would have taken her, and I would not confent to it, and this *Moore* faid I always hindred them making their Fortunes; was not that the Reafon I ftruck him? Was there not a Mutiny on Board.

Palmer. No. you chaced this *Dutchman*, and in the way took a *Malabar* Boat, and chaced this Ship all the whole Night; and they fhowed their Colours, and you put up your Colours.

Kidd. This is nothing to the Point, was there no Mutiny aboard?

Palmer. There was no Mutiny, all was quiet.

Kidd. Was there not a Mutiny, becaufe they would go and take that *Dutchman?*

Palmer. No, none at all.

Mr. *Coniers.* Call Robert *Bradinham.*

Jury. What was the Caufe that he ftruck him?

Palmer. A Fortnight before this was done, we met with this *Loyal Captain,* of which Captain *Hoar* was Commander, and he came on Board Captain *Kidd's* Ship, and Captain *Kidd* went on Board his, and then Captain *Kidd* let this Ship go. About a Fortnight after this, the Gunner was grinding his Chiffel on the Deck; and Captain *Kidd* faid to him *Which way could you have put me in a way to take this Ship, and been clear?* To which he reply'd, *I never faid fuch a Thing, nor thought of fuch a Thing.* Whereupon Captain *Kidd* called the Gunner *Loufie Dog.* And fays *Moore, if I am a Loufie Dog, you have made me fo; you have brought me to ruin, and a great many more.* And fays Captain *Kidd, Have I brought you to Ruin, you Dog?* and after ftruck him with the Bucket. Thefe were all the Words that paft.

Mr. *J. Powel.* Was Captain *Kidd* aboard that Ship?

Palmer. Yes, and Captain *Hoar* was aboard him.

Mr. *J. Powel.* Was there any Body nigh at that Time?

Palmer. Yes, there were eight or nine Men, that had Muskets and other Arms, and they were for taking the Ship, and Captain *Kidd* was againft it, fo it was not done.

Kidd. My Lord, I was in the Cabin, and heard a Noife, and came out; and *William Moore* faid, *You Ruin us becaufe you will not confent to take Captain* Hoar's *Ship.* Says a *Dutchman, I will put Captain* Kidd *in a way to take this Ship, and come off fairly.*

L. C. B. *Ward.* You may ask him any Questions you have a Mind to, but you muft referve what you have to fay for your felf till you come to make your Defence.

Mr. *Soll. Gen.* Mr. *Palmer,* Do you know of any other Provocation to ftrike him, befides thofe Words?

Palmer. I know of no other Provocation.

Mr. *Coniers.* Set up *Robert Bradinham. (who appeared.)*

Mr. *Bradinham,* In what Office was you in the Ship?

THE CAPTAIN KIDD HOME AT PEARL AND HANOVER STREETS
from a print in the April, 1927 Mentor Magazine

Bradinham. I was Surgeon of the Ship.

Mr. *Coniers.* Of what Ship?

Bradinham. The *Adventure* Galley; whereof Captain *Kidd* was Mafter.

Mr. *Coniers.* Was you there when the Blow was given?

Bradinham. No.

Mr. *Coniers.* Was you fent for when Captain *Kidd* had given the Gunner the Wound upon the Head.

Bradinham. I was fent for to his Affiftance after he was wounded, and I came to him, and asked him how he did; he faid, He was a dead Man, Captain *Kidd* had given him his laft Blow. And I was by the Gun-Room, and Captain *Kidd* was walking there, and I heard *Moore* fay, *Farewel, Farewel, Captain* Kidd *has given me my laft Blow;* and Captain *Kidd,* when he heard it, faid, *Damn him, he is a Villain.*

Mr. *Coniers.* Did you hear him fay fo?

Bradinham. I did hear it.

Mr. *Cowper.* Was it in a Way of Anfwer to what he faid?

Bradinham. Yes.

Mr. *Cowper.* How long did he live after the Blow?

Bradinham. He died the next day. The wound was but small, the Scull was fractured.

Mr. *Cowper.* Do you believe he died of that Wound?

Bradinham. Yes.

Mr. *Cowper.* Had you any Difcourfe with Captain *Kidd* after this, about this Man's Death?

Bradinham. Some Time after this, about two Months, by the Coast of *Malabar,* Captain *Kidd* faid, *I do not care fo much for the Death of my Gunner, as for other Paffages of my Voyage; for I have good Friends in* England, *that will bring me off for that.*

L. C. B. *Ward.* Mr. *Kidd,* Will you ask him any Questions?

Kidd. I ask him whether he knew of any difference between this Gunner and me before this happened.

Bradinham. I knew of no Difference between them before at all.

Mr. *Soll. Gen.* Mr. *Kidd,* Have you any Thing more to ask him?

Kidd. No.

Mr. *Coniers.* Then we have done for the King.

L. C. B. *Ward.* Then you may make your Defence, you are charged with Murther, and you have heard the Evidence that has been given, What have you to fay for your felf?

Kidd. I have Evidence to prove it is no fuch Thing, if they may be admitted to come hither. My Lord, I will tell you what the Cafe was, I was coming up within a League of the *Dutch*-man, and fome of my Men were making a Mutiny about taking her; and my Gunner told the People he could put the Captain in a Way to take the Ship, and be fafe. Says I, *How will you do that?* The Gunner anfwered, *We will get the Captain and Men aboard.* And what then? *We will go a-board the Ship, and plunder her, and we will have it under their Hands that we did not take her.* Says I, *This is Judas like, I dare not do fuch a Thing.* Says he, *We may do it, we are Beg-gars already.* Why fays I, *May we take this Ship becaufe we are Poor?* Upon that a Mutiny arofe, fo I took up a Bucket, and juft throwed it at him, and faid You are a Rogue to make fuch a Motion. This I can prove, my Lord.

L. C. B. *Ward.* Call your Evidence.

M r. *Cowper.* Mr. *Palmer,* Was there any Mutiny in the Ship, when this Man was killed?

Palmer. There was none.

L. C. B. *Ward.* Captain *Kidd,* Call what Evidence you Will.

Kidd. They are Prifoners I defire they may be called up.

L. C. B. *Ward.* Whatever other Crimes they may be guilty of, they may be Witneffes for him in this Cafe.

Mr. Baron *Harfell.* Mr. *Palmer.* Did he throw the Bucket at him, or ftrike him with it?

Palmer. He held it by the Strap in his Hand.

Kidd. Call *Abel Owens.* (*who appeared*) Can you tell which Way this Bucket was thrown?

Mr. *J. Powel.* What was the Provocation for throwing this Bucket?

Owens. I was in the Cook-room, and hearing fome Differ-ence on the Deck, I came out; and the Gunner was grinding a

Chiffel on the Grindftone, and the Captain and he had fome Words; and the Gunner faid to the Captain, *You have brought us to Ruin, and we are Defolate.* And fays he, *Have I brought you to Ruin? I have not brought you to Ruin, I have not done an ill Thing to Ruin you, you are a fawcy Fellow to give me thefe Words;* and then he took up the Bucket, and did give him a Blow.

Kidd. Was there not a Mutiny among the Men?

Owen. Yes, and the bigger Part was for taking the Ship; and the Captain faid, *You that will take the* Dutch-*man, you are the ftrongeft, you may do what you pleafe; if you will take her, you may take her; but if you go from aboard, you fhall never come aboard again.*

L. C. B. *Ward.* When was this Mutiny you fpeak of?

Abel Owens. When we were at Sea.

L. C. B. How long was it before this Man's Death?

Owens. About a Month.

Mr. *J. Powel.* At this time when the Blow was given, did *Moore* the Gunner endeavour to make any Mutiny?

Owens. No.

Mr. *J. Powel.* Was there any Mutiny then?

Owens. None at all.

Kidd. Did not he fay, he could put me in a way to take the *Dutchman*, and be clear?

Owens. I know there were feveral of them would have done it, but you would not give Confent to it.

Kidd. No, but this was the Reafon I threw the Bucket at him.

L. C. B. *Ward.* Captain *Kidd*, he tells you this was a Month before you ftruck him.

Jury. My Lord, we defire he may be asked, whether he did throw the Bucket, or ftrike him with it.

L. C. B. *Ward.* Anfwer the Jury to that Queftion.

Owens. He took it with the Strap, and ftruck him with it.

Kidd. Did not I throw it at him?

Owens. No, I was near you when you did it.

Mr. *Coniers.* Did you fee the Stroke given?

Owens. I did fee the Stroke given.

L. C. B. *Ward*. Captain *Kidd*, Will you call any more?

Kidd. Yes, my Lord. Call *Richard Barlicorn*.

Mr. *J. Powel*. What Questions would you have him ask'd?

Kidd. *R. Barlicorn*, what was the Reafon that Blow was given to the Gunner?

Barlicorn. At firft when you met the Ship there was a Mutiny, and Two or Three of the Dutchmen came aboard; and fome faid fhe was a rich Veffel, and they would take her: And the Captain faid, *No, I will not take her*. And there was a Mutiny in the Ship, and the Men faid, *If you will not, we will*. And he faid, *If you have a Mind, you may; but they that will not, come along with me*.

Kidd. Do you think *William Moore* was one of thofe that was for taking her?

Barlicorn. Yes.

L. C. B. *Ward*. How long was that before Moore died, do you know.

Barlicorn. No, I did not keep a Journal.

L. C. B. *Ward*. Was it after *Moore* died?

Barlicorn. No Sir, it was before *Moore* died.

Mr. *Coniers*. How long before?

Barlicorn. I believe it was about a Month or Three Weeks, I cannot tell which.

L. C. B. *Ward*. You fay there was a Mutiny in the Ship; what was the Mutiny about?

Barlicorn. About taking the Ship.

L. C. B. *Ward*. What was the Ship's Name?

Barlicorn. The *Loyal Captain*. And the Captain faid, *If they take the Ship, they fhall never come aboard again*.

L. C. B. *Ward*. Was you by when *Moore* received this Blow?

Barlicorn. No, I was not by then.

Kidd. Do you know of any Quarrel between this *Moore* and I before that Accident?

Barlicorn. No, I did not.

Mr. *J. Powel*. Was there any Mutiny in the Ship when this *Moore* died?

Barlicorn. They were talking of it.

Kidd. Was there not a Dutchman clofe by us, when this Blow was given?

Barlicorn. Yes, Sir.

Kidd. He was going to make another Mutiny, and I prevented him.

Mr. *J. Powel.* Did *Moore* endeavour to make any Mutiny at that time?

Barlicorn. The Ship was gone at that time.

Mr. *J. Powel.* How long had fhe been gone?

Barlicorn. About a Week.

Mr. B. *Hatfell.* Was there any Mutiny about the *Dutch* Ship you faw?

Barlicorn. The *Dutch* Ship? Not that I know of; but there was a Mutiny about the *Loyal Captain.*

Kidd. Do you not know of another Mutiny?

Mr. B. *Hatfell.* Do you know of any other Mutiny?

Barlicorn. No.

Kidd. At that very time they were going to make a Mutiny.

L. C. B. *Ward.* Will you ask him any more Queftions?

Kidd. What Difcourse had I with *Moore* at that time?

Barlicorn. I was aboard our Ship, but did not fee the Blow given.

Kidd. They were faying they would take her, and He faid, he could put me in a way to take her, without coming to any harm.

L. C. B. *Ward.* What occafion could thofe Words be of a Mutiny?

Barlicorn. There were many of the Men would have gone with Arms, and taken that Ship without the Captain's Confent.

L. C. B. *Ward.* At that Time when this Moore was killed was there any Mutiny?

Barlicorn. No.

L. C. B. *Ward.* When was it that *Moore* faid, they might have taken this Ship?

Barlicorn. At the fame time when the Ship was in Company with us.

L. C. B. *Ward.* That was a Week or Fortnight before?

Barlicorn. No, Sir, the *Loyal Captain* was within fight of us.

Mr. B. *Hatfell.* What, when *Moore* was killed?

Barlicorn. No, not then. *William Moore* lay fick a great while before this Blow was given; and the Doctor faid, when he vifited him This Blow was not the Caufe of his Death.

L. C. B. *Ward.* Then they must be confronted. Do you hear, *Bradinham,* what he fays? He fays you faid, That Blow was not the Caufe of his Death. Did you ever fay fo.

Bradinham. My Lord, I never faid fo.

L. C. B. *Ward.* Did you fee that young Man there?

Bradinham. Yes, he was aboard the Ship.

L. C. B. *Ward.* Was *Moore* fick before that Blow?

Bradinham. He was not fick at all before.

Barlicorn. He was fick fome time before, and this Blow did but juft touch him. and the Doctor faid, he did not die on the Occafion of this Blow.

Mr. *J. Gold.* Did you ever fay fo, Mr. *Bradinham?*

Bradinham. No, my Lord.

Mr. *Soll. Gen.* You fay he did but juft touch him, were you prefent when the Blow was given.

Barlicorn. No, but I faw him after he was dead, and I was by when the Doctor faid, he did not die of that Blow.

Mr. *Cowper.* What did he die of?

Barlicorn. I cannot tell, he had been fick before, we had many fick Men aboard.

Mr. *Soll. Gen.* How long did he lie after this Blow, before he died?

Barlicorn. I cannot tell juftly how long it was.

L. C. B. *Ward.* How long do you think? You took notice of the Blow, how long did he live after that?

Barlicorn. I believe about a Week.

L. C. B. *Ward.* And the two Witneffes fwore he died the next Day.

Barlicorn. I cannot tell juftly how long he lived afterwards.

Jury. We defire to know whether he knew what was the Occafion of this Blow.

Barlicorn. All the Reafon I can give is, becaufe it was thought he was going to breed a Mutiny in the Veffel.

L. C. B. *Ward.* Did you hear of that by any Body?

Kidd. Was *Bradinham* in the Mutiny? declare that.

L. C. B. *Ward.* Mr. *Kidd*, why do you ask that Queftion?

Kidd. I ask him whether *Bradinham* was not in any Mutiny in the Ship.

L. C. B. *Ward.* Why do you ask that?

Barlicorn. If any Thing was to be, he was as forward as any one.

L. C. B. *Ward.* You fay he was as forward as any, but it does not appear any one made a Mutiny at this time.

Barlicorn. I do not know, Sir.

L. C. B. *Ward.* Have you any more to call?

Kidd. My Lord, here is another Witnefs.

L. C. B. *Ward.* What is your Name?

Hugh Parrot. Hugh Parrot.

L. C. B. *Ward.* Mr. *Kidd*, what do you ask him?

Kidd. I ask you whether *Bradinham* was in a Mutiny in my Ship.

Hugh Parrot. I cannot fay whether he was or no.

L. C. B. *Ward.* Captain *Kidd*, you are tried for the Death of this *Moore*, now why do you ask this Queftion? what do you infer from hence? You will not infer, that if he was a Mutineer, it was lawful for you to kill *Moore*.

Kidd. Do you know the Reafon why I ftruck *Moore*?

Hugh Parrot. Yes, becaufe you did not take the *Loyal Captain*, whereof Captain *Hoar* was Commander.

L. C. B. *Ward.* Was that the Reafon he struck *Moore*, becaufe the Ship was not taken?

Hugh Parrot. I fhall tell you how it happened, according to the beft of my Knowledge. My Commander fortuned to come up with this Captain *Hoar's* Ship, and fome were for taking her, and fome not; and afterwards there was a little fort of Mutiny, and fome rofe in Arms, the greateft Part, and they faid they would take this Ship and the Commander was not for it; and fo they refolved to go away in the Boat, and take her. Captain *Kidd* faid, *If you defert my Ship, you fhall never come aboard again, and I will force you into* Bombay, *and I will carry you before fome of the Council there:* Infomuch as my Commander ftilled them again, and they remained on Board. And about a Fortnight afterwards there paffed fome Words between this *William Moore*, and my Commander; and then fays he, *Captain, I could have put you in a way to have taken this Ship, and been never the worfe for it.* He fays, *Would you have me take this Ship? I cannot anfwer it, they are our Friends,* and my Commander was in a Paffion; and with that I went off the Deck, and I underftood afterwards the Blow was given, but how I cannot tell.

Mr. *J. Powell.* Captain *Kidd,* have you any more to ask him, or have you any more Witneffes to call?

Kidd. I could call all of them to teftifie the fame thing, but I will not trouble you to call any more.

L. C. B. *Ward.* Have you any more to fay for yourfelf?

Kidd. I have no more to fay, but I had all the Provocation in the World given me; I had no Defign to kill him, I had no Malice or Spleen againft him.

L. C. B. *Ward.* That muft be left to the Jury to consider the Evidence that has been given; you make out no fuch Matter.

Jury-man. My Lord, I defire the Prifoner may give an Account whether he did do any Thing, in order to his Cure.

L. C. B. *Ward.* He is to be tried according to Law; the King's Evidence hath been heard, and he has the Liberty to produce what Evidence he can for himself; will you put him to produce more Evidence than he can? If he has any more to fay, it will be his Intereft to fay what he can, the Court is willing to hear him as long as he hath any thing to offer for himfelf, either upon that Account or any Thing elfe.

Kidd. It was not defignedly done, but in my Paffion, for which I am heartily forry.

L. C. B. *Ward.* Gentlemen of the Jury, the Prifoner at the Bar, *William Kidd,* is Indicted for the Murther of *William Moore;* and whether he be guilty of this Murther, or not guilty, it is your part to determine on the Evidence that has been given. The Fact charged againft him is this, That the Prifoner at the Bar, *William Kidd,* being the Commander of the Ship, called the *Adventure-Galley,* and the deceafed *Wil-*

liamMoore, the Gunner in that Ship; That upon the High Sea, near the Coaſt of *Malabar*, in the *Eaſt-Indies*, and within the Jurisdiction of the Admiralty of *England*, in *October*, in the Ninth Year of his Majesty's Reign, 1697, the Prisoner, *William Kidd*, out of his Malice fore-thought, did ſtrike the Deceaſed, *William Moore*, with a Bucket hoop'd with Iron, on the right Side of his Head, and that that Blow was the Occaſion of the Death of the ſaid *William Moore;* that this was done on the 30th of *October*, and that his Death enſued on the 31st of *October*, being the nect Day. This is the Fact charged upon him.

Now you have heard the Evidence that has been given on the King's Part, and you will weigh it well. You hear the firſt Witneſs that has Been produced on behalf of the King, is *Joseph Palmer*. He tells you he was preſent on board this Ship, at the time when this Blow was given. And he ſays there had been ſome Diſcourſe between the Prisoner *William Kidd*, and the Deceaſed *Moore*, concerning taking a Ship that was called the *Loyal Captain*, and that Captain *Kidd* ſaid to him, *How could you have put me in a way to take that Ship, and be clear?* No, ſays *Moore I ſaid no ſuch Thing.* The Reply Captain *Kidd* made to him was, *He was a Louſie Dog.* The Anſwer of the Deceaſed was this, *if I am ſo, you have made me ſo, you have ruined me and a great many others.* With that ſays Captain *Kidd, Have I ruined you, you Dog?* And up he took a Bucket, hoop'd with Iron, and gave him a Blow on the right ſide of his Head. And thereupon he complained and ſaid, *You have given me my laſt Blow.* And then *Moore* went down below Deck, and he ſaw him no more till the next Day, and then he was dead; and he felt upon his Head, and perceived a Bruiſe in one part of it, as broad as a Shilling, and he felt the Skull was broke; and he does take on him to ſay, that he believes that Blow was the occaſion of his Death. Being asked whether he knew in what State of Health he was before, he ſays, he was in a healthy Condition; he was grinding a Chiſſel at that time when the Blow was given; and that Blow he believes was the Occaſion of his Death. And being asked whether he heard any other Words, or ſaw or knew any

Thing that could be any Caufe of Provocation, he fays, he knew no more than the Reply of the Party deceafed, *If I am a Loufie Dog, you have made me fo, and have been my Ruin.* And then having taken two or three Turns upon the Deck, he gave him the Blow; and then *Moore* went down the Deck, and ufed thefe Words, *You have given me my laft Blow, or to that Effect.*

Gentlemen, You have heard the Surgeon alfo, *Robert Brad-inham,* and he tells you he did not fee the Blow given, but he was fent for after, and the Deceafed faid, Captain Kidd had given him his laft Blow: And thereupon he did examine him, as a Surgeon, and does believe that Blow on the Head was the Occafion of his Death, and he did obferve it as well as he could.

Jury-man. My Lord, I think *Bradinham,* faid he was not then by, when the Prifoner gave the Blow.

L. C. B. *Ward.* I did not fay he was: He fays he was fent for, after the Blow; and when he came, the Deceafed faid he gave it him, and what would be the Confequence.

Now thefe two being crofs-examined by the Prifoner *William Kidd,* whether they did not know of fome Mutiny in the Ship, that might be the occafion of his giving this Blow; they have told both their Stories, of what Difcourfe there was of taking this Ship the *Loyal Captain,* and of what Defign there was upon the *Dutch* Ship after. Now the firft of thefe was a Fortnight before this happen'd and the other a Week; fo that there was then no Occafion of Mutiny, nor do they know of any Mutiny at that time.

Now, Gentlemen, he has produced for himfelf Three Witneffes. The firft that he calls is *Abel Owens;* and this Witnefs has not in his Teftimony made for the Prifoner, but in effect confirmed what the other Witneffes for the King faid: For he tells you he was by when the Blow was given, and gives you an Account how this Thing was, That there was fome Difcourfe between them, much what to the Effect aforefaid, both as to what Capt. *Kidd* faid to *Moore,* and what *Moore* replyed; and that Capt. *Kidd* fhould fay to *Moore, You are a fawcy Fellow,* or to that purpofe; and *Moore* faid, *You have*

ruined me, and a great many others; and with that the Prifoner
took up the Bucket, and ftruck him with it. And he being
asked if there was any Provocation or Occafion why this
Blow was given. and whether there was any Mutiny at that
time, as pretended, he fays he knew of none, only he fpeaks
of one about a Month before.

They have call'd two other Witneffes, one is *Richard Barlicorn:* He is the Prifoner's Servant; and though he be his Servant, Yet the Law allows him to be a Witnefs for him, and
the Credit of his Teftimony is left to you. Now what has he
faid? He has told you fomething difierent Stories He thinks
there was a Mutiny in the Ship. And being ask'd about what
time, he thinks it was about a Month or three Weeks before;
and, upon a further Examination faith, there was no Mutiny
when *Moore* was killed. He is willing to fay what he can for
his Mafter, and believes Mr. *Kidd* did not defign to do any
harm to that Man; for he heard the Surgeon fay, that Blow
was not the Occafion of his Death. Now, in Contradiction to
that, Bradinham, the Surgeon fays he never did fay so, but
believes that this Blow was the Occafion of his Death. You
have heard what Objections the Young Man's Teftimony is
liable to, and you will confider his whole Evidence.

The laft Witnefs the Prifoner has called is *Hugh Parrot.*
He fays there was fomething of thefe Words, and that the
Deceafed did fay, he could have put the Captain in a way to
have taken the Ship, and thereupon Words arofe, and the
Captain was in a Paffion; and that he went away, and underftood afterwards the Blow was given, but how he could not
tell.

Now, Gentlemen, this being the Matter of Fact, the Prifoner is Indicted upon it for the Murther. Now to make the
killing of a Man to be Murther, there juft be Malice pre-
penfe, either exprefs or implied: The Law implies Malice,
when one Man, without any reafonable Caufe or Provocation,
kills another. You have had this Fact opened to you. What
Mutiny or Difcourfe might be a Fortnight or Month before,
will not be any Reafon or Caufe for fo long continuance of a
Paffion. But what did arife at that time, the Witneffes tell

you. The firſt Witneſs tells you, the firſt Words that were
ſpoken, were by Mr. *Kidd;* and upon his Anſwer, Mr. *Kidd*
calls him *louſie Dog.* The Reply was, *If I am ſo, you have
made me ſo; You have ruined me, and a great many more.* Now,
Gentlemen, I leave it to you to conſider whether that could
be a reaſonable Occaſion or Provocation for him to take a
Bucket and knock him on the Head, and kill him. You have
heard the Witneſſes have made it out that he was a healthy
Man, and they are of Opinion that the Blow was the Occaſion
of his Death. Now for the Priſoner, on ſuch a Saying, and
without any other Provocation, to take a Bucket and knock
the Deceaſed on the Head, and kill him, muſt be eſteemed
an unjuſtifiable Act. For, as I ſaid, if one Man kill another
without provocation, or reaſonable Cauſe, the Law preſumes
and implies Malice; and then ſuch killing will be Murther, in
the Senſe of the Law, as being done out of Malice prepenſe.
If there be a ſudden falling out, and fighting, and one is killed
in heat of Blood, then our Law calls it Manſlaughter: But in
ſuch a Caſe as this, that happens on ſlight Words, the Priſoner called the Deceaſed a *Louſie Dog;* and the Deceaſed ſaid,
If I be ſo, you made me ſo; Can this be a reaſonable Cauſe to
kill him? And if you believe them to be no reaſonable Cauſe
of Provocation, and that this Blow was given by the Priſoner,
and was the Occaſion of *Moore's* Death, as the Witneſſes al-
ledge, I cannot ſee what diſtinction can be made, but that
the Priſoner is guilty of Murther. Indeed, if there had been
a Mutiny at that time, and he had ſtruck him at the time of
Mutiny, there might have been a reaſonable Cauſe for him
to plead in his Defence, and it ought to have been taken into
Conſideration; but it appears, that what Mutiny there was
was a Fortnight at leaſt before. Therefore, Gentlemen, I muſt
leave it to you; if you believe the King's Witneſſes, and one
of the Priſoner's own, that this Blow was given by the Priſoner, in manner aforeſaid, and are ſatisfied that it was done
without reaſonable Cauſe or Provocation, then he will be
guilty of Murther; and if you do believe him guilty of Murther, upon this Evidence, you muſt find him ſo: If not, you
muſt acquit him.

Kidd. My Lord, I have Witneſſes to produce for my Reputation.

L. C. B. *Ward.* Mr. *Kidd,* we gave you Time to make your Defence; why did not you produce them? You were asked more than once, if you had any more to ſay; and you ſaid you would call no more Witneſſes.

Kidd. I can prove what Service I have done for the King.

L. C. B. *Ward.* You ſhould have ſpoken ſooner; but what would that help in this Caſe of Murther? You ſaid you had no more to ſay, before I began.

Then an Officer was ſworn to keep the Jury; and about an Hour after, the Jury returned, and gave in their Verdict.

Cl. of Arr. Gentlemen, anſwer to your Names. *Nath. Long.*

Nath. Long. Here, &c.

Cl. of Arr. Are you all agreed of your Verdict?

Omnes. Yes.

Cl. of Arr. Who ſhall ſay for you?

Omnes. Foreman.

Cl. of Arr. William Kidd, hold up thy Hand; (*which he did.*) Look upon the Priſoner. If he guilty of the Murther whereof he ſtands indicted, or not guilty?

Foreman. Guilty.

Cl. of Arr. Look to him, Keeper.

The TRYAL of *William Kidd, Nicholas Churchill, James Howe, Robert Lamley, William Jenkins Gabriel Loffe, Hugh Parrot, Richard Barlicorn, Abels Owen, and Darby Mullins,* for Piracy and Robbery on a Ship called the *Quedagh Merchant.*

The *Jurors for our Sovereign Lord the King, do, upon their Oath, preſent, That* William Kidd, *late of* London, *Mariner;* Nicholas Churchill, *late of* London, *Mariner;* James Howe, *late of* London, *Mariner;* Robert Lamley, *late of* London, *Mariner;* William Jenkins, *late of* London, *Mariner;* Gabriel Loffe, *late of* London, *Mariner;* Hugh Parrot, *late of* London, *Mariner;* Richard Barlicorn, *late of* London, *Mariner;* Abel Owens, *late of* London, *Mariner; and* Darby Mullins, *late of*

London, *Mariner; The 30th Day of* January, *in the Ninth Year of the Reign of our Soveriegn Lord,* William *the Third, by the Grace of God, of* England, Scotland, France, *and* Ireland, King, *Defender of the Faith,* &c *by Force and Arms,* &c. *upon the High Sea, in a ceratin Place diftant about Ten Leagues from* Cutfheen *in the* East-Indies, *and within the Jurifdiction of the Admiralty of* England, *did Piratically and Feloniously fet upon, board, break, and enter a certain Merchant-Ship called the* Quedagh Merchant, *then being a Ship of certain Perfons, (to the Jurors aforefaid unknown) and then and there Piratically and Feloniously did make an Affault in and upon certain Mainers (whofe Names to the Jurors aforefaid are unknown) in the fame Ship, in the Peace of God, and of our faid now Sovereign Lord the King, then and there being, Piratically and Feloniously did put the aforefaid Mariners of the fame Ship, in the Ship aforefaid then being, in corporal Fear of their Lives, then and there, in the Ship aforefaid, upon the high Sea, in the Place aforefaid, diftant about Ten Leagues from* Cutfheen *aforefaid, in the* East-Indies *aforefaid, and within the Jurifdiction aforefaid, Piratically and Feloniously did Steal, Take and carry away the faid Merchant Ship called the* Quedagh Merchant, *and the Apparel and Tackle of the fame Ship, of the Value of* 400£ *of lawful Money of* England; *Seventy Chefts of* Opium *of the Value of* 1400£ *of lawful Money of* England; *Two Hundred and Fifty Bags of Sugar, of the Value of* 100£ *of lawful Money of* England; *Twenty Bales of Raw Silk, of the Value of* 400£ *of lawful Money of* England; *an Hundred Bales of Callico's, of the Value of* 200£ *of lawful Money of* England; *Two Hundred Bales of Muflin's, of the Value of* 1000£ *of lawful Money of* England; *and three Bales of Romels, of the Value of* 30£ *of lawful Money of* England: *The Goods and Chattels of certain Perfons (to the Jurors aforefaid unknown;) then and there, upon the High Sea aforefaid, in the aforefiad Place, diftant about Ten Leagues from* Cutfheen *aforefaid, in the* Eaft-Indies *aforefaid, and within the Jurifdiction aforefaid, being found in the aforefaid Ship in the Cuftody and Poffeffion of the faid Mariners in the fame Ship, from the faid Mariners of the faid Ship, and from their Cuftody and Poffeffion, then and there, upon the High Sea aforefaid, in the Place aforefaid, diftant about Ten Leagues from* Cutfheen *aforefaid, in the Eaft-Indies aforefaid, and within the Jurifdiction aforefaid, againft the Peace of our faid now Sovereign Lord the King, his Crown and Dignity,* &c.

Cl. of Arr. Set *Will Kidd, Nicholas Churchill,* &c. *to the Bar; (and fo of the reft) Will. Kidd,* hold up thy Hand; (*which he did, and fo the reft*)

You the Prifoners at the Bar, thofe Men that you fhall hear called, and that perfonally appear, are to pafs between our Sovereign Lord the King and you, upon Tryal of your feveral Lives and Death: If therefore you, or any of you will Challenge any of them, your Time is to fpeak to them as they come to the Book to be fworn, and before they be fworn.

And there being no Challenges, the Twelve that were fworn on the Jury were as follows:

John Cooper,	*P. Walker,*
Jo. Hall,	*William Hunt,*
Jo. James,	*John Micklethwait,*
Peter Parker,	*Richard Chifwell,*
Caleb Hook,	*Abraham Hickman,*
R. Rider,	*George Grove.*

Cl. of Arr. Cryer, Count thefe; *John Cowper.*

Cryer. One, &c. Twelve good Men and true, ftand together, and hear your Evidence.

Then the ufual Proclamation for Information was made; and the Prifoners being bid to hold up their Hands, the Clerk of Arraignments charged the Jury with them thus:

Cl. of Arr. You of the Jury, look upon the Prifoners, and hearken to their Caufe. They ftand Indicted by the Names of *William Kidd,* &c. (as before in the Indictment). Upon this Indictment they have been Arraigned, and thereunto have feverally pleaded, not guilty; and for their Trial, put themfelves on God and their Country, which Country they are. Your Charge is, to enquire whether they be guilty of the Piracy and Robbery whereof they ftand Indicted, in Manner and Form as they ftand Indicted, or not guilty, &c.

Nic. Churchill. My Lord, I beg your Opinion, whether I may not plead the King's Pardon?

L. C. B. *Ward.* Let us fee your Pretences: You fhall have all legal Defences and Advantages allowed to you.

N. Churchill. I came in upon his Majefty's Proclamation.

L. C. B. *Ward.* Have you the King's Proclamation? If you have, let us fee it.

Churchill. We had notice of it at *Guiana,* and we delivered up our felves to Col. *Bafs,* Governour of *Eaft-Jerfey* and I have it under his Hand. I beg your Lordfhip would appoint me Council to plead my Cafe.

The Paper was fhown, and read.

Mr. *Crawley.* I know not when it was.

Churchill. I had notice of it at Guiana: I have been two Years in Cuftody.

L. C. B. *Ward.* How long have you been a Prifoner?

Churchill. Almoft two Years: Two Years next July.

L. C. B. *Ward. And the reft of the judges.* The Proclamation (*for which you fay your felf*) does not reach your Cafe.

Howe, Churchill, Mullins. We came in, upon the Proclamation, all the fame Day.

Mr. *J. Powell.* How can you make it appear you furrendred?

Prifoners. Here is an Affidavit made of it by the Governor's Secretary; and there's the Gentleman himfelf, Col. *Bafs.*

Mr. *J. Powell.* You muft make it out that you have came in within the Conditions of that Proclamation, if you have any Benefit by it.

L. C. B. *Ward.* Let the Proclamation be read, (*which was done accordingly, and it here follows:*)

By the KING, A Proclamation.

William R.

WHEREAS We being informed, by the frequent Complaints of our good Subjects Trading to the Eaft-Indies, of feveral wicked Piracies committed on thofe Seas, as well upon our own Subjects, as thofe of our Allies, have therefore thought fit (for the Security of the Trade of thofe Countries, by an utter Extirpation of the Pirates in all Parts Eaftward of the Cape of Good Hope, as well beyond Cape Comorin, as on

this fide of it, unlefs they fhall forthwith furrender themfelves as is herein after directed to fend out a Squadron of
Men of War, under the Command of Captain Thomas Warren. Now we, to the Intent that fuch who have been guilty
of any Acts of Piracy in thofe Seas, may have Notice of our
moft gracious Intention, of extending our Royal Mercy to
fuch of them as fhall furrender themfelves, and to caufe the
fevereft Punifhment according to Law to be inflicted upon
thofe who fhall continue obftinate, have thought fit, by the
Advice of our Privy Council, to Iffue this Proclamation; hereby Requiring and Commanding all perfons who have been
guilty of any Act of Piracy, or any ways Aiding of Affifting
therein, in any place Eaftward of the Cape of Good Hope, to
furrender themfelves within the feveral refpective Times
herein after limited, unto the faid Captain Thomas Warren,
and the Commander in chief of the faid Squadron for the
time being, and to Ifrael Hayes, Peter Dellanoye, and Chriftopher Pollard, Efquires, Commiffioners appointed by us for
the faid Expedition, or to any Three of them, or, in cafe of
Death, to the major part of the Survivors of them. And We
do hereby declare, That We have been Gracioufly pleafed to
Impower the faid Captain Thomas Warren, and the Commander in chief of the faid Squadron for the time being, Ifrael Hayes, Peter Dellanoye, and Chriftopher Pollard, Efquires, Commiffioners aforefaid, or any Three of them, or, in
cafe of Death, to the major part of the Survivors of them, to
give Affurance of our moft gracious Pardon unto all fuch Pirates in the Eaft-Indies, (Viz.) all Eaftward of the Cape of
Good Hope, who fhall fo furrender themfelves for Piracies or
Robberies committed by them upon the Sea or Land; except
neverthelefs fuch as they fhall commit in any Place whatfoever after Notice of our Grace and Favour hereby declared;
And alfo Excepting all fuch Piracies and Robberies as fhall
be committed from the Cape of Good Hope Eastward, to the
Longitude or Meridian of Socatora, after the laft Day of
April 1699, and in any Place from the Longitude or Merdian
of Socatora Eaftward, to the Longitude or Meridian of Cape
Comorin, after the laft Day of June, 1699. and in any Place

whatfoever Eaftward of Cape Comorin after the laft Day of July, 1699. And alfo excepting Henry Every alias Bridgman, and William Kidd.

Given at our Court at *Kenfington*, the Eighth Day of *December*, 1698. In the Tenth Year of our Reign.

God fave the King.

Cierk. There is no Day mentioned in this Paper when they furrendred themfelves.

Mr. *Moxon.* My Lord, about the Year 1697, there was a fpecial Commiffion given to Four Perfons, and they were to proceed in their Voyage to the *Indies*, and they carried a great Number of *Proclamations*, that all the Pirates in fuch and fuch Places fhould furrender themfelves. Now they came to St. *Helena* with them, and Captain *Warren* was fent to St. *Mary's*, and he was to deliver fome of thefe *Proclamations* there, and the Commiffioner had then the Embaffador to the *Great Mogul* on Board, and this Captain *Warren* thefe *Proclamations, Warren* comes and delivers the *Proclamations out*, and among the reft the Prifoners at the Bar having notice of this, he goes to the Governor, and Confeffes he had been a Pirate, and defired them to take notice that he furrendred himfelf; and we have the Governor here, to give an Account of this Matter.

L. C. B. *Ward.* The *Proclamation* fays they muft furrender themfelves to fuch and fuch Perfons by Name. See if it be not fo. (*Then the* Proclamation *was read again.*) Here are feveral Qualifications mentioned; you must bring your felves under them, if you would have the Benefit of it.

Dr. *Newton.* Let them fhow that they furrendred themfelves to the Perfons they were to furrender to.

Mr. *Moxon.* My Lord, we will prove we gave Notice within the Time, by this Paper.

Mr. *Soll. Gen.* There is no Time mentioned in it. (*The Affidavit was read.*) Charles Hally, *Gent. Maketh Oath, That in the Year 98, there being Notice of his Majefty's gracious Pardon to fuch Pirates as fhould furrender themfelves,* James Howe, Nicholas Churchill, *and* Darby Mullins, *in* May 1699, *did furrender themfelves to* Jeremiah Bafs, *and he did admit them to Bail.*

L. C. B. *Ward.* There are Four Commiffioners named in the Proclamation: There is no Governor mentioned that is to receive them, only thofe Four Commiffioners.

Mr. *Moxon.* But, my Lord, confider the Nature of this *Proclamation*, and what was the Defign of it, which was to invite Pirates to come in.

Mr. *Coniers.* We muft keep you to the *Proclamation.* Here is not enough to put off the Tryal.

L. C. B. *Ward.* If you had brought your felves within the Cafe of the *Proclamation*, we fhould be very glad. You that offer it, muft confider it is a Special *Proclamation*, with divers Limitations; and if you would have the Benefit of it, you muft bring your felves under the Conditions of it. Now there are Four Commiffioners named, that you ought to furrender to; but you have not furrendered to any one of thefe, but to Colonel *Bafs*, and there is no fuch Man mentioned in this *Proclamation.*

Mr. *Knapp.* My Lord, and Gentlemen of the Jury, The Indictment fets forth, That the Prifoners at the Bar, on the 30th of *January*, in the Ninth Year of his Majefty's Reign, ten Leagues diftant from *Cutfheen*, did Piratically feize and rob a certain Ship called the *Quedagh Merchant*, and put Men in fear of their Lives; and the faid Ship, with her Apparel, Tackle, and Goods, did then and there, upon the High Sea, take and carry away, againft the Peace of our Sovereign Lord the King, his Crown and Dignity. To this Indictment they have Pleaded, Not guilty. If we prove it upon them, you muft find them guilty.

Dr. *Newton, Advocate of the Admiralty.* My Lord, and Gentlemen, The Prifoners at the Bar, Captain *Will. Kidd*, late Commander of the *Adventure Galley*, and nine other Mariners in the fame Veffel, ftand Indicted for Felonioufly and Piratically Affaulting and taking a Ship called the *Quedagh Merchant*, on the High Sea near *Cutfheen*, in the *Eaft-Indies*, about the 30th of *January*, in the Ninth Year of his Majefty's Reign: The Ship was confiderable for its Force and

Bulk, being about 400 Tun; and more confiderable for its Lading, having on Board to the Value of many Thoufand Pounds.

This Cap. *Kidd*, who thus acted the Pirate himfelf, went from *England* in *April* 1696, with a Commiffion dated the 26th of *January* preceeding to take and feize Pirates in the *Indian Seas*, which were then very much and very dangerously infefted by them, to the great Hazard, and Lofs, and Ruine of the Merchant.

The Ship carried 30 Guns, and there were on Board about 80 Men; but the Captain being come to *New-York* in *July* 96, pretending, as indeed it was defigned he fhould, and he had undertaken to make that Defign good, that he was going to Madagafcar, (which was the known and common Receptable of the Pirates in thofe Seas) to take Pirates, and free the Seas from thofe Difturbers of the Commerce of Mankind; fo many came in to him, being invited by Articles publickly fet up by him in that Place, that his Number quickly encreafed to 155 Men; a Force fufficient, if he had meant well, to have made him ufeful to the Publick; and to prove as mifchievous, if his Defigns were otherwife: And what thofe were will quickly appear.

After calling in at feveral Places for Provifions, and among others at *Madagafcar*, in *July* 97, he failed to *Babs-key*, a fmall Ifland at the Entrance of the *Red-Sea*, and a convenient Station for the obferving what Veffels went from thence to the *Indies;* and now inftead of taking Pirates, he becomes one himfelf, and the greateft and the worft of all. Here he ftaid three Weeks, in expectation of the *Mocca* Fleet, to make his Benefit and his Fortune out of it: For whatever he had before pretended, this was his real Defign, and now fo poffefled his Mind, that he could not refrain from declaring, and that often, to his Men, That now he fhould make his Voyage and balaft his Ship with Gold and Silver. After long Expectation, the Fleet, on the 14th of *August*, to the Number of 14, came by: He fell in with the middle of them, fired feveral Guns at them; but finding they had an *Englifh* and *Dutch* Convoy, that Defign happily fail'd of the wifh'd for Succefs.

This Difappointment however did not difcourage him, but that he proceeded on for the Coaft of *Malabar*, where he knew the Trade was confiderable, and hoped his advantage would be proportionable in the difturbing it; and there accordingly, for feveral Months, he committed many great Piracies and Robberies, taking the Ships and Goods of the *Indians* and others at Sea, *Moors* and *Christians*, and torturing cruelly their Perfons, to difcover if any thing had efcaped his Hands; burning their Houfes, and killing after a barbarous manner the Natives on the Shore; equally cruel, dreaded and hated both on the Land and at Sea.

Thefe Criminal Attempts and Actions had rendered his Name (to the Difgrace and the Prejudice of the *Englifh* Nation) too well known, and defervedly detefted, on thofe Parts of the World; and he was now looked upon as an Arch-Pirate, and the Common Enemy of Mankind; and accordingly two *Portuguefe* Men of War went out in purfuit of him, and one met with him and fought him for feveral hours; but *Kidd's* Fortune then referved him for another Place, and another manner of Tryal.

Amongft the great number of Veffels he took on that Coaft, was the Ship he now ftands Indicted for, the *Quedagh Merchant*, being then on a Trading Voyage from *Bengal* to *Suratt*, the Commander *Englifh*, Captain *Wright*, the Owners *Armenian* Merchants, and others; he had taken Moors before, but *Moors* and *Chriftians* are all alike to Pirates, they diftinguifh not Nations and Religions.

Thofe on Board the Veffel offered 30000 *Rupees* for her Ranfom; but the Ship was too confiderable to be parted with, even for fo great a Sum: So *Kidd* fold Goods out of her, on the Neighbouring Coaft, to the Value of Ten or Twelve Thoufands Pounds, out of which he took whatever he could pretend to for Ammunition and Provifions, with Forty Shares for himfelf; and the Remainder was difposed of amongft the Crew, and particularly thofe who are here Indicted with him, who accompanied him, who affifted him throughout in all his Piracies, and who now too fhare the Spoils and the Guilt with him.

With this Ship and another, and the Remainder of the Goods not fold on the Coaft, he failed one more for Madagafcar, where he arrived in the beginning of May 98, and there again, what was left on Board, was divided according to the fame Proportions, and amongft the fame Perfons as before, each Mariner having about three Bales to his share.

Then the Jury brought in their Verdict againft William Kidd *for Murther: And Dr. Newton proceeded;*

It is not to be omitted, That at his return to *Madagafcar*, there came on board him fome Perfons from the Ship *The Refolution*, formerly the *Mocca Frigat*, (for the Piratical feizing of which Veffel there have been formerly Tryals and Convictions in this Place) of which Captain *Culliford*, a notorious Pirate, now in Cuftody, and againft whom two Bills have been found for Piracy, by the Grand Jury, was the Commander: They at firft feemed to be afraid of *Kidd*, but without any Ground, as his former Actions had demonftrated, and the Sequel fhewed. They who were hardened Pirates, and long injured to Villanies, could fcarce think that any Man could fo betray the Truft and Confidence the Publick had placed in him, and faid, They heard he was come to take and hang them. But Captain Kidd affured them, That he had no fuch Defign, and that he had rather his Soul fhould broil in Hell, than do them any Harm; bid them not be afraid, and fwore he would be true to them. And here indeed he did not break his Word: This was his way of being True to his Truft, and making good the Ends of his Commiffion, in acting with the greateft Treachery and the greateft Falfenefs that ever Man did. And to make all that has been reprefented of him true, Captain *Kidd* and Captain *Culliford* went on Board, Treated, and prefented each other; and inftead of taking Culliford, as it was his Duty to have done, and his Force was fufficient to have performed it, he gave him Money and Ammunition, two great Guns and Shot, and other Neceffaries to fit him out to Sea, that he might be in a Condition the better to take and feize other Innocent Perfons.

His own Ship he now left, and went on Board the *Quedagh Merchant*; feveral of his Men then went from hin, but not the Prifoners, they were all along Well-wifhers and Affiftants to him, fought for him, divided the Plunder with him, and are now come to be tryed with him. This, Gentlemen, is the Crime he is Indicted for, Piracy; the growing Trouble, Dif-turbance and Mifchief of the Trading World, and the peace-able of Mankind, the Scandal and Reproach of the *European* Nations, and the Chriftian Name, (Iwifh I could not fay, that the *Kidd's* and the *Avery's* had not made it more par-ticualrly fo of the *Englifh*) amongft *Mahometans* and *Pagans*, in the extreameft Parts of the Earth; which turns not only to the Difadvantage of the immdeiate Sufferers, but of all fuch as traffick In thofe Countries, whether Companies or fingle Merchants, who are to fuffer for the Misfortunes of others, with whom, it may be, they have no Dealings; and for the Villanies of fuch, whom they and all Mankind equally and juftly deteft and abhor.

This is the Perfon that ftands Indicted at that Bar, than whom no one in this age has done more Mifchief, in this worft kind of Mifchief; or has occafioned greater Confufion and Diforder, attended with all the Circumftances of Cruelty and Falfehood, and a Complication of all manner of Ill.

If therefore thefe Facts fhall be proved upon him you will then Gentlemen, in finding him Guilty, do Juftice to the in-jured World, the *Englifh* Nation, (our Common Country) whofe intereft and Welfare fo much depend on the Encreafe and Security of Trade; and, Laftly, to your felves, whom the Law has made Judges of the Fact.

Mr. *Soll. Gen.* My Lord, and Gentlemen of the Jury, I am of Council for the King, with the Doctor that has opened the Matter from the beginning. Thefe Prifoners at the Bar went out with Commiffions for good Purposes, though they made ufe of them to very bad ones. Gentlemen of the Jury, I muft tell you, The Charge upon which you are to enquire, is only upon a certain Ship called the *Quedagh Merchant,* and to that we fhall apply our Evidence. What was taken in her, has been opened already: All we will do now, is to call our Wit-neffes, and make out to your Satisfaction the Things charged upon them.

Mr. *Coniers.* My Lord, we fhall prove this Charge by the Perfons that were Evidence before, *Robert Bradinham,* and *Joseph Palmer.* They went out with Captain *Kidd* in his Voyage, and he began it in April 1696. I believe it will be neceffary that they give fome Account before this Piracy was committed, which was not in Time till February 1697. They will give you account of fome Plunders that happened before this, and then of the taking of this Ship, and the dividing it amongft them.

Mr. Juftice *Powell.* When went they out?

Mr. *Coniers.* They began their Voyage in *April* 1696, and took this Ship in February 1697. They did all along that Voyage commit feveral Plunders on feveral Ships they thought a Prey. Their Defign was, not to take Pirates, but to take what they could get out of any Ships, Friends or Enemies: For in this Ship, the *Quedagh Merchant,* which was a *Moorifh* Ship, there were feveral *Armenians;* and they offered them a great Sum of Money to redeem the Ship, but they refufed it; and they difpofed of the Goods, and divided the Money: And for the Proof of that, we will call Mr *Bradinham.*

Mr. *J. Powell.* I underftand that he had a Commiffion; therefore if any one has a Commiffion, and he acts according to it, he is not a Pirate; but if he take a Commiffion for a Colour, that he may be a Pirate, it will be bad indeed: And there fore if you can prove that he was a Pirate all along, this will be a great Evidence againft him.

Mr. *Coniers.* My Lord, We will prove that; fo that the Commiffion was but a Colour. Mr *Bradinham,* Pray give my Lord and the Jury an Account when you began your Voyage, and your Proceedings afterwards.

Bradinham. Sometime in the Year 1696; about the beginning of *May.* I and others, were with Capt. *Kidd:* And we failed from *Plymouth,* defigning for *New-York;* and in the Way to *New-York* we met with a *French* Banker, and took her.

Mr. *Coniers.* Tell the Court what Ship it was you went in, and with whom.

Bradinham. We went with Captain *Kidd*, in the *Adventure-Galley*.

Mr. *Coniers.* What Number of Men had you when you went firſt out?

Bradinham. About Seventy or Eighty Men.

Mr. *Coniers.* What Force of Guns had you?

Bradinham. We had thirty Guns.

Mr. *Coniers.* In what Office was Captain *Kidd* in the Ship?

Bradinham. He was the Commander of her.

Mr. *Coniers.* Now tell my Lord, and the Jury, what time you left *England*, and how you proceeded.

Bradinham. In *May* 1696, we left Plymouth, and went to *New York*, and in the way met with a *French* Ship, and took her; And when we came to *New York*, Captain *Kidd* put up Articles, That if any Men would enter themſelves on Board his Ship, they ſhould have their Shares of what ſhould be taken and he himſelf was to have Forty Shares.

Mr. *Coniers.* What Number of Men did he get after theſe Articles were Publiſhed?

Bradinham. He carried from *New-York* an Hundred and fifty-five Men.

Mr. *Coniers.* Whither did he ſail then?

Bradinham. To the *Madera's*, from thence to *Bonavis*, from thence to St. *Jago*, from thence to *Madagaſcar*, from thence to *Joanna*, from thence to *Mahala* to *Joanna* again, and from thence to the *Red-Sea;* and there we waited for the *Mocca* Fleet. They paſſed us one Night, and he purſued them, and went among them, and was deſigned to take what he could of them; but he found they were too ſtrong for him, and was fain to leave them.

Mr. *Cowper.* How long did you lie in wait for that Fleet?

Bradinham. A Fortnight or Three Weeks.

Mr. *Cowper.* Did he expreſs himſelf ſo, that he did lie in wait for that Fleet?

Bradinham. Yes; he ſaid that he did deſign to make a Voyage out of them.

Mr. *Cowper.* Did he not lie in wait for any French Effects in that Fleet?

Bradinham. No, only for the *Moorifh* Fleet.

Mr. *Cowper.* What do you mean by the Moorifh Fleet?

Bradinham. The Natives of *India,* the *Mahometans.*

Mr. *Cowper.* Where did you lie in wait for that Fleet?

Bradinham. In the *Red-Sea.*

Mr. *Cowper.* In the Mouth of it?

Bradinham. Yes.

Mr. *Cowper.* Is it a fit Place for that Purpofe?

Bradinham. Several Sail of Ships may lie there.

Mr. *Cowper.* Did you expect them?

Bradinham. Yes; Capt. *Kidd* waited for them?

Mr. *Coniers.* How long did ylou ftay there?

Bradinham. About a Fortnight.

Mr. *Coniers.* Did you do any thing in that time to get Intelligence?

Bradinham. Captain *Kidd* fent his Boat three times to
Mocca, to fee if they could make any Difcovery; and the two
firft times they could make none; but the third time they
brought word the Ships were ready to fail: And accordingly
they came, and we failed after them, and fell in with them,
and Captain *Kidd* fired at them.

Mr. *Cowper.* You fay, he fent his Boat three times for Intelligence; Can yoɪ remember what Anfwer they brought?

Bradinham. The two firft time they brought no Intelligence, but the third time they brought Word that fourteen
or fifteen Ships were ready to fail.

Mr. *Cowper.* What Colours did they fay they had?

Bradinham. I cannot tell that. When Captain *Kidd* had
fetched them up, he found they were under Convoy, and fo
he left them: And then he was going to the Coaft of *Malabar,*
and by the Way met with Captain *Parker.*

Mr. Juftice *Powel.* Did they fire any Guns at the *Mocca*
Fleet?

Bradinham. Yes; Captain *Kidd* fired divers Guns at them.

Mr. *Coniers.* After fuch time as you left the *Mocca* Fleet,
What happened after that? Recollect your felf.

Bradinham. We took a Ship that Capt. *Parker* was Commander of, between *Carawar* and the *Red-Sea.*

Mr. *Coniers.* What Ship was this that Captain *Parker* was Commander of?

Bradinham. A *Moorifh* Ship, fhe came from *Bombay,* and Captain *Parker* was the Mafter.

Mr. *Coniers.* What did you take from this Ship?

Bradinham. Captain *Kidd* took out *Parker,* and a *Portuguefe* for a *Linguifter.*

Mr. *Coniers.* A *Linguifter;* What do you mean by that?

Bradinham. An Interpreter. He took out of her a Bail of Coffee, a Bail of Pepper, about twenty Pieces of *Arabian* Gold, and ordered fome Men to be taken and hoifted up by the Arms, and drub'd with a naked Cutlace.

Mr. *Coniers.* Why did he do that?

Bradinham. That they might Confefs what Money they had.

Mr. *Coniers.* Were thofe Men *Frenchmen* that were thus ufed?

Bradinham. No; they were *Moors.*

Mr. *Coniers.* Was there any Demand made of thofe Men, Captain *Parker* and the *Portuguefe*?

Bradinham. Yes; The *Englifh* Factory fent for this *Parker* and the *Portuguefe,* and he deny'd that he had any fuch Perfons on Board, for he kept them in a Hole.

Mr. *Coniers.* Do you know any thing more?

Bradinham. Then he went to Sea, and that Night he met with a *Portuguefe* Man of War; the next Morning he came up with her, and the *Portuguefe* firft fired at Captain *Kidd,* and he at him again; they fought four or five Hours; Captain *Kidd* had ten Men wounded.

Mr. *Coniers.* So that there was nothing more than Fighting.

Bradinham. No.

Mr. *Coniers.* Go on; What did you do next?

Bradinham. We went to the Coaft of *Malabar.*

Mr. *Coniers.* What did you go thither for?

Bradinham. We went to one of the *Malabar* Iflands for Wood and Water, and Captain *Kidd* went a-fhore, and feveral of his Men, and plundered feveral Boats, and burnt feveral Houfes, and ordered one of the Natives to be ty'd to a Tree, and one of his Men to fhoot him.

Mr. *Coniers.* Pray go on: What was the Reafon of his fhooting this *Indian*?

Bradinham. One of his Men, that was his Cooper, had been a-fhore, and fome of the Natives had cut this Man's Throat, and that was the Reafon he ordered his Men to ferve this Man fo.

Mr. *Coniers.* Pray go on, and give an Account what happened afterwards.

Bradinham. Then we came back again to the *Malabar* Coaft, and cruifed; and in *October* he killed his Gunner, *William Moore.*

Mr. *Coniers.* Tell what happened next after that.

Mr. *Cowper.* Was this the *October* next after he left *England*, or the Year following.

Bradinham. It was in *October* 1697.

Mr. *Coniers.* Well, Go on.

Bradinham. Sometime in November he took a *Moorifh* Ship belonging to *Suratt*, there were two *Dutchmen* belonging to her, the reft were *Moors.* Captain *Kidd* chafed this Ship under *French* Colours; and when the *Dutchman* faw that, he put out *French* Colours too. And Captain *Kidd* came up with them, and commanded them on Board; and he ordered a *Frenchman* to come upon Deck, and to pretend himfelf Captain. And fo this Commander comes aboard, and comes to this Monfieur *Le Roy* that was to pafs for the Captain; and he fhows him a Paper, and faid it was a *French* Pafs. And Captain *Kidd* faid, *By God, Have I catch'd you? You are free Prize to* England. We took two Horfes, fome Quilts, &c and the Ship he carried to *Madagafcar.* In December he took a *Moorifh* Ketch, she was taken by the Boat, we had one Man wounded in taking of her.

Mr. *Coniers.* When was this done?

Bradinham. In *December* 1697.

Mr. *Cobiers.* What did you plunder then?

Bradinham. Our People took the Veffel a-fhore, and Captain *Kidd* took out of the hirty Tubs of Sugar, a Bail of Coffee, &c and then he ordered the Veffel to be turned a-drift.

Mr. Coniers. What followed in *January*?

Bradinham. January the 20th, Captain *Kidd* took a *Por-tuguefe* that came from *Bengal:* He took out of her two Chefts of *Opium*, fome *Eaft-India* Goods, and Bags of Rice, &c.

Mr. Coniers. How long did you keep this Ship?

Bradinham. He kept this *Portuguefe* Ship about feven Days; He took out of her fome Butter, Wax, and *Eaft-India* Goods; He kept her till he was chafed by feven or eight Sail of *Dutch*, and then he loft her.

Mr. Coniers. My Lord, Now we are come to that on which the Indictments is founded. Mr. *Bradinham*, give a particular Account of that.

Bradinham. Some time in January, Captain *Kidd* took the *Quedagh-Merchant:* He gave her chafe under *French* Colours: He came up with her, and commanded the Mafter aboard: And there came an old *Frenchman* in the Boat; and after he had been aboard a while, he told Captain *Kidd* he was not the Captain, but the Gunner. And Captain *Kidd* fent for the Captain on board his Ship.

Mr. Coniers. Who was that?

Bradinham. Mr. *Wright.*

Mr. Coniers. What Countryman was he?

Bradinham. An *Englifhman.* He was fent for aboard, and came; and Captain *Kidd* told him, he was his Prifoner. And he ordered his Men to go a-board, and take Poffeffion of the Ship, and difpofed of the Goods on that Coaft to the Value of Seven or Eight Thoufand Pounds.

Mr. Coniers. What Perfons were a-board her?

Bradinham. There was Captain *Wright*, and two *Dutch-men*, and a *Frenchman*, and fome *Armenians*, and the reft *Moors.*

Mr. Coniers. Did thefe Armenians make any Offer of any Money for their Ranfom?

Bradinham. Captain *Kidd* told them, They fhould be ran-fomed, if they made an Offer that he liked of. So they offered him twenty thoufand *Rupees.* He told them, That was but a fmall parcel of Money, and the Cargo was worth a great deal more.

Mr. *Coniers.* Who did the Cargo belong to?

Bradinham. To thofe *Armenians,* as I was informed by Captain *Wright.*

Mr. *Coniers.* What did he do with them?

Bradinham. He difpofed of fome of them on the Coaft of *India.*

Mr. *Coniers.* What did he do with the Proceed of the Goods he fold?

Bradinham. He fhared the Money.

Mr. *Coniers.* Had thefe Men (the other Prifoners) any of the Shares?

Bradinham. Yes, all of them. You were a Half-fhare Man, and you a Half-fhare Man, (pointing to two of them.)

Mr. *Coniers.* Mr. *Bradinham,* You fay Capt. Wright came a-board *Kidd's* Ship.

Bradinham. Yes.

Mr. *Coniers.* Did he difcourfe with him?

Bradinham. I was not with him, for he kept his Cabin to himfelf.

Mr. *Coniers.* But you are fure he came a-board?

Bradinham. Yes.

Mr. *Coniers.* And that he was an *Englifhman?*

Bradinham. Yes.

Mr. *Coniers.* How did Captain *Kidd* behave himfelf to the Ships or Boats there?

Bradinham. He boarded feveral Ships, and took out of of them what was for his turn.

Mr. *Coniers.* How did he ufe thofe that he traded with?

Bradinham. Some of them came a-board feveral times, and he traded with them: But fome of them came a-board when he was going away, and he plundered them, and fent them a-fhore without any Goods.

Mr. *Coniers.* What Country Men were thofe he ferved thus?

Bradinham. Mahometans: They had dealt with him before confiderably.

Mr. *Coniers*. How much did he take from them.

Bradinham. About Five Hundred Pieces of Eight.

Mr. *Coniers*. How do you know that?

Bradinham. I faw it told afterwards. We went to *Mada-gafcar* afterwards, and by the Way met with a *Moorifh* Ship, and took out of her feveral Casks of Butter, and other Things.

Mr. *Cowper*. What were the Crew of this Ship?

Mr. *J. Powell*. They are Indicted for the *Quedagh-Merchant*; Were all the Prifoners in that Action? You have given an Hiftorical Account from the Beginning, that he was a meer Plunderer; But now you are come to the *Quedagh*, for which they are Indicted; Go not beyond it.

Mr. *Coniers*. Look on the feveral Prifoners at the Bar, and tell whether any of the Prifoners were at the taking of the *Quedagh- Merchant*.

Cl. of Arr. Was *William Kidd* there, at the time the Ship was taken?

Bradinham. Yes.

Cl. of Arr. Was Nicholas Churchill there?

Bradinham. Yes.

Cl. of Arr. Do you know *James Howe?* Was he there?

Bradinham. Yes.

Cl. of Arr. Had he a Share?

Bradinham. Yes.

Cl. of Arr. Had Robert Lamley a Share?

Bradinham. Yes. He was a Servant, and had but a share of the Money, and a whole Share of the Goods.

Cl. of Arr. William Jenkins, was he there, and had a Share?

Bradinham. Yes.

Cl. of Arr. Gabriel Loffe, did you know what he had?

Bradinham. He had half a Share of the Money, and a whole Share of the Goods.

Cl. of Arr. Hugh Parrot, what had he?

Bradinham. Half a Share.

Cl. of Arr. Had *Richard Barlicorn* a Share?

Brad.nham. He had half a Share of Money, and a whole Share of Goods.

Cl. of Arr. Had *Abel Owens* any?

Bradinham. He had half a Share.

Abel Owens. Had I any of it?

Bradinham. You had it: You took it.

Cl. of Arr. What had *Darby Mullins*?

Bradinham. He had half a Share of the Money, and a whole Share of Goods.

Mr. *Coniers.* Now We have fully proved this as to the *Que-dagh-Merchant.*

Dr. *Newton.* When you came to *Madagascar* what was done there?

Bradinham. There came a *Canooe* to us with some Englifh Men in her, they were formerly acquainted with Captain *Kidd,* and they told him, They had heard, that he was come to take them, and hang them.

Dr. *Newton.* Who were they?

Bradinham. They belonged to the *Moco* Frigate.

Mr. *Coniers.* Give a particular Account of that Matter.

Bradinham. When we came to *Madagascar,* there came a *Canooe* off to us.

Mr. *Coniers.* From whom?

Bradinham. From the *Moco* Frigate, Captain Culliford was the Commander. And there were some white Men in her, that had formerly been acquainted with Captain *Kidd;* they heard that he was come to take them, and hang them. He told them, it was no such thing for he was as bad as they.

Mr. *Coniers.* Were they thought to be Pirates?

Bradinham. They were so.

Mr. *Coniers.* What was it that Captain Kidd said?

Bradinham. He assured them it was no such thing. And afterwards went aboard with them, and swore to be true to them; and he took a Cup of Bomboe, and swore to be true to them, and assist them; and he assisted this Captain *Culliford* with Guns, and an Anchor, to fit him to Sea again.

L. C. B. *Ward.* How came you to know all this? Was you aboard them?

Bradinham. I was aboard then, and I heard the Words.

Dr. *Newton.* Were any of the Goods divided at *Madagascar*?

Bradinham. Yes.

Mr. *Coniers.* Now look on the Prifoners again, you fay after he met with this Captain *Culliford*, you went and had a Divifion made; pray give details.

Bradinham. When we came to *Madagafcar*, Captain *Kidd* ordered the Goods to be carried a-fhore, and fhared. And he had forty Shares himfelf.

Cl. of Arr. Had *Nicholas Churchill* a Share?

Bradinham. Yes.

Cl. of Arr. Had *James Howe* a Share?

Bradinham. Yes.

Cl. of Arr. Had *Robert Lamley* a Share?

Bradinham. Yes.

Cl. of Arr. Had *William Jenkins* a Share?

Bradinham. Yes.

Cl. of Arr. Had *Gabriel Loffe* a Share?

Bradinham. Yes.

Cl. of Arr. Had *Hugh Parrot* a Share?.

Bradinham. Yes.

Cl. of Arr. Had *Richard Barlicorn* a Share?

Bradinham. Yes.

Cl. of Arr. Had *Abel Owens* a Share?

Bradinham. Yes.

Cl. of Arr. Had *Darby Mullins* a Share?

Bradinham. Yes.

Cl. of Arr. So that you fay, every one of the Prifoners at the Bar had a Share.

Bradinham. Yes.

Mr. *Coniers.* What become afterwards of the *Adventure-Ga\ley?*

Bradinham. She was fo leaky, that fhe had two Pumps going; and when they came to fhore, they left her, becaufe fhe was not fit to go to Sea again. And fo Captain *Kidd* went aboard the *Scuddee Merchant*, and defigned to make a Man of War of her.

Mr. *Coniers.* What is that *Scuddee-Merchant?* Do you mean the *Quedagh-Merchant?*

Bradinham. Yes.

L. C. B. *Ward.* What became of that Ship afterwards?

Bradinham. I left him at *Madagafcar,* after the Money and Goods were divided; and can give no Account afterwards.

Dr. *Newton.* But you fay, Captain *Kidd* went a-board the *Quedagh.*

Bradinham. Yes.

Mr. *Coniers.* My Lord, we have done as to this Witnefs; if they will ask him any Thing they may.

Cl. of Arr. Will any of you ask him any Queftions?

Kidd. He fays, when we went out firft from *England,* we went out of *Plymouth* in *May,* which we did not; for we went in April, therefore this is a Contradiction.

L. C. B. *Ward.* Mr. *Kidd,* if you will ask him any Question, you may. Do you defire he fhould be pofitive when you went from *Plymouth?*

Bradinham. It was about the firft of *May,* my Lord.

L. C. B. *Ward.* What Year?

Bradinham. In the Year, 1696.

Cl. of Arr. Nicholas Churchill, will you ask him any Queftions?

Churchill. I would have went a-fhore at *Carawar,* but the Captain would not let me.

L. C. B. *Ward.* It is proved, that you was at the taking of the *Quedagh-Merchant,* and dividing the Goods.

Churchill. Yes, my Lord, but I could not help it, I was forced to do what the Captain ordered me.

Cl. of Arr. James Howe, will you ask any Questionf?

James Howe. Have I not obeyed my Captain in all his Commands?

L. C. B. *Ward.* There is no doubt made of that. If any of you will ask him any Queftions, you may.

Kidd. Did you not fee any French Paffes aborad the *Queda* Merchant?

Bradinham. You told me you had *French* Paffes, I never did fee them.

Kidd. Did you never declare this to any body, that you faw thefe *French* Paffes?

Bradinham. No, I never did fee any; but I only faid, I heard you fay you had them.

Churchill. Had I any ſhare?

Bradinham. Yes.

Churchill. How will you prove that?

Jenkins. My Lord, I ask him, Whether I was not a Servant?

L. C. B. *Ward.* Ask the Witneſs what Qeuſtions you will.

Bradinham. My Lord he was a Servant.

L. C. B. *Ward.* Who was he a Servant to?

Bradibham. To *George Bullen.*

Jenkins. My Lord, I beg you will examine my Indenture; for I have it in my Pocket, I had nothing aboard that Ship, but what my Maſter had.

Bradinham. But you had a ſhare of the Goods, I cannot tell whether your Maſter had it afterwards.

Cl. of Arr. Gabriel Loff. Have you any Queſtion to ask him?

Gab. Loff. I have nothing to ſay to him, but to ask him, Whether I did ever diſobey my Captain's Commands, or was any ways mutinous on Board the Ship?

Bradinham. No, I cannot ſay you did.

Cl. of Arr. Hugh Parrot, do you ask him any Queſtions?

Parrot. No.

Cl. of Arr. Richard Barlicorn, do you ask him any Queſtions?

Barlicorn. I ask him, Whether I was not the Captain's Servant?

L. C. B. *Ward.* Yes, he ſays he was.

Cl. of Arr. Abel Owens, will you ask him any Queſtions?

Owens. I have nothing to ſay; but depend upon the King's Proclamation.

Cl. of Arr. Darby Molins, have you any Queſtions to ask him?

Molins. My Lord, he knows I had nothing but what Capt. *Kidd* was pleas'd to give me.

L. C. B. *Ward.* Was he a Servant to Capt. *Kidd* or no?

Bradinham. He had a half ſhare of Money, and a whole ſhare of Goods.

Mr. *J. Powel.* What was the reaſon ſome had whole ſhares, and ſome half ſhares?

Bradinham. Some were able Seamen, and ſome Landmen, or Servants. There were in all 160 ſhares, whereof Capt. *Kidd* had 49; and fome of the Men had whole fhares, and fome only half fhares.

Mr. *Cowper*. You told us at firft, That in your paffage to *New-York*, you took a *French* Banker, and that he condemned her at *New-York*.

Bradinham. Yes.

Mr. *Cowper*. Did he offer to carry any other Ships he took, to be condemned?

Bradinham. No, Sir, never.

Mr. *Coniers*. Call *Jofeph Palmer*. (who appeared.) Mr. *Palmer*, Give my Lord, and the Jury an account, whether you were one of the Men that went with Capt. *Kidd* in the *Adventure-Galley*.

Palmer. Yes, I was.

Mr. *Coniers*. Then give an account when you left *England;* and of your proceedings in your Voyage.

Palmer. About the laft of *April*, or the beginning of *May*, 1696, we went out of *Plymouth* to *New-York;* and by the Way took a *French* Banker. And in *July* we came to *New-York*. About the 6th of *February* we went to *Maderas*.

Mr. *Coniers*. When you were at *New York*, was there any publication of any Thing to invite Men to come in to Captain *Kidd?*

Palmer. Yes, there were Articles fet up for Men to come aboard Captain *Kidd's* Ship. He was to have Forty Shares for his Ship, and every Man was to have a Share. And they were to give him Six Pounds a Man for their Arms.

Mr. *Coniers*. How many Men was his Complement?

Palmer. When he came from *New-York*, he had between 150 and 160 Men.

Mr. *Coniers*. Give an Account what you did after this. Whither did you go then?

Palmer. We went from *New-York* to *Maderas*, and from thence to *Bonavift*, and there we took in Salt; and from thence we went to St. *Jago*, and there we bought Provifions; and from thence we went to *Madagafcar*. When we were not far from the *Cape of good hope*, he met with Capt. *Warren*, with three Sail of Men of War befides himfelf; there was the *Tyger*, and the *King-fifher*, and another Ship. And Capt. *Kidd* kept them company about three or four Days, and after that went to *Madagafcar*, and fometime in *February* arriv'd there; and there we watered and victualled. We came to *Malabar* about the firft of *June*. Then we went to *Joanna*, and from thence to *Mahala;* and from thence to *Joanna*, and from thence to *Mahala;* and from thence to *Joanna* again. And then we met with fome *Indian* Merchants, fo we watered the Ship there, and did them no harm. And from thence we went to *Mahala*, where Captain *Kidd* graved his Ship; We had a great ficknefs in the Ship, and fometimes we loft four or five Men in a Day. And afterwards we went to *Joanna* again, and there came aboard feveral *French* Men, and feveral *Englifh* Men that had loft their Ship. Thofe *French* Men lent Captain *Kidd* fome Money to mend his Ship. And after this, we went to a Place called *Mabbee* in the *Red-Sea*, and took in Water, and *Guiny* Corn that he took from the Natives. And from thence we went to *Babs* Key.

Mr. *Coniers*. What Time was it that you came to that *Babs* Key?

Palmer. In *July* 1697.

Mr. *Coniers*. Now pray tell us what paffed there.

Palmer. When Captain *Kidd* came to *Babs* Key, ftayed there about three Weeks.

Mr. *Coniers*. Why did you ftay there? Tell us the Reafon of it.

Palmer. I heard him fay, *Come Boys, I will make Money enough out of that Fleet.*

Mr. *Coniers*. Out of what Fleet?

Palmer. The *Mocco* Fleet. When he came to the Key, he ordered fome of his Men to look out as Spies. He fent his Boat three times to make Difcovery, and he gave Orders either to take a Prifoner, or to get an Account what Ships lay there. And the Boat went twice, and brought no News; but the third Time they brought Word, that there were Fourteen or Fifteen Ships lying there ready to Sail; fome of them had *Englifh* Colours, fome *Dutch* Colours, and fome *Moorifh* Colours; and that there was a great Ship with Red

Colours, with her Fore-top-fail loofe, ready to Sail. And Captain *Kidd* ordered his Men to take care thefe Ships did not pafs by in the Night.

Mr. *Coniers.* You fay, he ordered his Men to watch this Fleet, How did he order them?

Palmer. He ordered them by a lift in their Turns, to look out for the coming of this Fleet. And fo after four or five Days the Fleet came down in an Evening, about the 14th or 15th of *Auguft;* the next Morning Captain *Kidd* went after them, and he fell into the Midft of the Fleet, and there was a *Dutch* Convoy, and an *Englifh* one among them. He went into the midft of the Fleet, and fired a Gun after a *Moorifh* Ship. And the two Men of War fired at us, but did no harm, for they did not reach us. So he left the Fleet, and from thence went to *Carawar.*

Mr. *Coniers.* Tell what paffed there.

Palmer. Then we met with a fmall Veffel belonging to Aden.

Mr. *Coniers.* What Country did it belong to?

Palmer. Black People, only there was one Thomas *Parker,* and a *Portuguefe Don Antonio* on board.

Mr. *Coniers.* Was he the Commander of the Ship?

Palmer. I cannot tell.

Mr. *Coniers.* What did Captain *Kidd* do with this Ship?

Palmer. He took this *Parker* for a Pilot, and the *Portuguefe* for a Linghuifter.

Mr. *Coniers.* What do you mean by that Word Linguifter?

Palmer. An interpreter to fpeak *Spanish* and *Portuguefe.*

Mr. *Coniers.* Did he take any thing out of the Ship befides the Men?

Palmer. He took a Bail of Pepper, and a Bail of Coffee, and let the Ship go. But after this we came to *Carawar.*

Mr. *Coniers.* Before you let the Ship go, how were the Men ufed by him?

Palmer. He ordered fome of the men to be hoifted up by their Arms, and rubb'd with a naked Cutlafs. They were laid with their Hands backward.

Mr. *Coniers.* When they were hoifted up, give an Account how they were ufed, and for what Reafon.

Palmer. They were beat with a naked Cutlſas to make them diſcover what Money was aboard.

Mr. *Coniers.* What was the next Thing?

Palmer. He took out this *Parker* for a Pilot, and *Antonio* the *Portugueſe* for a Linguiſter. I heard there was Money taken, but I did not ſee it.

Mr. *Coniers.* What did he do with thoſe Men?

Palmer. He kept them as the other Men were kept.

Mr. *Coniers.* Was there any Demand made of theſe Men?

Palmer. When we came to *Carawar*, the Factory demanded them, and he denied them.

Mr. *Coniers.* What Factory is this?

Palmer. An *Engliſh* Factory. There was one *Harvey* and *Maſon* came to demand theſe Men.

Mr. *Coniers.* And what ſaid Capt. *Kidd* to them?

Palmer. He deny'd that he had any ſuch Men, and he kept them in the Hold, I believe a Week. Several of his Men would have left him if they could.

Mr. *Coniers.* What did he do after this?

Palmer. He put to Sea, and met with a *Portugueſe* Man of War, and fought her; he engaged her five or ſix Hours, and afterwards left her, and then he bought ſome Hogs of the Natives. After he went from this *Carawar*, he went to *Porco*, and took in ſome Hogs there. And then went to the Iſland of *Malabar*, and watered his Ship. And his Cooper went a-ſhore, and the Natives cut his Throat. And after this, Capt. *Kidd* ſent ſome Men aſhore, and ordered them, That if they ſhould meet any of the Natives, they ſhould kill 'em, and plunder 'em.

Mr. *Coniers.* Go on, Sir.

Palmer. After That, they went to the Coaſt of *Malabar* again, and in *November* met with a Ship, and took her. One *Schipper Mitchet* was the Commander: She was a *Mooriſh* Ship.

Mr. *Coniers.* What became of her?

Palmer. Capt. *Kidd* carried her to *Madagaſcar*.

Mr. *Coniers.* What Goods were in her?

Palmer. There were two Horſes, and [ten Bails of Cotton, that he ſold to the Natives.

Mr. *Coniers.* Did he ſend for any aboard at this Time?

Palmer. There was a *Frenchman* that was to pretend him-ſelf the Captain. He took her under *French* Colours, and haled the Ship in *French.* And this *Monſieur le Roy* was to paſs for Captain, and he ſhewed his *French* Paſs, and . . .

Mr. *Coniers.* Give an Account of his perſonating the Cap-tain. Who order'd him to do ſo?

Palmer. Capt. *Kidd* ordered him to do ſo; and they haled him in *French*, and he came aboard, and he had a *French* Paſs. And then Capt. *Kidd* told him, he was Captain.

Mr. *Coniers.* And he took the Ship?

Palmer. Yes the Cotton, and Horſes, and ſold them after-wards.

Mr. *Coniers.* Whither went you next?

Palmer. We coaſted about the Coaſt of *Malabar.*

Mr. *Coniers.* Did you meet with any Boats there?

Palmer. Yes, ſeveral.

Mr. *Coniers.* What did you do with them?

Palmer. Capt. *Kidd* robb'd and plundered them, and turn'd them adrift again.

Mr. *Coniers.* What was the next Thing you did?

Palmer. About the Firſt of *January* we met with a *Portu-gueſe* Ship.

Mr. *Coniers.* Where?

Palmer. On the ſame Coaſt. We took her.

Mr. *Coniers.* What did you do with that Ship?

Palmer. He kept her a Week, and took out two Cheſts of *Indian* Goods, and thirty Jars of Butter and a Tun of Wax, and half a Tun of Iron, and an hundred Bags of Rice.

Mr. *Coniers.* Did you take thoſe Goods you mention?

Palmer. Yes, and carried them aboard the *Adventure-Gally.*

Mr. *Coniers.* What was the next Ship you met with?

Palmer. The *Queda Merchant.*

L. C. B. *Ward.* Be very plain and particular in this, and

how She was taken; for this is the Ship in the Indictment, and for taking of which the Prifoners are tryed.

Palmer. About the laſt of January ſhe was taken; I was not then aboard the Gally, for then I was aboard the *November*, and was ordered to get Water. After three or four Days I went aboard; but I was not aboard at the Time ſhe was taken. About three or four Days after, I ſaw her, and Capt. *Kidd* was aboard; and I believe there were taken out of her, Goods, to the Value of Ten or Twelve Thouſand Pounds; which were ſold, ſome before they were put aſhore, and ſome after.

Mr. *Coniers.* To whom were they ſold?

Palmer. To the *Banians.* Capt. *Kidd* kept the Seamen to help to ſail the Ships.

L. C. B. *Ward.* What became of the Money the Goods were ſold for?

Palmer. It was ſhared.

L. C. B. *Ward.* What Share had the Captain?

Palmer. He had forty Shares.

Cl. of Arr. In Goods, or Money?

Palmer. In both Goods and Money.

Cl. of Arr. Look upon *Nich. Churchill,* What had he?

Palmer. He had near Two Hundred Pounds of each, which was a Man's Share.

Cl. of Arr. Look upon *James Howe,* Had he any Share?

Palmer. Yes, a whole Share.

Cl. of Arr. Had *Robert Lamley* any Share?

Palmer. He had half a Share of the Money, and a whole Share of the Goods.

Cl. of Arr. Will. Jenkins, Had he any Share?

Palmer. He had half a Share of the Money, and a whole Share of the Goods.

Cl. of Arr. Had *Gabriel Loff* any Share?

Palmer. He had half a Share of the Money, and a whole Share of the Goods.

Mr. *Coniers.* Why had they no more?

Palmer. They were Land-men.

Cl. of Arr. Hugh Parrot. Had he any?

Palmer. He had a whole Share.

Cl. of Arr. Had *Richard Barlicorn* any Share?

Palmer. He had half a Share.

Cl. of Arr. Had *Abel Owens* any?

Palmer. He had a whole Share.

Cl. of Arr. Had *Darby Mullins* any Share?

Palmer. He had a whole Share.

Mr. *Coniers.* What became of the reſt of the Goods?

Palmer. They were carried to *Madagaſcar.*

Mr. *Coniers.* Who ordered the Goods to be hoiſted out, and ſhared? Who ordered that?

Palmer. At the Beginning I was not there.

Mr. *Coniers.* Who ordered it?

Palmer. Captain *Kidd.* And moſt of the Goods were a-ſhore before I came back, and before I came back he had his Share, and moſt of the reſt.

Mr. *Coniers.* How many of the Prisoners at the bar, had their Shares of the Goods?

Palmer. All theſe Men.

Cl. of Arr. Whoſe Shares were divided to them before you went away?

Palmer. None; but only they were prepared in order to be divided.

L. C. B. *Ward* Did you hear any ot them ſay They had any Shares?

Palmer. Yes, *Hugh Parrot,* and *Gabriel Loffe.*

Cl. of Arr. What ſay you to *Will. Kidd?* Did he own he had any Share?

Palmer. No.

Cl. of Arr. Did you hear *Nich. Churchill* ſay he had any?

Palmer. No, I did not; I cannot ſay, I heard them ſay ſo.

Cl. of Arr. Did you hear *Gabriel Loffe* and *Hugh Parrot* ſay, they had any Shares?

Palmer. Yes, I heard them ſay ſo.

Mr. *Coniers.* Whither did you proceed next?

Palmer. We left Captain *Kidd* there, I went on further with him.

Mr. *Coniers*. I ask you, whether you met with any Ships, befides what you mentioned?

Palmer. When we came to *Madagafcar*, in the latter end of *April*, or beginning of *May* 1696, there was a Ship called the *Refolution*, which was formerly called the *Moco* Frigate; feveral of the Men came off to Captain *Kidd*, and told him, they heard he came to take, and hang them. He faid that it was no fuch thing, and that he would do them all the Good he could. And Captain *Culliford* came aboard of Captain *Kidd*, and Captain *Kidd* went aboard of *Culliford*.

Mr. *Coniers*. Who was that *Culliford*?

Palmer. The Captain of the Ship. And on the Quarter-deck they made fome Bomboo, and drank together, and Captain Kidd faid, before I would do you any harm, I would have my Soul fry in Hell-fire; and wifhed Damnation to himfelf feveral times, if he did. And he took the Cup, and wifhed that might be his laft, if he did not do them all the Good he could.

Mr. *Powell*. Did you take thefe Men to be Pirates?

Palmer. They were reckoned fo.

Dr. *Newton*. Did Captain *Kidd* make *Culliford* any Prefents?

Palmer. Yes, he had four Guns of him.

Dr. *Newton*. Of whom?

Palmer. Of Captain *Kidd*, he presented him with them.

Mr. *Powell*. Was there not a Prefent on the other Side?

Palmer. I believe there was, I have heard fo; I heard *Culliford* fay, I have prefented Captain *Kidd* to the Value of four or five Hundred Pounds.

Mr. *Cowper*. Were thefe Kindneffes done to *Culliford* after *Culliford's* Men faid, they heard that Captain *Kidd* was come to hang them?

Palmer. Yes.

Mr. *Cowper*. What did Captain *Kidd* do after that?

Palmer. He went aboard the *Quedagh* Merchant.

Mr. *Cowper*. What did he do with his own Ship?

Palmer. She was leaky, and he left her.

Mr. *Cowper*. Did he carry, or attempt to carry, any of the

Ships he took, in order to condemn them, befides that *French* Banker?

Palmer. He never did, nor talked of any fuch thing.

L. C. B. *Ward.* Mr. *Kidd,* Will you ask this Witnefs any Queftions?

Kidd. I ask him, Whether I had no *French* Paffes?

Palmer. Indeed Captain *Kidd,* I cannot tell. I did hear him fay, that he had *French* Paffes, but I never faw them.

L. C. B. *Ward.* Thofe Goods that were taken out of the *Quedagh* Merchant, whofe Goods were they fuppofed to be?

Palmer. The *Armenian* Merchants. I have heard Captain Kidd fay feveral times, he had *French* Paffes.

Kidd. And did you hear no-Body elfe fay fo?

Palmer. No.

Cl. of Arr. Churchill. Will you ask him any Queftions?

Churchill. My Lord, I have no Queftions to ask him.

Cl. of Arr. James Howe, Will you ask him any Queftions?

J. Howe. No.

Cl. of Arr. Robert Lamley, Will you ask him any Queftions?

Robert Lamley. No.

Cl. of Arr. Will. Jenkins, Will you ask him any Questions?

William Jenkins. Had I half a Share?

Palmer. You received half a Share of Money, and a whole Share of Goods.

Will. Jenkins. You know that I was a Servant, and had nothing in this Voyage but what my Mafter had.

C. of Arr. Gabriel Loffe, Will you ask him any Queftions?

Gabriel Loffe. No.

Cl. of Arr. Hugh Parrot, Will you ask him any Queftions?

Hugh Parrot. No.

Cl. of Arr. Richard Barlicorn, Will you ask him any Toing?

Richard Barlicorn. No.

Cl. of Arr. Abel Owens, Will you ask him any Thing?

Abel Owens. No.

Cl. of Arr. Darby Mullins, Will you ask him any Thing?

Darby Mullins. No.

Kidd. It is in vain to ask any Queftions.

L. C. B. *Ward.* Then you may make your own Defence.

Come Mr. *Kidd*, what have you to fay in your own Defence?

Kidd. I had a Commiſſion to take the *French*, and Pirates, and in order to that, I came up with two Ships, that had *French* Paſſes both of them. I called you all a Deck to confult; and did not a great many of the Men go aboard? Did not you go? You know, Mr. *Palmer*, I would have given thefe Ships to them again, but you would not; you all voted againft it.

Palmer. This man (*pointing to the* Armenian, *that was in Court*) offered you twenty thouſand Rupees for the Ship, and you refuſed it.

Kidd. Did not I ask, Where will you carry this Ship? And you ſaid, we will make a Prize of her, we will carry her to *Madagaſcar*.

Palmer. Says Captain *Kidd* to his Men, Thefe *Armenians* make ſuch a Noiſe for the Ship, that there was not a quarter part of the Men concerned in it. The *Arnemians* came crying and wringing their Hands; Upon which, ſays Captain *Kidd*, I muſt ſay, my Men will not give them the Ship. And ſo ſome of the Men went on the Fore-caſtle, and pretended, they would not give them the Ship; but there was not a quarter part of the Men concerned in it.

L. C. B. *Ward.* Did thoſe Goods belong to *Frenchmen*, or *Armenians*?

Palmer. To *Armenians*.

L. C. B. *Ward.* What was the Pretence of a French Paſs that was on Board the *Quedagh Merchant*?

Palmer. I ſaw none.

Kidd. But you have heard of it.

Palmer. I have heard of it, but never ſaw it.

L. C. B. *Ward.* Mr. *Kidd*, have you any more to ſay? You ſpeak of a Commiſſion that you had, you may have it read if you pleaſe.

Kidd. I defire to have them both read.

L. C. B. *Ward.* Yes, they ſhall.

Then his Commiſſion for Repriſals upon the *French* was Read.

WILLIAM the Third, *By the Grace of God, of* England,

Scotland, France *and* Ireland, *King, Defender of the Faith,
&c. Whereas We having taken into Our Confideration, the In-
juries, Spoils, and Acts of Hoftility committed by the French
King and his Subjects, unto, and upon the Ships, Goods and
Perfons of our Subjects extending to their grievous Damages, and
amounting to great Summs; and that notwithftanding the many
and frequent Demands made for redrefs and reparation, yet none
could ever be obtain'd. We did therefore with the Advice of our
Privy Council, think fit, and ordered, that general Reprizals be
Granted againft the Ships, Goods, and Subjects of the Frcnch
King; fo tha{,} as well Our Fleets and Ships, an alfo all other
Ships, and Veffels that fhall be Commiffioned by Letters of
Marque, or general Reprizals, or otherwife, fhall and may lawfully feize, and take all Ships, Veffels, and Goods belongong ti
the French King, or his Subjects, or Inhabitants within any of
the Territories of the French King: And fuch other Ships, Veffels, and Goods, as are, or fhall be liable to Confifcation, and
bring the fame to Judgment in our High Court of Admiralty of
England, or fuch other Court of Admiralty of* England, *or fuch
other Court of Admiralty as fhall be lawfully Authorized in that
behalf, according to the ufual courfe and Laws of Nations. And
Whereas William* Kid *is thought fitly qualified, and hath Equipped, Furnifhed, and Victualled a Ship called,* The Adventure
Gally, *of the burthen of about Two Hundred eighty feven Tunns
whereof the faid* William Kid *is Commander. And whereas, he
the faid* William Kid *hath given Security with Secureties by
Bond to Us, in Our faid High Court of Admiralty according to
the effect and form fet down in certain Inftructions made the
fecond Day of* May, *One thoufand fix hundred ninety three, and
in the Fifth Year of Our Reign, a Copy whereof is given to the
faid Capt.* William Kid. *Know ye therefore, That we by thefe
prefents, grant Commiffion to, and do Licence and Authorize the
faid* William Kid *to fet forth in warlike manner the faid Ship
call'd,* The Adventure Gally, *under his own Command, and
therewith by force of Arms to Apprehend, Seize and take the
Ships, Veffels and Goods belonging to the French King and his
Subjects, or Inhabitants within the Dominions of the faid French
King; and fuch other Ships, Veffels, and Goods, as are, or fhall*

*be liable to Confiscation, and to bring the same to such Port as
shall be most convenient, in order to have them legally adjudged
in Our High Court of Admiralty, or such other Court of Admiralty as shall be lawfully Authorized in that behalf; which
being Condemned, it shall and may be lawful for the said* William
Kid, *to sell and dispose of such Ships, Vessels, and Goods, so
adjudged and condemned, in such sort and manner as by the
course of Admiralty hath been accustomed (except in such Cases,
where it is otherwise directed by the said Instructions and the
Act of Parliament thereunto annexed) Provided always, that the
said* William Kid, *keep an exact Journal of his proceedings, and
therein particularly take notice of all Prizes which shall be taken
by him, the nature of such Prizes, the times, and places of their
being taken, and the values of them, as near as he can judge; as
also of the station, motion, and strengh of the Enemy, as well as
he or his Mariners can discover by the best Intelligence he can
get; and also whatsoever else, shall come unto him, or any of his
Officers, or Mariners, or be discovered or declared unto him or
them, or found out by examination, or conference with any Mariners or Passengers of, or in any of the Ships or Vessels taken
or by any other person, or persons, or by any other ways or
means whatsoever touching or concerning the Designs of the Enemy, or any of their Fleets, Vessels, or Parties, and of their Stations, Ports, and Places, and of their intents therein; and of
what Merchants Ships or Vessels of the Enemy's bound out, or
home, or to any other place, as he, or his Officers, or Mariners
shall hear of, and of what else material in those Cases may ar-
rive to his, or their knowledge, of all which he shall from time
to time, as he shall, or may have opportunity, transmit an account to our Commissioners for executing the Office of Lord
High Admiral of* England, *or their Secretaries, and to keep a
Correspondence with them by all opportunities that shall present.
And further, Provided that nothing be done by the said* William
Kid, *or any of his Officers, Mariners, or Company, contrary to
the true meaning of Our aforesaid Instructions, but that the said
Instructions shall be by them, and each and every of them, as far
as they, or any of them are therein concern'd, in all particulars
well and duly perform'd and observed. And We pray and desire*

*all Kings, Princes, Potentates, Eſtates, and Republicks, being
Our Friends and Allies, and all others to whom it ſhall apper-
tain, to give the ſaid* William Kid *all aid, aſſiſtance and ſuccour
in their Ports with his ſaid Ship, Company and Prizes, without
doing, of ſuffering to be done to him any wrong, trouble, or hindrance; We offering to do like when We ſhall be by them thereunto desired. And We will and require all Our own Officers
whatſoever, to give him ſuccour and aſſiſtance as occaſion ſhall require This Our Commiſſion to continue in force till further order
to the contrary from Us, or Our Commiſſioners for executing the
Office of Lord High Admiral of* England. *In Witneſs whereof
We have cauſed the Great Seal of Our High Court of Admiralty of*
England *to be hereunto affixed.* Given at *London* the Eleventh
Day of *December,* in the Year of Our Lord One Thouſand ſix
hundred ninety five, and in the Seventh Year of Our Reign.

Orlando Gee, Reg.

Mr. *Juſt. Powel.* Capt. *Kidd,* Can you make it appear there
was a *French* Paſs aboard the *Queda* Merchant?

Will. Kidd. My Lord, theſe Men ſay, They heard ſeveral
ſay ſo.

Mr. *Coniers.* But all came from you.

L. C. B. *Ward.* If there was a French Paſs in the Ship, you
ought to have condemned her as Prize.

Then his other Commiſſion was Read for Cruiſing againſt
the Pirates.

WILLIAM *Rex,*

WILLIAM III. *By the Grace of God, King of* England,
Scotland, France *and* Ireland, *Defender of the Faith,* &c. *To
our truſty and well beloved Capt.* William Kid, *Commander of
the Ship* Adventure Gally, *or to any other, the Commander of
the ſame for the time being,* Greeting, *Whereas, We are inform'd,
that Capt.* Thomas Too, John Ireland, *Capt.* Thomas Wake,
and Capt. William Maze, *or* Mace, *and other Our Subjects,
Natives, or Inhabitants of* New England, New York, *and elſe-
where, in Our Plantations in* America, *have aſſociated themſelves with divers other wicked and ill-diſpoſed Perſons, and do
againſt the Law of Nations, daily commit many and great Piracies, Robberies, and Depradations upon the Seas in the parts*

R. LIVINGSTON

of America, *and in other parts, to the great hindrance and dif-
çouragement of Trade and Navigation, and to the danger and
hurt of our Loving Subjects, Our Allies, and all others Navigating the Seas upon their lawful Occaſions:* Now Know Ye, *That
We being deſirous to prevent the aforeſaid Miſchiefs; and as far
as in Us lyes, to bring the ſaid Pirates, Freebooters, and Sea-
Rovers to Juſtice, have thought fit, and do hereby Give, and Grant
unto you the ſaid Capt.* William Kid (*to whom Our Commiſſioners for Exerciſing the Office of Our Lord High Admiral of*
England, *have Granted a Commiſſion as a private Man of War
bearing date the Eleventh day of* December, 1695.) *and unto
the Commander of the ſaid Ship for the time being, and unto
the Officers, Mariners and others which ſhall be under your Command, full Power and Authority, to Apprehend, Seize, and take
into your Cuſtody, as well the ſaid Capt.* Thomas Too, John
Ireland, *Capt.* Thomas Wake, *and Capt.* William Maze, *or*
Mace, *as all ſuch Pirates, Freebooters, and Sea-Rovers, being
either Our own Subjects, or of other Nations aſſociated with them,
which you ſhall meet with upon the Coaſts or Seas of* America,
*or in any other Seas, or Ports, with their Ships and Veſſels, and
alſo ſuch Merchandizes, Money, Goods and Wares, as ſhall be
found on board, or with them, in caſe they willingly yield themſelves. But if they will not submit without fighting; then you are
by force to compel them go yield: And we do alſo require you
to bring, or cauſe to be brought ſuch Pirates, Freebooters, and
Sea-Rovers as you ſhall ſeize to a legal Tryal; to the end that
they may be proceeded againſt according to the law in ſuch Caſes.
And We do hereby charge, and command all Our Officers, Min-
iſters, and other Our loving Subjects whatſoever, to be Aiding and
Aſſiſting to you in the Premiſes. And We do hereby enjoin you
keep an exact Journal of your proceeding in the Execution of
the Premiſes, and therein to ſet down the Names of ſuch Pirates,
and of their Officers and Company, and the Names of ſuch Ships
and Veſſels as you ſhall by virtue of theſe Preſents ſeize and take,
and the true value of the ſame, as near as you can judge. And
We do hereby ſtrictly charge, and command you, as you will
anſwer the ſame at your utmoſt peril, that you do not in any manner offend, or moleſt any of Our Friends or Allies, their Ships,*

or *Subjects, by colour or pretence of thefe Prefents, or the. Au-thority thereby Granted. In Witnefs whereof, We have caufed Our Great Seal of England to be affixed to thefe Prefents.* Given at Our Court at Kenfington, the 26th Day of *January,* 1695, in the Seventh Year of our Reign.

L. C. B. *Ward.* Now you have had the Commiffions Read, What do you excufe your felf by? What ufe do you make of them to juftifie or defend your felf?

Will. Kidd. About this *Queda* Merchant.

L. C. B. *Ward.* What would you have her a *French* Ship?

Will. Kidd. Under a *French* Commiffion. The Mafter was a Tavern-keeper at *Suratt;* Do you not know that, Mr. *Palmer?*

Jof. Palmer. I was not on board when this Pafs came, I never faw it.

L. C. B. *Ward.* But then you fhould have Condemned this Ship, if fhe had been a *French* Ship, or had a *French* Pafs.

Will. Kidd. The Evidence fays, it was by my order that the Goods were taken out; I was not at the fharing of the Goods, I knew nothing ot if.

L. C. B. *Ward.* Out of the Goods that were taken, fome were fold in the Country there, and the produce of them was fo much money; it is proved, that that money was divided; and purfuant to the Articles fet up, you were to have forty Shares, and the reft of the Men whole, or half Shares as they deferved. Now this money both thefe Men Swear, it was taken by you. And the firft Swears, That the Goods not fold then, that remained in the Ship were alfo divided, and that you had forty fhares of them. And the other fays, he did not fee the Goods divided, but two of the Men acknowledged it.

Will. Kidd. My Lord, this *Frenchman* was board five or fix Days before I understood there was any *Englifhman* a-board. Well, faid I, What are you? An *Englifhman,* I am Mafter. What have you to fhew for it? Nothing (fays he.) When they fee a *French* Pafs, they will not let the Ship go.

Mr. *J. Powel.* You have produced Letters Patents that im-powered you to take Pirates, why did you not take *Culliford?*

Will. Kidd. A great many of the Men were gone a-fhore.

Mr. *J. Powel.* But you prefented him with great Guns, and fwore you would not meddle with them.

L. C. B. *Ward.* When the Queftion was put, Are you come to take us, and hang us? You anfwered, I will fry in Hell before I will do you any harm.

Will. Kidd. That is only what thefe Witneffes fay.

L. C. B. *Ward.* Did you not go aboard *Culliford?*

Will. Kidd. I was not aboard *Culliford.*

L. C. B. *Ward.* Thefe things prefs very hard upon you. We ought to let you know what is obferved, that you make you Defence as well as you can.

Will. Kidd. I defire Mr. *Davis* may be called (he was called accordingly, and appeared) Mr. Davis, pray give an account whether you did not fee a *French* Pafs?

L. C. B. *Ward.* You are his Witnefs, you muft anfwer what he asks you.

Mr. *Davis.* I came a Paffenger from *Madagafcar.* and from thence to *Amboyna,* and there he fent his Boat a-fhore, and this Man was a-fhore; and there was one faid, Capt. *Kidd,* was publifhed a Pirate in *England;* and he gave thofe Paffes to him to Read. The Captain faid, they were *French.*

L. C. B. *Ward.* Who gave them?

Mr. *Davis.* Captain *Kidd* gave them.

L. C. B. *Ward.* Did you know any thing of taking the *Queda* Merchant?

Mr. *Davis.* No, no.

L. C. B. *Ward.* Then you cannot fay, they have any relation to the *Queda* Merchant.

Mr. *Davis.* No, not I.

Will. Kidd. You heard Capt. *Elms* fay, They were *French* Paffes.

Mr. *Davis.* Yes, I heard Capt. *Elms* fay, They were *French* Paffes. Says he, if you will, I can turn them into Latin.

Mr. *B. Hatfel.* Have you any more to fay, Capt. Kidd?

Will. Kidd. I have fome Papers, but my Lord *Bellamont* keeps them from me, that I cannot bring them before the Court.

Cl. of Arr. Have you any more to fay?

Will. Kidd. I have fome to call, that will bear teftimony to my Reputation.

L. C. B. *Ward.* Call whom you pleafe, we will not abridge you.

Kidd. Call Mr. *Bradinham.* I defire this of him, whether he never faw the *French* Paffes, and whether he did not Coll. *Bafs* fo.

R. Bradinham. I never faw a *French* Pafs, I only heard fo.

Coll. *Bafs.* I have heard Mr. *Bradinham* fay, he heard Capt. *Kidd* fay he had *French* Paffes on Board, but I never heard him fay he faw them Paffes.

Kidd. He juft now denied that he ever faw the *French* Paffes, or heard of them.

L. C. B. *Ward.* He fays fo now, that he never faw them, only he heard you fay fo. Coll. *Bafs*, have you heard him fay the Paffes related to the *Quedah* Merchant?

Coll. *Bafs.* He has often faid he heard Kidd fay the *French* Paffes were aboard.

Cl. of Arr. Have you any more Witneffes to call?

Kidd. I defire Mr. Say may be called, he is in the Prifon, I defire he may be fent for.

L. C. B. *Ward.* We will give you all the liberty you can expect, if you have any more, you were beft call them all together. In the mean time what fay you, *Churchill?*

N. Churchill. I defire Coll. *Bafs*, may be called, and that this Affidavit may be read.

L. C. B. *Ward.* Colonel *Bafs*, what have you to fay for *N. Churchill?*

Coll. *Bafs.* My Lord, I only wait for his Queftion.

L. C. B. *Ward. Churchill*, what will you ask Coll. *Bafs?*

N. Churchill. Whether I did not Surrender my felf to him.

L. C. B. *Ward.* If you can make your Cafe come within the Proclamation, you muft make it appear that you Surrendered according to the Directions of it.

N. Churchill. My Lord, we came in, in the Year 1699, and Surrendered our felves to Coll. *Bafs.*

L. C. B. *Ward.* If you can make it appear that you Sur-rendered your felves in purfuance of that, to the Perfons appointed to receive your Surrender, that will be fomewhat to the Point; but Colonel *Bafs*, had not Power by that Proclamation to receive your Surrender, and therefore you cannot have any Benefit by it, unlefs you can bring your Cafe within it. But you may call Col. *Bafs*, if you will.

Churchill. My Lord, we came in upon that Proclamation, and might have gone away any Day if we would; but we ftay'd in the Country, and we never offered to go away till it was my Lord *Bellamont's* Pleafure to fend for us.

L. C. B. Ward. You may call Coll. *Bafs*, and hear what he fays.

Churchill. Col. *Bafs*, will you be pleafed to tell my Lord whether we did not furrender our felves to you in purfuance of the King's Proclamation.

Col. Bafs. My Lord, about the 29th of *May*, 1699, I had an Account of fome Perfons, that were fuppofed Pirates, that were come to furrender themfelves; and on my landing, thefe two Perfons came to me, and furrendered to me the 4th of June, 1699. And I told them I muft refer their Cafe to his Majefty at home.

L. C. B. Ward. Who were they that furrendered to you?

Coll. *Bafs*. *Nicholas Churchill*, and *James Howe*.

L. C. B. Ward. Where were you Governour?

Coll. *Bafs*. At the Province of *Weft-Jerfey*.

Dr. Oxenden. How came they here?

Coll. *Bafs*. I left them under Bail.

L. C. B. Ward. Did you fend them over?

Col. Bafs. No, my Lord, I came to *England* before: I left them in Cuftody. They were fent over Prifoners by my Succeffor.

L. C. B. Ward. What did they fay to you when they furrendered themfelves to you?

Col. Bafs. They faid they had been in the Indies, and that they had committed feveral Piracies, and defired they might have the Benefit of his Majefty's Proclamation.

L. C. B. Ward. What Pirates did they mention to you?

Col. Bafs. They mentioned the *Moco Frigate*, and Capt. *Kidd*.

Dr. *Oxenden.* Had you the Proclamation?

Col. *Bafs.* No, but I had feen one of them.

L. C. B. *Ward.* Did you take yourfelf allowed to receive their Surrender?

Col. *Bafs.* No, my Lord, I did not.

Cl. of Arr. *Nicholas Churchill,* have you quite done?

N. Churchill and *James Howe.* Yes, Sir, we came in upon his Majefty's Proclamation.

Cl. of Arr. *Robert Lamley,* what have you to fay?

Robert Lamley. My Lord, I was but a Servant.

L. C. B. *Ward.* Who was you a Servant to?

Robert Lamley. To Mr. *Owen.*

L. C. B. *Ward.* How does that appear?

Robert Lamley. The Surgeon knows it.

Bradinham. My Lord, he was concerned with the Cook.

Robert Lamley. My Lord, here is my Indenture (*which was read.*)

Cl. of Arr. *William Jenkins,* What have you to fay?

William Jenkins. I have nothing to fay, but I was a Servant to Mr. *Bullen.*

L. C. B. *Ward.* Where is your Witnefs to prove it?

Jenkins. Both the King's Witneffes know it.

Bradinham and *Palmer.* My Lord, he was his Servant.

Cl. of Arr. *Gabriel Loff,* what fay you for your felf?

Loff. My Lord, about the Year 1696, I entered my felf on Board Captain *Kidd,* and went out with him, and I never difobeyed his Command in any Thing.

L. C. B. *Ward.* Did he go out under the firft Commiffion?

Palmer. He came aboard at New-York.

L. C. B. *Ward.* Did you take him in before, or after the Articles were fet up.

Palmer. After the Articles were fet up.

L. C. B. *Ward.* Did Captain *Kidd* take any Notive of his Commiffions in the Articles?

Palmer. Yes, my Lord, he did mention them. I have a copy of the Articles.

Mr. *Crawley.* Mr. *Palmer,* are thefe Articles the Copy of the Articles fet up by Captain *Kidd,* at *New-York?*

Palmer. Yes.

Mr. *J. Gould.* Did you examine them?

Palmer. To the beft of my knowledge they were a true copy.

Mr. *J. Turton.* Did you compare them with the Original?

Palmer. No, my Lord.

Cl. of Arr. *Gabriel Loff,* Have you any more to fay?

Loff. Yes, a great deal more to ask the Evidence.

Cl. of Arr. What will you ask them?

Loff. Whether I did not obey the Captain.

Mr. *J. Tourton.* There is no fcruple to be made of that.

Loff. I went out to ferve his Majefty under his Commiffion.

L. C. B. *Ward.* But how came you to take part of the Money?

Loff. I had what they pleafed to give me.

L. C. B. *Ward.* You muft needs imagine, that when Captain *Kidd* did thefe extravagant Things, and divided the Money and Goods, that he did not act according to his Commiffion. What could you think of it?

Cl. of Arr. *Hugh Parrot,* what have you to fay for yourfelf?

Parrot. My Lord, in the Year 1695, in the Month of *October,* I failed out of *Plymouth* in a Merchant-man, bound for *Cork* in *Ireland,* there to take in Provifions; thence to the Ifland of *Barbadoes;* and in fight of the Ifland of *Barbadoes,* I was taken by a *French* Privateer, and carried to *Martinico;* and thence coming in a Tranfport-Ship, I was brought to *Barbadoes,* there I Ship'd my felf in a Veffel bound to *Newfoundland,* and thence to *Maderas.* And then I went to *Madagafcar;* and there I stay'd fome fhort time after, and came in Company with Captain *Kidd,* and then the Commander and I had a falling out, and fo I went afhore at that Ifland. And underftanding that Captain *Kidd* had a Commiffion from the King, I came aboard Captain *Kidd's* Ship, and ever fince have been with him.

L. C. B. *Ward.* Did you come to him after he had been at *New-York?*

Parrot. This was in the Year 1697.

L. C. B. *Ward.* You have acted with him, and fhared with

him. Could you imagine he was acting according to his Commiffion, when he was doing thefe Things?

Parrot. I thought I was fafe where the King's Commiffion was.

L. C. B. *Ward.* The Commiffion was to take Pirates, and not to turn Pirates.

Parrot. Mr. *Palmer,* did you ever fee me guilty of an ill Thing? Did I ever difobey my Captain?

Palmer. You were always obedient to your Commander.

Parrot. Then I came to *Madagafcar* with Captain *Kidd,* where I might have gone aboard a known Pirate, but I refufed it, and kept clofe to my Captain: And when I came to *New-England,* I might have gone away as others did; but I had my Liberty at *Bofton* for above a Week, and went up and down, and I furrendered my felf.

L. C. B. *Ward.* You did not furrender your felf; but only you had a liberty to go away, and did not.

Parrot. I thought there was no need of it. My Lord, I defire you will ask the Witnefs whether I ever difobeyed the Captain's Commands.

L. C. B. *Ward.* They fay no otherwife, but that you went willingly.

Cl. of Arr. *Richard Barlicorn.* what have you to fay?

Barlicorn. My Lord, I beg leave that I may produce fome Evidence for my Reputation. Here is a Certificate from the Parifh where I was born.

L. C. B. *Ward.* That will fignify nothing, we cannot read Certificates, they must fpeak *Viva Voce.*

Barlicorn. Call *Benjamin Bond, Daniel Phillips,* and *James Newton.*

L. C. B. *Ward.* What do you call thefe Witneffes for?

Barlicorn. To give an Account of my Reputation, what they know of me.

Benj. Bond. I knew him when he was a Child, and he was very civil and honeft; I lived near him till he was 13 or 14 Years old. And he came of honeft Parents, and behaved himfelf very civilly all that time.

L. C. B. *Ward.* Have you known any Thing of him fince?

Bond. No, my Lord.

L. C. B. *Ward.* What have you to fay further?

Barlicorn. My Lord, I was a Servant to Captain *Kidd,* and I have been with him fix Years; and I have a Certificate from feveral of my Relations that will teftify it.

Cl. of Arr. *R. Barlicorn,* have you any Thing more to fay?

Barlicorn. I am a Servant to Captain Kidd.

L. C. B. *Ward.* How long have you been fo? Where was it that you came firft to be his Servant?

Barlicorn. At *Carolina.*

Cl. of Arr. *Abel Owens,* what fay you for your felf?

Owens. My Lord, I defire the Privilege of the Proclamation. I entered my felf into the King's Service. I have been in the King's Service, according to his Majefty's Proclamation. I defire it may be read. (*which was done.*)

L. C. B. *Ward.* You defire the Benefit of this Proclamation, but you muft bring your felf under the Qualifications it requires, if you would have any Benefit by it.

Mr. *Crawley.* He has a Certificate of it.

L. C. B. *Ward.* Is it within the Proclamation?

Mr. *Crawley.* The Certificate is dated the 13th of *March,* 1700, from Mr. Riches, a Juftice of the Peace in *Southwark.*

L. C. B. *Ward.* Mr. *Riches,* I fuppofe, did believe he was within this Proclamation.

Mr. *J. Gould.* The Pardon extends to all Perfons for Piracies committed before that Time, if they furrender themfelves to fuch and fuch, and enter themfelves on Board one of his Majefty's Ships.

Mr. *Coniers.* A Juftice of the Peace is not within the Proclamation.

Cl. of Arr. Have you any more to fay?

Owens. Only to defire the Benefit of that Proclamation.

L. C. B. *Ward.* He furrendered himfelf to Juftice *Riches,* and then entered himfelf aboard one of his Majefty's Ships; and then there was Evidence againft him, when on board, and he was feized. This may be fit to recommend him to the King's Mercy, but it is not a Defence againft the Accufation.

Cl. of Arr. *Darby Mullins,* what do you fay for your felf?

Mullins. I came in upon the King's Act of Grace, I came afhore with the reft of the People.

L. C. B. Ward. What have you to fhew, to intitle you to the Benefit of this Proclamation.

Mullins. I was ready to die of the Bloody Flux, and no able to go my felf, but I fent my Name in to the Governour.

L. C. B. Ward. Where was you when you was fo fick?

Mullins. In *Weft-Jerfey.* I came afhore in *Cape May.* I was fick like to die all the Way from *Madagafcar,* expecting every Minute to die with the Bloody Flux.

Dr. Oxenden. How came you to leave Captain *Kidd?*

Mullins. He ufed me very hardly, and therefore I left him.

L. C. B. Ward. You had a Dividend of the Money and Goods.

Mullins. He gave it me, and afterwards took it from me.

L. C. B. Ward. Was he your Mafter?

Mullins. I had no Mafter.

Dr. Oxenden. How did you come to *Jerfey?*

Mullins. I came here with Captain *Shelly,* he is in Court.

Dr. Oxenden. You were aboard Captain *Cullifbrd.*

Mullins. I came home in hopes to get the King's Pardon.

L. C. B. Ward. That which you fay is very odd, though you quitted Captain *Kidd's* Ship, you went into *Culliford's.*

L. C. B. Ward. Captain *Kidd,* you faid you had more to fay juft now; if you have, let us hear it.

Kidd. I defire this Man may be heard two or three Words.

L. C. B. Ward. What is his Name?

Kidd. Mr. *Say.*

Mr. *Say.* I happened to be at the *Treafury-Office* in *Broad-ftreet* to receive fome Maney, and Mr. *White* was there; and he asked me, will you go along with me, and fee one *Elbury* that is in the *Marfhalfea* for Debt? fays I, I am a Stranger to him I do not care to go. Says he, bear me Company. So I went with him, and when I came there, I faw Captain *Kidd's* Men. And this Mr. *Elbury* was in Company with Captain *Kidd's* Surgeon. Says I, I am a Brother of the Quill, I fhould be glad to drink a Glafs with you. We ftayed there but a little while, and asked what that Man was; fays he, he is Captain *Kidd's* Surgeon. Upon this I faid, here is a mighty Noife about Capt. Kidd; fays he, I believe he has done nothing but what ge can anfwer, or that can do him any hurt, Says I, where have you been with him? He faid, at *Madagafcar*.

L. C. B. *Ward*. Mr. *Bradinham* was with them, there is no doubt of that. It is not to be queftioned that he would not fay any Thing Ill of them then. Captain Kidd, have you any Thing more to fay?

Kidd. Call Captain *Humphrys*, (*who appeared*.)

L. C. B. *Ward*. What Queftions would you ask him?

Kidd. What do you know of me?

Capt. *Humphrys*. I knew you, Sir, in the *Weft-Indies* in the beginning of the late War, and I know you had the Applaufe of the General, as I can fhew by the General's Letter. I know nothing further of you.

Kidd. Did you know any Thing that I was Guilty of any Piracies?

Humphrys. No, but you had a general Applaufe for what you had done from time to time.

L. C. B. *Ward*. How long was this ago?

Humphrys. Twelve Years ago.

L. C. B. *Ward*. That was before he was turned Pirate.

Kidd. Call Captain *Bond*, (*who appeared*.)

L. C. B. *Ward*. What do you call him for?

Kidd. Capt. *Bond*, pray will you give an Account what you know of me.

Capt. *Bond*. I know you was very ufeful at the beginning of the War in the *Weft-Indies*.

Mr. *B. Hatfell*. To be fure they had a good Opinion of him in 1695, when they granted him the Commiffion.

Kidd. There is nothing in the World cam make it appear I was guilty of Piracy, I kept Company with Captain *Warren* for fix Days.

Mr. *Coniers*. I believe you kept Company more with Captain *Culliford*, than with Captain *Warren*.

Kidd. I never defigned to do any fuch Thing.

Mr. *Coniers.* My Lord, we will fay nothing at all, but leave it to your Lordfhip to direct the Jury.

Kidd. I have many Papers for my Defence, if I could have had them.

L. C. B. *Ward* What Papers were they?

Kidd. My *French* Paffes.

L. C. B. *Ward.* Where are they?

Kidd. My Lord *Bellamont* had them.

L. C. B. *Ward.* If you had had the *French* Paffes, you fhould have condemned Ships.

Kidd. I could not becaufe of the Mutiny in my Ship.

L. C. B. *Ward.* If you had any Thing of Difability upon you, to make your Defence, you fhould have objected it at the beginning of your Trial; what you mean by it now, I cannot tell. If you have any Thing more to fay, you may fay it, the Court is ready to hear you.

L. C. B. *Ward.* Gentlemen of the Jury, the Prifoners at the Bar, *W. Kidd, N. Churchill, J. Howe, R. Lamley, Will. Jenkins, Gabriel Loff, Hugh Parrot, Rich. Barlicorn, Abel Owens,* and *Darby Mullins,* in Number Ten; ftand all here Indicated for the Crime of Piracy, charged to be committed by them. And the Instance of the Crime, is for Felonioufly and Piratcally Seizing and Taking the Ship called the *Quedagh* Merchant, with the Apparel and Tackling thereof, to the value of 400£ and divers Goods mentioned in the Indict- to the value of 4500£ the Goods of the feveral Perfons unknown, from the Mariners of the faid Ship, and this at High Sea, within the Jurifdiction of the Court of Admiralty, about ten Leagues from *Cutfheen* in the *Eaft-Indies* the 30th of *January,* 1697, and in the 9th Year of his Majefty's Reign. Now whether all, or any, and which if thefe Prifoners are guilty of this Crime of Piracy laid in this Indictment, or not guilty, it is your Part to determine according to the Evidence that has been given on both Sides. The Crime charged on them is Piracy, that is, Seizing and Taking this Ship and Goods in it Piratically and Felonioufly, the Time and Place is laid alfo in the Indictment. To make good this Accufation, the King's Council have produced their Evidence; and two Witnesses have been examined in this Cafe, each of them were in the Ship which took the *Quedagh Merchant*, and very well acquainted with all the Proceedings, that is, *Robert Bradinham*, and *Joseph Palmer*. The firft has given you an Hiftorical Account of the whole Proceedings of Captain *Kidd*, from his firft going out of *England* in the *Adventure Galley*, to the Time of this Fact charged on them. They tell you, that about *May* 1696, the King inftructed this Captain *Kidd* with two Commiffions, and they were both read to you. By one of them, under the Admiralty Seal, he was Authorized to fet out as a Privateer the *Adventure Galley*, and therewith to Take and Seize the Ships and Goods belonging to the *French* King, or his Subjects, and fuch other as were liable to Confifcation. And by the other Commiffion under the Broad Seal of *England*, Authority was given for the taking of fome Pirates by Name, and all other Pirates in the feveral Places therein mentioned. But in no fort to offend or moleft any of the King's Friends or Allies, their Ships or Subjects by Colour thereof. And by both Commiffions command was given to bring all fuch Ships and Goods, as fhould be taken to legal Trials and Condemnations. They tell us, that this Ship fet out from *Plymouth* about *May*, 1696, and that in their Paffage, they did take a *French* Ship, and they did condemn that Ship. Now Gentlemen, you muft bear this in your Minds, that to make it Piracy, it muft be the taking Piratically and Felonioufly upon the High Seas, within the Jurifdiction of the Admiralty of *England*, the Goods of a Friend, that is fuch as are in Amity with the King. Now you fee what Way they went to work, and what Meafures they took. Captain *Kidd* goes out, and goes to *New-York;* and when he was there, he has a Project in his Head of fetting up Articles between himfelf and the People that were willing to be concerned with him: For now whether it feems more probable from what followed that Captain *Kidd* defigned to manage himfelf according to the Meafures given him, and the Powers of his Commiffions, or another Way, you muft confider; for it is told you that between 150, and 160 Men came in under thofe Articles, whereof the other Prifoners were part and concerned in them. And as to thofe Articles, the Import of them was, that whatever fhould be taken by thefe People in their Expeditions, fhould be divided into 160 Parts, whereof Captain *Kidd* was to have 40 Shares for his Part, and the reft were to have according to the Merit of each Party, fome whole Shares, and fome half Shares.

Now after thefe Articles, you perceive what Progrefs they made, and what Courfe they took. They went from one place to another, and ufed a pretty deal of Severity where ever they came. A defign they had to go into the Red-Sea, and they had expectations of the *Moco* Fleet that lay at *Moco*, and they fent their Spies three times to get Intelligence. The two times they could make no Difcovery; but the third time they made an effectual Difcovery that the Fleet was ready to Sail; and in the mean time Capt. *Kidd* lay there in expectation of this Fleet; and as the firft Witnefs tells you, Capt. *Kidd* faid he intended to make a Voyage out of this Fleet. Well, he had a Difcovery of this Fleet, and they came accordingly, and they tell you, that he and his Men in the Ship did attack one of the Ships: But thefe Ships being guarded by two Men of War, he could make nothing of them, however he fhewed what his intention and defign was. Could he have proved that what he did was in purfuance of his Commiffions, it had been fomething: But what had he to do to make an attack on thefe Ships, the Owners and Freighters whereof, were in Amity with the King; this does not appear to be an action fuitable to his Commiffion. After he had done this, he came to Land, and there, and afterwards at Sea, purfued ftrange Methods, as you have heard. The feeming juftification he depends on, is his Commiffions; now it muft be obferved how he acted with relation to them, and what irregularities he went by. He came to a place in the Indies, and fent his Cooper afhore, and that Cooper was killed by Natives; and he ufes Barbarity, and ties an *Indian* to a Tree, and fhoots him to death. Now he went from place to place and committed Hoftilities upon feveral Ships, dealing very feverely with the People.

But this being fomething foreign to the Indictment, and

not the Facts for which the Prifoners at Bar are Indicted, we are confined to the *Quedagh Merchant;* but what he did before fhews his Mind and Intentions not to act by his Commoffions, which warrant no fuch things. Gentlemen, you have an account that he met with this Ship the *Quedagh Merchant* at Sea, and took her; that this Ship belonged to People in Amity with the King of *England;* that he feized this Ship, and divers Goods were taken out of her, and fold, and the Money divided purfuant to the heads contained in thofe Articles fet up at *New York.* The Witneffes that fpeak to that, come home to every one of the Prifoners: They tell you that this Dividend was made, that Capt. *Kidd* had 40 Chares of the Money, and the reft of the Prifoners had their proportions according to the Articles, fome whole Shares, and fome a half Share of that Money. After they had feized on the Ship, you hear of a certain fort of project, that a *French* Man fhould come and pretend himfelf the Mafter, and produce, or pretend to produce a *French* Pafs, under a colour that thefe Peoples Ship and Goods, who were Moors, fhould be *French* Men's Ship and Goods, or Sailed under a *French* Pafs, and fo juftify what they did under the colour of his Commiffion from the King. Now no Man knows the Mind and Intention of another, but as it may be difcovered by his Actions. If he would have this to be underftood to be his Intention, or that it was a reality, that he tcok this as a *French* Ship, or under a *French* Pafs, then he ought to have had the Ship and Goods inventoried, and Condemned, according to Law, that he might have had what proportion belonged to him, and that the King might have had what belonged to him, as his Commiffions directed. But here was nothing of that done, but the Money and Goods that were taken were fhared; and you have an account likewife how fome of the Goods were fold and the Money difpofed of, and how the remaining Goods were difpofed of; and one Witnefs fpeaks pofitively of the diftribution of the Goods that remained unfold, that they were divided according to the fame proportions as the Articles mentioned, and every one of the Prifoners had his Share.

There belonged 40 Shares to Capt. *Kidd*, and Shares and half Shares to the reſt.

Now this is the great Caſe that is before you on which the Indictment turns. The Ships and Goods, as you have heard, are ſaid by the Witneſſes, to be the Goods of the Armenians, and other People that were in Amity with the King; and Capt. *Kidd* would have them to be the Goods of *French* Men, or at leaſt that the Ship was Sailed under *French* Paſſes. Now if it were ſo, as Capt. *Kidd* ſays, it was a lawful Prize, and liable to Confiſcation, but if they were the Goods of Perſons in Amity with the King, and the Ship was not Navigated under *French* Paſſes, it was very plain it was a Piratical taking of them. Gentlemen, it is to be conſidered what Evidence Capt. *Kidd*. hath given to prove that Ship and Goods to belong to the *French* King, or his Subjects, or that the Ship was Failed under a *French* Paſs, or indeed that ever there was a *French* Paſs ſhewn or ſeen. He appeals indeed to the Witneſſes over and over again, Did you never ſee it? No, ſay they: Nor did not you, ſaith he, ſay you ſaw it? No. ſaith the Witneſs, I ſaid that Capt. *Kidd* ſaid he had a *French* Paſs, but I never ſaw it. Now after all, the taking of the *Quedagh Merchant* is brought down to Mr. *Kidd*, and the Priſoners with others, and the diſtribution of the Money produced by the Sale of the Goods among Mr. *Kidd*, and his Crew, whereof every one of theſe Priſoners were preſent at the ſame time, and had Proportions.

Now Gentlemen, this muſt be obſerved, if this was a Capture on the High Sea, and these were the Goods of Perſons in Amity with the King, and had no *French* Paſs, then it is a plain Piracy. And if you believe the Witneſſes, here is a taking of the Goods and Ship of Perſons in Amity, and converting them to their own Uſe. Such a taking at Land as this would be Felony, and being at Sea it will be Piracy: For this is a taking the Ship from the right Owners, and turning it to their own uſe. So that you have Evidence as to the Seizing of the Ship, and dividing the Money riſing from the Goods ſold, and ſharing the remainder according to the Articles.

Now, what does Capt. *Kidd* ſay to all this? He has told

you he acted purfuant to his Commiffion; but that cannot be, unlefs he gives you fatisfaction that the Ship and Goods belonged to the *French* King, or his Subjects, or that the Ship had a *French* Pafs, otherwife neither of them will exfuce him from being a Pirate; for if he takes the Goods of Friends he is a pirate, he had no Authority for that: There is no colour from either of his Commiffions for him to take them. And as to the *French* Paffes, there is nothing of that appears by any Proof, and for ought I can fee, none faw them but himflef, if there were ever any. It is proved that the People that were Owners of the Goods, made him very large Offers to redeem the Ship (Twenty Thoufand Ruppees, as I remember) but he would not accept their Propofal; but faid, That is a fmall Summ, the Cargo is worth a great deal more, or to that effect: And further faid, he muft anfwer thefe People, that his Men will not part with it. And a *French* Man was to be fet up for a Mock bufinefs, as you have heard; and if the Witneffes fay true, they were faid by the Captain of the Ship to be, and were reputed to be, the Ship and Goods of Friends, and not of Enemies; and if they were fo, and had no *French* Pafs, then is he, and thofe that were concerned with him, guilty of Piratically taking this Ship, and of Piratically feizing the Goods in the Ship; and neither of his Commiffions will juftify fuch an Action as this. If he had acted purfuant to his Commiffion, he ought to have condemned the Ship and Goods, if they were a *French* Intereft, or Sailed under a *French* Pafs; but by his not condemning them, he feems to fhew his Aim, Mind and Intention, that he did not act in that Cafe by virtue of his Commiffion, but quite contrary to it; for he takes the Ship, and fhares the Money and Goods, and is taken in that very Ship by my Lord *Bellamont*, and he had continued in that Ship till that time, fo that there is no colour or pretence appears, that he intended to bring this Ship to *England*, to be condemned, or to have condemned it in any of the Englifh Plantations, having difpofed of the whole Cargo, as aforefaid. Here I muft leave it to you, to confider whether, according to the Evidence that appears, there is any Ground for him to fay, he has acted by his Commiffion in taking the *Quedagh Merchant* and Goods in her, or whether he has not acted contrary thereunto.

Now for himfelf he has called fome Perfons here, to give an account of his Reputation, and of his Services done in the *Weft-Indies;* and one of them fays, about 10 or 12 Years, he did good Service there. Why fo he might, and might have, and 'tis very like he had fuch Reputation, when the King trufted him with thefe Commiffions, elfe I believe he had never had them; fo what thatever he might be fo many Years ago, that is not a matter to be infifted on now, but what he hath been fince, and how he hath acted in this matter charged againft him. So that, Gentlemen, as to Mr. *Kidd,* I muft leave it to you, whether he is Guilty of Piracy, or no, and if you believe him Guilty upon the Evidence, you will find him fo, if not you will acquit him.

Now for the other Prifoners, it is proved they were all concerned in taking and fharing the Ship and Goods in the Indictment; yet their Circumftances differ pretty much among themfelves. There are three of them, that it has been made out to you, and owned by the King's Witneffes that they were Servants. *Robert Lamley, William Jenkins, Richard Barlicorn.* All thefe are made out to be Servants, and you have had the Indentures of two of them produced, and the King's Witneffes prove them fo, and they were admitted to be Servants. Now, Gentlemen, there muft go an Intention of the Mind, and a Freedom of the Will, to the committing a Felony or Piracy. A Pirate is not to be underftood to be under conftraint, but a free Agent; for in this Cafe, the bare Act will not make him Guilty, unlefs the Will make it fo. Now a Servant, it is true, if he go voluntarily, and have his Proportion, he muft be accounted a Pirate, for then he acts upon his own account, and not by Compulfion. And thefe perfons, according to the Evidence, received their Part, but whether they accounted to their Mafters for their Shares afterwards, yea or no, as they pretend, but make no proof of it, I muft leave that to you; and therefore there is a confideration to be had of them. For if thefe Men did go under the Compulfion of their Mafters, to whom they were Servants, and not vol-

untarily, and upon their own Accounts, it may difference their
Cafe from others, who went and acted willingly in this matter,
and upon their own Accounts. So that as to thofe that were
Servants under the command of their Mafters that were prefent with them, I must leave it to you, whether you will diftinguifh between them and the others that were not Servants,
but free Agents. It is true, a Servant is not bound to obey
his Mafter, but in lawful things, which they fay they thought
this was, and that they knew not to the contrary, but that
their Mafters acted according to the King's Commiffion; and
therefore their Cafe muft be left to your confideration, whether you think them upon the whole matter Guilty or no. If
you believe them Guilty, you will find them fo, other wifeyou
will Acquit them.

For the other Perfons, fome of them pretend they came in
on his Majefty's Proclamation, and for that you muft confider the Evidence, and take it all together, and confider
whether you are fatisfied by what they have faid or proved,
that they have brought themselves within the benefit of the
King's Favour by that Proclamation. You have heard it read,
and obferved the Qualifications and Directions by it, and the
Terms upon which the Pardon was promifed, which are not
made out to you, to be complied with by them; they may
apply another way, for the King Mercy; this Court muft proceed according to the Rules of Law and Juftice. But then all
of them hold on this: We were, fay they, under the Captain,
and acted under him as their Commander; and, Gentlemen,
fo far as they acted under his lawful Commands, and by Virtue, and in Purfuance of his Commiffions, it muft be admitted
they were Juftifyable, and ought to be Juftify'd. But how
far forth that hath been, the Actions of the Captain and their
own, will beft make it appear. It is not contefted, but that
thefe Men knew, and were fenfible of what was done and
acted, and did take part in it, and had the benefit of what
was taken, fhared amongft them. And if the taking of this
Ship and Goods was Unlawful, then thefe Men can claim no
advantage by thefe Commiffions, becaufe they had no Authority by them to do what they did, but acted quite con-

trary to them. What had they to do to enter into fuch Articles, and to act as they did? You muft confider the Evidence given here, according to the Rules of the Law, and if you are fatisfy'd that they have Knowingly and Wilfully been concerned of partaken with Capt. *Kidd*, in taking this Ship, and dividing the Goods and that Piratically and Felonioufly, then they will be Guilty with in this Indictment. It is worthy of Confideration what appears upon the Evidence, that they met with one reputed to be a Notorious Pirate, call'd *Culliford*; he was efteemed an Arch-Pirate, and known to be fo, yet this Capt. *Kidd*, that was Commiffioned to take Pirates, enftead of taking, grows to fuch an Intimacy with him, that he faid he would have his Sould fry in Hell, before he would hurt him, or to that effect, and fo they made Prefents one to another; and Capt. *Kidd* left three of his Men with him. Whilft Men purfue their Commiffions, they muft be Juftify'd, but when they do things not Authorized, or never acted by them, it is as if there had been no Commiffion at all. I have diftinguifhed the Evidence as well as my memory ferves me, and muft leave it to you to determine upon the whole matter, who are Guilty, and who not; and fuch as you are fatisfied to be Guilty, you will find fo, and fuch as you are not fatisfy'd to be Guilty, you will acquit.

Then the Jury withdrew, and *after half an hour's ftay, brought in their Verdict.*

Cl. of *Arr.* Gentlemen of the Jury, Anfwer to your Names, *John Cooper,* &c.

J. Cooper. Here, &c.

Cl. of *Arr.* Are you agreed of your verdict?

Omnes. Yes.

Cl. of *Arr.* Who fhall fay for you?

Omnes. Foreman.

Cl. of *Arr. Will. Kidd,* hold up thy Hand. (which he did.) How fay you, Is he Guilty of the Piracy whereof he ftands Indicted, or not Guilty? And fo of the reft.

Foreman. Guilty.

Cl. of *Arr.* Is *Nich. Churchill* Guilty, or Not Guilty?

Foreman. Guilty.

Cl. of *Arr.* Is *James Howe* Guilty, &c?
Foreman. Guilty.
Cl. of *Arr.* Is *Rob. Lamley* Guilty, &c?
Foreman. Not Guilty.
Cl. of *Arr.* Is *Will. Jenkins* Guilty, &c?
Foreman. Not Guilty.
Cl. of *Arr.* Is *Gabriel Loff* Guilty, &c?
Foreman. Guilty.
Cl. of *Arr.* Is *Hugh Parrot* Guilty, &c?
Foreman. Guilty.
Cl. of *Arr.* Is *R. Barlicorn* Guilty, &c?
Foreman. Not Guilty.
Cl. of *Arr.* Is *Abel Owens* Guilty, &c?
Foreman. Guilty.
Cl. of *Arr.* Is *Darby Mullins* Guilty, &c?
Foreman. Guilty.

Then Will. Kidd, *and the other Nine Perfons, were further Arraigned upon four Indictments, in manner following.*

Cl. of *Arr. Will. Kidd,* hold up thy Hand. (which he did.) And fo the other Nine.

You ftand Indicted by the Name of *Will. Kidd,* late of *London* Mariner, &c.

The Jurors for our Sovereign Lord the King, do upon their Oath, prefent that *William Kidd,* late of *London,* Mariner, *Nicholas Churchill,* late of *London,* Marriner, *James Howe,* late of *London,* Marriner, *Robert Lamley,* late of *London,* Marriner, *William Jenkins,* late of *London,* Marriner, *Gabriel Loff,* late of *London,* Marriner, *Hugh Parrot,* late of *London,* Marriner, *Richard Barlicorn,* late of *London,* Marriner, *Abel Owens,* late of *London,* Marriner, and *Darby Mullins,* late of *London,* Marriner, the 20th Day of *September,* in the Ninth Year of the Reign of our Sovereign Lord *William* the Third, by the Grace of God, of *England, Scotland, France* and *Ireland,* King, Defender of the Faith, &c. By Force and Arms, &c. upon the High Sea, in a certain place, diftant about Fifty Leagues from the Port of *Carrawar,* in the *Eaft-Indies,* and within the Jurifdiction of the Admiralty of *England,* did Piratically, and Feloniously fet upon, board, break and enter a certain Ship call'd a *Moorifh* Ship, then being a Ship of certain perfons (to the Jurors aforefaid unknown) and then and there Piratically and Feloniously did make an affault, in and upon certain Marriners (whofe Names to the Jurors aforefaid are unknown) in the fame Ship in the Peace of God, and of our faid now Sovereign Lord the King, then and there being, Piratically and Felonioufly did put the aforefaid Marriners of the fame Ship, in the Ship aforefaid then being, in corporeal fear of their Lives, then and there in the Ship aforefaid upon the High Sea, in the place aforefaid, diftant about Fifty Leagues from the Port of *Carrawar* aforefaid, in the Eaft-Indies aforefaid, and within the Jurifdiction aforefaid, Piratically and Felonioufly did Steal, take and carry away One Hundred Pound weight of Coffee, of the value of Five Pounds of lawful Money of *England*, Sixty Pound weight of Pepper, of the value of Three Pounds of lawful Money of *England*, One Hundred weight of *Myrrh*, of the value of Fie Pounds of lawful Money of *England*, and Twenty pieces of *Arabian* Gold, of the value of Eight Pounds of lawful Money of *England*, the Goods, Chattels and Moneys of certain perfons (to the Jurors aforefaid unknown) then and there upon the high Sea aforefaid, in the aforefaid place, diftant about Fifty Leagues from the Port of *Carrawar* aforefaid, in the *Eaft-Indies* aforefaid, and within the Jurifdiction aforefaid, being found in the aforefaid Ship, in the Cuftody and poffefifon of the faid Marriners in the fame Ship, from the faid Marriners of the faid Ship, and from their cuftody and poffeffion then and there upon the High Sea aforefaid, in the place aforefaid, diftant about 50 Leagues from the Port of *Carrawar* aforefaid, in the *Eaft-Indies* aforefaid, and within the Jurifdiction aforefaid, againft the Peace of our faid now Sovereign Lord the King, his Crown and Dignity, &c.

How fay'ft thou, *William Kidd*, art thou Guilty of this Piracy and Robbery, whereof thou ftandeft Indicted, or not Guilty?

Will. Kidd. Not Guilty.

Cl. of *Arr. Culprit*, how wilt thou be Tried?

Will. Kdd. By God and my Country.

Cl. of *Arr*. God fend thee a good Deliverance. (And fo the other Nine.)

Cl. of *Arr*. *Will*. *Kidd*, hold up thy Hand. (Which he did.) And fo the other Nine.

You ftand Indicted, by the Name of *Will*. *Kidd*, late of London, Marriner, (and fo the reft.)

The Jurors for our Sovereign Lord the King, do upon their Oath prefent, that *William Kidd*, late of *London*, Marriner, *Nicholas Churchill*, late of *London*, Marriner, *James Howe*, late of *London*, Marriner, *Robert Lamley*, late of *London*, Marriner, *William Jenkins*, late of *London*, Marriner, *Gabriel Loffe*, late of *London*, Marriner, *Hugh Parrot*, late of *London*, Marriner, *Richard Barlicorn*, late of *London*, Marriner, *Abel Owens*, late of *London*, Marriner, and *Darby Mullins*, *late* of *London*, Marriner, the 27th Day of *November*, in the 9th Year of the Reign of our Sovereign Lord *William* the Third, by the Grace of God, of *England*, *Scotland*, *France* and *Ireland*, King, Defender of the Faith, &c, by Force and Arms, &c. upon the High Sea, in a certain Place, diftant about four Leagues from *Callicut*, in the *Eaft-Indies*, and within the Jurifdiction of the Admiralty of *England*, did Piratically, and Felonioufly fet upon, board, break, and enter a certain Ship, call'd a *Moorifh* Ship; then being a Ship of certain Perfons (to the Jurors aforefaid unknown) and then and there Piratically and Felonioufly, did make an affault in and upon certain Marriners (whofe Names to the Jurors aforefaid are unknown) in the fame Ship in the peace of God, and of our faid now Sovereign Lord the King, then and there being, Piratically and Felonioufly did put the aforefaid Marriners of the fame Ship, in the Ship aforefaid then being, in corporal fear of their Lives, then and there in the Ship aforefaid, upon the High Sea, in the Place aforefaid, diftant about four Leagues from *Callicut*, aforefaid, in the *Eaft-Indies* aforefaid, and within the Jurifdiction aforefaid, Piratically and Felonioufly did Steal, take and carry away the faid Ship, and the Apparel and Tackle of the fame Ship, of the value of Five Hundred Pounds of lawful Money of *England*; Eleven Bales of Cotton, of the value of Sixty Pounds of lawful Money of *England*; Two Horfes, each

of them of the Price of Twenty Pounds of lawful Money of
England, and Fifty *Indian* Quilts, of the Value of Five Pounds
of lawful Money of *England*, the Goods and Chattels of certain Perſons (to the Jurors aforeſaid unknown) then and
there upon the High Sea aforeſaid, in the aforeſaid Place,
diſtant about four Leagues from *Callicut* aforeſaid, i n the
Eaſt-Indies aforeſaid, and within the Juriſdiction aforeſaid,
being found in the aforeſaid Ship, in the Cuſtody and Poſ-
feſſion of the ſaid Marriners, in the ſame Ship, from the ſaid
Marriners of the ſaid Ship, and from their Cuſtody and Poſ-
ſeſſion, then and there upon the High Sea aforeſaid, in the
Place aforeſaid, diſtant about four Leagues from *Callicut*
aforeſaid, in the *Eaſt-Indies* aforeſaid, and within the Juriſdiction aforeſaid, againſt the Peace of our ſaid now Sovereign
Lord the King, his Crown and Dignity, &*c.*

How ſay'ſt thou, *Will. Kidd*, art thou Guilty of this Piracy and Robbery whereof thou ſtandeſt Indicted, or not
Guilty?

Will. Kidd. Not Guilty.

Cl. of Arr. Culprit, How wilt thou be try'd?

Will. Kidd. By God and my Country.

Cl. of Arr. God ſend thee a good Deliverance. (And ſo of
the other Nine.)

Cl. of Arr. Will. Kidd, Hold up thy Hand (which he did.)
And ſo the other Nine.

You ſtand Indicted by the Name of *Will. Kidd*, late of
London, Marriner. (And ſo of the reſt.)

"The Jurors for our Sovereign Lord the King, do, upon
"their Oath preſent, That *William Kidd*, late of *London*, Mar-
"riner, *Nicholas Churchill*, late of *London*, Marriner, *James*
"*How*, late of *London*, Marriner, *Robert Lamley*, late of *Lon-*
"*don*, Marriner, *William Jenkins*, late of *London*, Marriner,
"*Gabriel Loff*, late of *London*, Marriner, *Hugh Parrat*, late of
"*London*, Marriner, *Richard Barlycorne*, late of *London*, Mar-
"riner, *Abel Owens*, late of *London*, Marriner, and *Darby*
"*Mullins*, late of *London*, Marriner; the Twenty Eighth Day
"of *December*, in the Ninth Year of the Reign of our Sover-
"eign Lord, *William*, the Third, by the Grace of God, of

"England, Scotland, France, and Ireland, King Defender of
"the Faith &c. by Force and Arms, &c. upon the High Sea,
"in a certain Place, diftant about four Leagues from *Callicut,*
"in the *Eaft-Indies,* and within the Jurifdiction of the Admir-
"alty of England, did Piratically and Felonioufly fet upon,
"board, break, and enter a certain Ketch, call'd a *Moorifh*
"Ketch, then being a Ketch of certain Perfons (to the Jurors
"aforefaid unknown) and then and there, Piratically and Fel-
"onioufly did make an Affault, in and upon certain Marriners
"(whofe Names to the Jurors aforefaid are unknown) in the
"fame Ship, in the Peace of God, and of Our faid now Sover-
"eign Lord the King, then and there being, Piratically and
"Felonioufly, did put the aforefaid Marriners of the fame
"Ketch, in the Ketch aforefaid then being, in corporal Fear of
"their Lives then and there in the Ketch aforefaid, upon the
"High Sea, in the Place aforefaid, diftant about four Leagues
"from *Callicut* aforefaid, in the Eaft-Indies aforefaid, and
"within the Jurifdiction aforefaid, Piratically and Felonioufly
"did fteal, take and carry away the faid Ketch, and the Ap-
"parel and Tackle of the fame Ketch, of the Value of fifty
"Pounds of lawful Money of *England,* fix Bales of Sugar, of
"the Value of fix Pounds of lawful Money of *England,* and
"ten Bales of Tobacco, of the Value of ten Pounds of lawful
"Money of *England,* the Goods and Chattels of certain Per-
"fons (to the Jurors aforefaid unknown) then and there upon
"the High Sea aforefaid, in the aforefaid Place, diftant about
"four Leagues from Callicut aforefaid, in the Eaft-Indies
"aforefaid, and within the Jurifdiction aforefaid, being found
"in the aforefaid Ketch, in the Cuftody and Poffeffion of the
"faid Marriners in the fame Ketch, from the faid Marriners
"of the faid Ketch, and from their Cuftody and Poffeffion,
"then and there upon the High Sea aforefaid, in the Place
"aforefaid, diftant about four Leagues from *Callicut* afore-
"faid, in the *Eaft-Indies* aforefaid, and within the Jurifdiction
"aforefaid, againft the Peace of Our faid now Sovereign Lord
"the King, his Crown and Dignity, &c.
How fay'ft thou, *Will. Kidd,* art thou Guilty of the Pi-

racy and Robbery whereof thou ſtandeſt Indicted, or not
Guilty?

Will. Kidd. Not Guilty.

Cl. of Arr. How wilt thou be try'd?

Will. Kidd. By God and my Country.

Cl. of Arr. God ſend thee a good Deliverance. (And ſo of
the other Nine.)

Cl. of Arr. Will. Kidd, Hold up thy Hand (which he did.)
And ſo the other Nine.

You ſtand Indicted by the Name of *Will Kidd,* late of
London, Marriner, &c. (And ſo of the reſt.)

"The Jurors for our Sovereign Lord the King, do, upon
"their Oath, preſent, That *William Kidd,* late of *London,*
"Mariner, *Nicholas Churchill,* late of *London,* Mariner; *James*
"*How,* late of *London,* Mariner; *Robert Lamley,* late of *Lon-*
"*don,* Mariner; *William Jenkins,* late of *London,* Mariner;
"*Gabriel Loff,* late of *London,* Mariner; *Hugh Parrot,* late of
"*London,* Mariner; *Richard Barlycorne,* late of *London,* Mar-
"iner; *Abel Owens,* late of *London,* Mariner; and *Darby Mul-*
"*lins,* late of *London,* Mariner; the Twentieth Day of *Jan-*
"*uary,* in the Ninth Year of the Reign of Our Sovereign Lord,
"*William* the Third, by the Grace of God, of *England, Scot-*
"*land, France,* and *Ireland,* King, Defender of the Faith,&c.
"by Force and Arms, &c. upon the High Sea, in a certain
"Place, diſtant about twelve Leagues from *Callicut,* in the
"*Eaſt-Indies,* and within the Juriſdiction of the Admiralty of
"*England,* did Piratically and Feloniouſly ſet upon, board,
"and enter a certain Ship, call'd a *Portugueze* Ship, then being
"a Ship of certain Perſons (to the Jurors aforeſaid unknown)
"and then and there Piratically and Feloniouſly did make
"an Aſſault in and upon certain Mariners, Subjects of the
"King of *Portugal* (whoſe Names to the Jurors aforeſaid are
"unknown) in the ſame Ship, in the Peace of God, and of
"our ſaid now Sovereign Lord the King, then and there being,
"Piratically and Feloniouſly did put the aforeſaid Mariners
"of the ſame Ship, in the Ship aforeſaid then being, in cor-
"poral Fear of their Lives, then and there in the Ship afore-
"ſaid, upon the High Sea, in the Place aforeſaid, diſtant about

"twelve Leagues from *Callicut* aforefaid, in the *Eaſt-Indies*
"aforeſaid, and within the Jurifdiction aforeſaid, Piratically
"and Felonioufly did ſteal, take, and carry away two Chefts
"of Opium, of the Value of Forty Pounds of lawful Money
"of *England*, eighty Baggs of Rice of the Value of Twelve
"Pounds of lawful Money of *England*, ⸨ne Tun of Bees-Wax,
"of the Value of Ten Pounds of lawful Money of *England*,
"thirty Jarrs of Butter of the Value of Ten Pounds of lawful
"Money of *England*. and half a Tun of Iron of the Value of
"Four Pounds of lawful Money of *England*, the Goods and
"Chattels of certain Perſons (to the Jurors aforeſaid un-
"known) then and there upon the High Sea aforeſaid, in the
"aforeſaid Place, diftant about twelve Leagues from *Callicut*
"aforeſaid, in the *Eaſt-Indies* aforeſaid, and within the Jurif-
"diction aforeſaid, being found in the aforeſaid Ship, in the
"Cuftody and Poffeffion of the ſaid Mariners in the ſame
"Ship, from the ſaid Mariners of the ſame Ship, and from
"their Cuftody and Poffeffion, then and there upon the High
"Sea aforeſaid, in the Place aforeſaid, diftant about twelve
"Leagues from *Callicut* aforeſaid, in the *Eaſt-Indies* aforeſaid,
"and within the Jurifdiction aforeſaid, againft the Peace of
"our ſaid now Sovereign Lord the King, his Crown and Dig-
"nity, &c.

How ſay'ſt thou, *William Kidd*, art thou guilty of the Piracy and Robbery whereof thou ftandeft Indicted, or not
Guilty?

William Kidd. Not Guilty.

Cl. of Arr. How wilt thou be try'd?

William Kidd. By God and my Country.

Cl. of Arr. God ſend thee a good Deliverance. (And ſo the
other Nine.)

(*Then the Court adjourned till to Morrow Morning eight
a Clock*.)

The further Proceedings againſt William Kidd, *and the other
nine Prifoners, on the four indictments*, May *the 9th, 1701*.

Cl. of Arr. Call *William Kidd, Nicholas Churchill, James
How, Robert Lamley, William Jenkins, Gabriel Loff, Hugh Parrot, R. Barlicorn, Abel Owens,* and *Darby Mullins* to the Bar.

You the Prifoners at the Bar, *William Kidd*, &c. thofe Men
that you fhall hear called, and perfonally appear, are to pafs
between our Sovereign Lord the King and you, upon Tryal
of your feveral Lives and Deaths; of therefire you, or any of
you, will challenge them, or any of them your Time is to
fpeak unto them as they come tothe Book to be Sworn, and
before they be Sworn. Call *William Smith*, who appeared, and
there being no Challenges, the Twelve that were Sworn, are
as follows.

The JURY.

Will. Smith,	*Peter Gray,*
Benj. Hooper,	*Rob. Comfort,*
Jo. Hibbert,	*Tho. Hollis,*
Jo. Pettit,	*Will. Ford,*
Will. Hatch,	*Tho. Stephens,*
Jof. Chaplain,	*Jo. Dodfon.*

Cl. of Arr. Cryer, count thefe, *Will. Smith.*
Cryer. One, &c.
Cl. of Arr. Benj. Hooper.
Cryer. Two, &c. Twelve good Men and true, ftand to-
gether, and hear your Evidence.
(*Then the ufual Proclamation for Information was made, and
the Prifoners being bid to hold up their Hands, the Clerk of
Arraignments charged the Jury with them thus:*)
Cl. of Arr. "You of the Jury, look upon the Prifoners, and
"hearken to their Caufe. They ftand indicted by the Names
"of *William Kidd*, &c. (*as before in the Indictment*) upon this
"Indictment they have been arraigned, and thereunto have
"feverally pleaded, not guilty, and for their Tryal put them-
"felves on God and their Country, which Country you are.
"Your charge is to enquire, Whether they be guilty of the
"Piracy and Robbery whereof they ftand Indicted, or not
"guilty, &c.
Nich. Churchill. May it pleafe you, my Lord, I came in upon his Majefty'f Proclamation, and if that do not do, I throw
my felf upon the Mercy of the Honourable Bench.

Mr. Bar. *Hatfell.* If they will withdraw their Plea, and confefs the Indictment, they may.

Nich. Churchill and *James How.* We refer our felves to the King's Proclamation.

Dr. *Oxenden.* But do you confefs the Matter of the Indictment? You may do that if you will, and then you need not be tryed.

Abel Owens. My Lord, I came in upon the King's Proclamation, and enter'd my felf aboard one of the King's Ships.

Dr. *Oxenden.* You muft anfwer firft, and come to your Defence afterward.

Abel Owens. I hope your Honours will grant it me as well as the reft, I enterd my felf into the King's Service.

Cl. of Arr. You of the Jury, look on the Prifoners, and hearken to their Caufe. They ftand Indicted by the Name of *William,* &c.

Mr. J. *Turton.* You may try all the Indictments together, if they are the fame Perfons concerned.

Cl. of Arr. They are the fame that are concerned in the two firft Indictments.

Mr. J. *Turton.* Then proceed upon thefe two together.

Cl. of Arr. They ftand a fecond Time indicted by the Name of *William Kidd,* late of *London,* Mariner, (*and fo of the reft.*) Upon thefe two Indictments they have been Arraigned, and thereto have feverally pleaded, not guilty; and for their Tryals have put themfelves on God and their Country, which Country you are. Your Charge is to enquire, Whether they are guilty of the faid Piracies and Robberies whereof they ftand Indicted, or not guilty, &c.

Mr. *Knapp.* May it pleafe your Lordship, and Gentlemen of the Jury, thefe are two feveral Indictments againft William *Kidd,* &c. and they are both for Piracy. One fets forth, That the Prifoners at the Bar, on the Twentieth of *September,* in the ninth Year of his Majefty's Reign, fifteen Leagues from *Carawar,* did Piratically invade and take a Ship called the *Moorifh Ketch,* and put the Mariners in Fear of their Lives. The other Indictment fets forth, That on the 27th of *November,* in the ninth Year of his Majefty's Reign, four Leagues

from *Callicut*, the Prifoners at the Bar did feize and take another Moorifh Ship, to both which Indictments they have
pleaded, not guilty. If we prove the Fact, you muft find them
guilty. We will call our Witneffes. The Witneffes are the fame.
The whole Story you have heard before, and we will apply
our felves now to thefe Facts mentioned in thefe two Indictments.

Mr. J. *Turton*. You muft open your Matters firft, becaufe
there is a new Jury.

Mr. *Knapp*. Then, my Lord, and Gentlemen of the Jury,
this Capt. Kidd went out of *England* in a Ship called the
Adventure-Galley. He firft went to *New York*, and there he
fet out Articles to procure Men, and promifed them that
would come in to him a Share in the Adventures they fhould
get. From thence he goes to *Babs-Key* and lies about three
Weeks there, watching for the *Moco* Fleet: He fent his Boat
out three Times to fee in what Condition the Ships were. He
could get no Intelligence the firft two Times, but the third
Time he did; they brought him Word, there were fourteen or
fifteen Ships ready to fail, and that their Colours were *Englifh* and *Dutch*, and *Moorifh*. He lay in wait for thefe Ships,
and watched them; and when they came down, he fell in
with them, and fired at them; but he found they were under
an *Englifh* and *Dutch* Convoy, and fo away he went and left
them. And then he came to cruife on the Coaft of *Malabar*,
and there he met with his firft Prize, and that is the Moorifh
Ship mentioned in the firft Indictment: They feized and took
this *Moorifh* Ship, and entred her, and took feveral Goods
out of her, and then let the Ship go away. We will call our
Witneffes as to this Ship firft. Call *Robert Bradinham* and
Jofeph Palmer, (*who appeared and were fworn.*) Mr. *Bradinham*, What have you to fay as to this Matter?

Mr. Bar. *Hatfell*. Tell it from the Beginning; from the Time
that you went out of *England*, to the Time of taking this
Ship, becaufe there is a new Jury.

Bradinham. About the Beginingn of *May*, 1696, we went
out of *England*, and went to New-York, in the *Adventure-
Galley*, whereof Capt. *Kidd* was Commander.

Mr. *Knapp*. Whither did you go?

Bradinham. To *New-York:* We took the Ship by the Way, and carried her to *New-York*, where we condemn'd her.

Mr. *Knapp*. What Ship was that?

Bradinham. A *French* Banker. At *New-York* Capt. *Kidd* put up his Articles, that if any would come aboard his Ship they fhould be welcome, no Purchafe no Pay, mentioning that he had the King's Commiffion. From thence we went to St. Jauger, then to *Maderas*, then to *Madagafcar*, then to *Bonavis*, then to *Joanna*, and then to the *Red-Sea*, and then to *Babs-Key:* There he lay three Weeks looking for the *Moco* Fleet.

Mr. *Knapp*. Where?

Bradinham. In *Babs-Key*.

Mr. *Knapp*. You fay he lay there about a Fort-night or or three Weeks, how did he behave himfelf there?

Bradinham. He fent out his Boat three Times; and the two firft Times they could get no Intelligence.

Mr. J. *Turton*. Tell whofe that *Moco* Fleet was.

Bradinham. They belong'd to the Moors; they were Merchant-men belonging to the Moors.

Mr. *Knapp*. What News did they bring the third Time?

Bradinham. The third Time they brought Word that there were fourteen or fifteen Ships in the Harbour ready to fail.

Dr. *Newton*. What did he fay them?

Bradinham. That he would take as many of them as he could, and did not doubt but to make a Voyage out of them.

Mr. J. *Turton*. What Account did the two firft Boats bring?

Bradinham. No Account at all, my Lord.

Mr. J. *Turton*. What Notice did they bring the third Time?

Bradinham. They brought Word, that there were about fourteen or fifteen Ships in the Harbour ready to fail.

Mr. J. *Turton*. Which Time was it that they brought that Word?

Bradinham. The third Time. Then the Fleet came down and Capt. *Kidd* followed them.

Mr. *Knapp*. Were there any on Shoar to watch this Fleet?

Bradinham. There were fome fent to the high land of the

Ifland to fee if the Fleet came; and when they faw it, they were to give a Sign with a Half-Pike and Flag, and then the Boat was to fetch them off. At laft the Fleet came down, and Capt. *Kidd* went among them, and fired at them; but finding they were under a Convoy, and too ftrong for him, he was forced to leave them.

Mr. *Knapp.* Whither did you go then?

Bradinham. From thence we went to *Carawar*, and by the Way we met with a *Moorish* Ship, of which Capt. *Parker* was Commander.

Mr. *Knapp.* My Lord, that is the Ship that they are In-dicted for. Where was it that you met with that Ship?

Bradinham. About fifty Leagues from *Carawar*.

Mr. *Knapp.* Pray, what did they do with that Ship?

Bradinham. We took Capt. *Parker's* Ship, and took him aboard, and the *Portugueze* for a Linguifter: And he took out fome of the Men, and bound their Hands behind them, and ordered them to be drub'd with a naked Cutlace. And he took out of her fome Pepper, and Coffee, and *Arabian* Gold, and wearing Apparel, and feveral other Things.

Mr. *Knapp.* What did he do with thefe Men, after he had plundered the Ship?

Bradinham. He let the Ship go, and kept *Parker* and the *Portugueze* aboard.

Dr. *Newton.* How many Men were there aboard the Ship?

Bradinham. About Thirty.

Dr. *Oxenden.* What Countryman was this *Parker?*

Bradinham. He was an *Englifh-man.*

Dr. *Oxenden.* How do you know That?

Bradinham. He told me fo.

Mr. *Knapp.* What Ship was it?

Bradinham. A Moorifh Ship.

Mr. *Knapp.* What Time was this done?

Bradinham. In *September,* 1697.

Mr. *Knapp.* What did he do with the two Men he took out of this Ship?

Bradinham. He kept them aboard his Veffel.

Mr. *Knapp.* What Ship was Captain *Kidd* in then?

Bradinham. He was in the *Adventure-Galley*.

Mr. *Knapp*. Tell us whether any other of thefe Prifoners at the Bar were in that Ship when this was done.

Bradinham. Every one of them.

Cl. of Arr. Was Captain *Kidd* himfelf there?

Bradinham. Yes.

Cl. of Arr. Was *Nicholas Churchill* there?!

Bradinham. Yes.

Cl. of Arr. Was *James Howe* there?

Bradinham. Yes.

Cl. of Arr. Was *Robert Lamley* there?

Bradinham. Yes.

Cl. of Arr. Was *William Jenkins* there?

Bradinham. Yes.

Cl. of Arr. Was *Gabriel Loffe* there?

Bradinham. Yes.

Cl. of Arr. Was *Hugh Parrot* there?

Bradinham. Yes.

Cl. of Arr. Was *Richard Barlicorn* there?

Bradinham. Yes.

Cl. of Arr. Was *Abel Owens* there?

Bradinham. Yes.

Cl. of Arr. Was *Darby Mullins* there?

Bradinham. Yes.

Cl. of Arr. You fay you are fure they were all there?

Bradinham. Yes, I am fure they were.

Mr. J. *Turton*. What Goods did they take out of that Ship?

Bradinham. Several Bales of Pepper, Several Bales of Coffee, and fome Myrrh, which is a Gum.

Mr. *Soll. Gen*. What did they do with it?

Bradinham. Capt. *Kidd* made ufe of the Myrrh to make Pitch of.

Mr. *Soll. Gen*. What was the Value of the Myrrh?

Bradinham. About fifteen Pounds.

Mr. *Soll. Gen*. Where did they go after the Taking of this Ship?

Bradinham. To *Carawar*.

Mr. *Soll. Gen*. What did they do there?

Bradinham. There the Captain wooded and watered his Ship.

Dr. *Oxenden.* What is *Carawar?* Tell the Court.

Bradinham. There is an *Englifh* Factory. They fent fome Men aboard, and demanded this *Parker,* and the *Portugueze;* and the Captain denyed them, and kept them in the Hold, and would not let them know he had them on board.

Dr. *Oxenden.* Had they any notice of *Parker's* being on board Capt. *Kidd's* Ship.

Bradinham. I fuppofe they had Information from *Bombay* by the Marriners that went away, for Capt. *Parker's* Veffel belonged to that Place.

Mr. *Soll. Gen.* How far is that *Carawar* from *Bombay?*

Bradinham. About 40 Leafues.

Mr. *Soll. Gen.* Where did you go after that?

Bradinham. They crufed on that Coaft, and went to one of the *Malabar* Iflands.

Mr. *Soll. Gen.* What was done there?

Bradinham. We wooded and watered our Ship.

Mr. *Soll. Gen.* Did they take any Ships there?

Bradinham. Capt. *Kidd* went afhore there, and burnt fome Houfes, and plundered feveral Boats.

Mr. *Soll. Gen.* Was there any Ship taken there?

Bradinham. Yes.

Mr. *Soll. Gen.* What Ship?

Bradinham. Some time in *November;* about the 17th of *November,* they took a *Moorifh* Ship, Skipper *Mitchel* was the Commander.

Mr. B. *Hatfell.* You need go no further now.

Mr. *Knapp.* We will call the other Evidence, if you pleafe, Mr. Sollicitor.

Mr. *Soll. Gen.* We will give our Evidence upon both Indictments together.

Mr. *Knapp.* They ftand charged with taking another Ship. You have heard how far we have carry'd it: Now they went and took another Ship about the 17th of *November.*

Bradinham. They took a *Moorifh* Ship four Leagues from *Callicut.*

Mr. J. Turton. Now go on.

Bradinham. Capt. *Kidd* took this *Moorifh* Ship on the Coaft of *Malabar*, Skipper *Mitchel* was the Commander; fhe was a *Moorifh* Ship. He took out of her two Horses, fome Bails of Cotton, fome Quilts.

Mr. B. Hatfell. What Country-man was this Skipper *Mitchel*?

Bradinham. A *Dutch-man*.

Mr. B. Hatfell. What Ship was it?

Bradinham. A *Moorifh* Ship, fhe belong'd to *Surat*.

Mr. Soll. Gen. What Burden was fhe?

Bradinham. About 150 Tun.

Mr. Soll. Gen. What was found in her?

Bradinham. Two Horfes, about eleven or twelve Bales of Cotton.

Mr. J. Turton. Was this on the Coaft of *Callicut*?

Bradinham. It was on the Coaft of *Malabar*.

Mr. Knapp. How far from *Malabar*?

Bradinham. Seven or eight Leagues.

Mr. Soll. Gen. What did they do after this with the Ship, and Goods, and People?

Bradinham. The People they fet fahore, and kept the Ship, and carry'd her to *Madagafcar*.

Mr. Soll. Gen. What was the Value of the Horfes taken out of her?

Bradinham. The Horfes were worth about 40£.

Mr. Soll. Gen. What the Cotton?

Bradinham.   About an Hundred Pounds.

Mr. B. Hatfell. How do you know this Skipper *Mitchel* was a *Dutchman*?

Bradinham. He told me fo, he came, afterwards aboard Capt. *Kidd*, and took Arms under him.

Mr. Soll. Gen. Were all thefe Perfons aboard this Ship when fhe was taken?

Bradinham. Yes, my Lord.

Mr. B. Hatfell. You fay this Ship was about 150 Tuns; What might fhe be worth?

Bradinham. About 500£.

Mr. B. *Hatfell.* To whom did fhe belong.

Bradinham. To the *Moors.*

Mr. *Hatfell.* What *Moors.*

Bradinham. The *Moors* that belonged to *Suratt*, as I was informed by the *Moors.*

Mr. *Soll. Gen.* What did he do with the Ship afterwards?

Bradinham. She was carried to *Madagafcar.*

Mr. *Soll. Gen.* What did they do with the Ship?

Bradinham. They funk her.

Mr. *Soll. Gen.* Do you know why they funk her?

Bradinham. She was funk voluntarily.

Kidd. This Man contradicts himfelf in an hundred places.

Bradinham. The Ship was funk purpofely.

Dr. *Newton.* What was done when you came to Madagafcar?

Bradinham. When we came to *Madagafcar*, there came off a Canooe with white Men aboard that belong'd to the *Moco* Frogat. Some of thefe Men belong'd formerly to Capt. *Kidd.* She was fuppos'd to be a Pirate-Ship.

Mr. *Soll. Gen.* What was the reafon of finking that Ship?

Bradinham. They funk her in the Harbour, that fhe might be convenient for Veffels to Careen by. Some Men came off in this Canooe, and they told him, they heard he was come to take them, and hang them. He faid it was no fuch thing.

Dr. *Newton.* Who was the Captain of the *Moco* Frigat?

Bradinham. Captain *Culliford.*

Dr. *Newton.* Was he a Pirate?

Bradinham. Yes, he was reputed fo.

Mr. *Soll. Gen.* Well, go on.

Bradinham. Capt. *Kidd* fwore he would be true to them, and that he would do them no harm.

Mr. *Soll. Gen.* Did you hear all this?

Bradinham. Yes, he fwore to be true to them.

Mr. *Knapp.* Was there any thing faid about Capt. *Kidd's* taking her?

Bradinham. Nothing.

Dr. *Newton.* What paffed afterwards between Captain *Kidd* and *Culliford*?

Bradinham. They were very friendly together, and they made Prefents to one another.

Dr. *Newton.* What Prefents were there made?

Bradinham. Culliford gave to Capt. *Kidd* fome Pieces of *China*-Silk, and *Kidd* bid *Culliford* take any thing he had.

Mr. *Soll. Gen.* Did Capt. *Kidd* give *Culliford* any Guns?

Bradinham. He fuplpy'd him with two Guns.

Dr. *Newton.* Was there any Divifion of Goods or Money?

Bradinham. After we came to *Madagafcar*, Captain *Kidd* ordered the Goods to be hoifted out, and fhared, and Captain *Kidd* had forty Shares for himfelf.

Mr. *Soll. Gen.* What became of the Goods of thofe Ships?

Bradinham. They were fold.

Mr. *Soll. Gen.* What was done with the Product of the Goods?

Bradinham. Captain *Kidd* kept it, and when there was fomething worth fharing, he fhared it, and he had forty Shares for himfelf.

Cl. of Arr. Had *N. Churchill* any Share?

Bradinham. He had a whole Share.

Cl. of Arr. Had *James Howe* and Share?

Bradinham. He had a whole Share.

Cl. of Arr. Had *R. Lamley* any Share?

Bradinham. He had a half Share.

Cl. of Arr. Had *W. Jenkins* any Share?

Bradinham. He had half a Share.

Jenkins. How can you atteft thefe wicked lies? I had nothing.

Mr. B. *Hatfell.* Who fhared it?

Bradinham. The Captain.

Kidd. He tells a thoufand Lies.

Cl. of Arr. Look on *Hugh Parrot*, had he any Share?

Bradinham. No, half a Share of Money, and a whole Share of Goods.

Cl. of Arr. Had *R. Barlicorn* any Share?

Bradinham. He had half a Share.

Cl. of Arr. Had *Abel Owens* any Share?

Bradinham. He had a whole Share.

Cl. of Arr. Had *Darby Mullins* any Share?

Bradinham. He had half a Share.

Mr. *Soll. Gen.* Now if any of you will ask him any Queſtions you may?

Kidd. Mr. *Bradinham.* Pray what Share had you?

Bradinham. If my Lord ask me, I will anſwer him.

Kidd. Had you any Share?

Bradinham. Yes.

Kidd. Did you not come aboard my Ship, and rob the Surgeon's Cheſt?

Bradinham. No, I did not.

Kidd. Did not I come to you, when you went away, and met you on the Deck, and ſaid, why do you take the Cheſt away?

Bradinham. No, I did not do it.

Kidd. You are a Rogue.

Mr. J. *Turton.* It were the ſame thing for him to confeſs it, as to deny it, if he had done it.

Kidd. He did certainly do it.

Mr. B. *Hatfell.* But he ſays he did not.

Mr. J. *Turton.* Would any of you ask him any Queſtions?

Cl. of Arr. *Nich. Churchill*, will you ask him any Queſtionſ?

Churchill. I came in on the King's Proclamation, and depend wholly on it.

Kidd. Were there not any *French* Paſſes aboard that Ship?

Bradinham. I heard ſay there were, I did never ſee them.

Kidd. I did not divide the Things, but the Men did what they pleaſed, and you took your Share, and ſaw the *French* paſſes.

Mr. B. *Hatfell.* What Ship is that you mean, that taken in *September* or that in *November*?

Bradinham. The Mooriſh Ship, that *Parker* was Commander of.

Mr. B. *Hatfell.* There were two mentioned.

Kidd. Juſt now he told you of two in *November*, now he ſays one in *November*, another in *September*.

Mr. B. *Hatfell.* He ſays that in *September*, that *Parker* was Commander of.

Kidd. There was no fuch Thing in *November;* he knows no more of thefe Things than you do. This Fellow ufed to fleep 5 or 6 Months together in the Hold.

Mr. J. *Turton.* I affure you he gives a very good Account of the Matter.

Mr. B. *Hatfell.* Why did you give him a Share then?

Kidd. Becaufe he was Surgeon. As for the Goods they took it amongft them, and did what they pleafed, I was never near them. They laid wait for me to kill me. They took away what they pleafed, and went to the Ifland; and I, with about 40 Men, was left in the Ship, and we might go whither we pleafed.

Mr. *Soll. Gen.* Mr. *Kidd,* will you ask him any Queftions?

Kidd. No, no, fo long as he fwears it, our Words or Oaths cannot be taken.

Cl. of Arr. Will you ask him any more Queftions?

Kidd. No, no, it fignifies nothing.

Cl. of Arr. *N. Churchill.* Will you ask him any Queftions?

Churchill. I came in on his Majefty's Proclamation, and rely upon that.

Cl. of Arr. *J. Howe,* Will you ask him any Queftions?

Howe. I furrendred my felf upon the King's Proclamation, and plead guilty.

Cl. of Arr. *R. Lamley,* Will you ask this Witnefs any Quef-tions?

Lamley. Do you fay I had half a Share of Money?

Bradinham. Yes.

Lamley. No, I had none.

Cl. of Arr. It was your Share, and you muft make it ap-pear if you accounted for it to your Mafter.

Lamley. If your Lordship plaefe, I was an Apprentice.

Mr. B. *Hatfell.* To whom was you a Servant?

Lamley. I was an Apprentice to *A. Owens.*

Mr. J. *Turton.* Was *Lamley* an Apprentice to *Owens?*

Bradinham. My Lord, he was a Servant to *Owens,* who was a-board then.

Mr. J. *Turton.* He had half a Share, but perhaps he might account for it to his Mafter afterwards.

Cl. of Arr. *W. Jenkins*, Will you ask the Witnefs any Queftions?

Jenkins. My Lord, I beg he may fpeak the Truth, whether
I was a Servant.

Bradinham. My Lord, he was a Servant to *George Bullen*.

Mr. J. *Turton*. Was this *Bullen* aboard then?

Bradinham. Yes.

Mr. J. *Turton*. When both Ships were taken?

Bradinham. Yes.

Cl. of Arr. Will you ask the Witnefs any Queftions, *G.
Loff*.

Loff. My Lord, when I came aboard, the Captain opened
his Commiffion there. Did I ever difobey his Commands.?

Bradinham. Not that I know of.

Loff. Did you fee me receive any Share?

Bradinham. Yes, half a Share of Money, and whole Share
of Goods.

Loff. Where?

Bradinham. In the great Cabin.

Cl. of Arr. What Queftions will you ask him *Hugh Parrot*?

Parrot. May it pleafe your Lordship, I will give you an
exact Account from the Time of my going out of *England*.
In the Month of *October*, 1695. - - - -

Cl. of Arr. You may make your Defence afterwards, in the
mean time will you ask him any Queftionf now?

Parrot. I appeal to him, whether he ever faw me do any
fuch Cruelty as he mentions.

Mr. J. *Turton*. You hear what he fays, anfwer him.

Bradinham. I cannot fay you were the very Man that did
it. But thofe Men were ufed fo, they were hoifted up, and
drubb'd with a Naked Cutlace.

Parrot. And then I ask him, whether I ever went any further than my Commander ordered me, or againft the King's
Commiffion as I thought.

Bradinham. I cannot fay you did any Thing contrary to
your Commander's Orders.

Parrot. I ask him, whether, when I might have went a-
board this Pirate, I did not ftick clofe to my Captain, and

come home with him, and whether I had any Inclination to leave him.

Mr. J. Turton. He knows not your Inclination. Where did you leave Captain *Kidd*? will you ask him that?

Parrot. I came home to Boſton with Captain *Kidd.* Doctor, did I go away with them that left Captain *Kidd.*

Bradinham. You went with Captain *Kidd* to *Madagaſcar.*

Parrot. I came home with Captain *Kidd*, and ſurrendred my ſelf to my Lord *Bellamont.*

Cl. of Arr. Abel Owens, will you ask the Witneſs any Queſtions?

Owens. I ask the Witneſs, whether I did not ſurrender my ſelf.

Bradinham. I cannot ſay any Thing to that.

Cl. of Arr. Will you ask him any more Queſtions?

Owens. No, I ſtand to his Majeſty's Proclamation, and the Mercy of the Honourable Bench.

Cl. of Arr. Darby Mullins. will you ask the King's Witneſs any Queſtions?

Mullins. No. May it pleaſe you, my Lord, I came in upon the King's gracious Proclamation, as the King's Evidence knows. Do you not know I came a-ſhore with you about the 28th of *May*?

Bradinham. I know he went a-ſhore.

Mullins. I went a-ſhore. I came home upon the King's Proclamation. We went a-ſhore at Cape May. I was very ſick of the Bloody-Flux, and not able to travel, and was like to die every Day.

Bradinham. My Lord, I know this Man was very ſick in the Paſſage.

Mullins. I was a Paſſenger aboard Captain *Shelly's* Ship.

Mr. J. Turton. How came he to come aboard Captain *Shelly*? Where did he leave Captain *Kidd*?

Bradinham. He left Captain *Kidd* at *Madagaſcar*, and took his Paſſage with Captain *Shelly* afterwards, after theſe Ships were taken.

Mr. Soll. Gen. How came he to leave Captain *Kidd* at *Madagaſcar*?

Bradinham. He went aboard Captain *Culliford's* Ship. There was about 60 or 70 Men went aboard *Culliford*.

Mr. *Knapp*. Call *Jofeph Palmer*.

Dr. *Oxenden*. He fays he came in upon the King's Proclamation, to Cape *May*, do you know any Thing of that?

Bradinham. Yes.

Dr. *Oxenden*. Where is that Cape *May*?

Bradinham. Off of Maryland; where Captain *Shelly's* Ship was at Anchor; and Captain *Gravenport* came on Board Captain *Shelly's* Ship, and faid he heard his Majefty's Proclamation was out to receive Pirates that would come in; and the Men rejoiced that there was fuch a Thing, and they went afhore, and furrendered themfelves.

Dr. *Oxenden*. Where?

Bradinham. At *Cape May*.

Dr. *Oxenden*. Did he go to the Govenour?

Bradinham. I did not fee him go a-fhore.

Cl. of Arr. *D. Mullins*, will you ask him any more Queftions?

Mullins. You was aboard when I went a-fhore.

Bradinham. I did not fee you go a-fhore.

Mr. *Soll. Gen*. Was he fick when he went a-fhore?

Bradinham. He was fick.

Mullins. I was fick, and expected to die every Moment.

Cl. of Arr. All was done before that Time.

Mr. *Soll. Gen*. Did he rejoice, when he heard the King's Proclamation was out?

Bradinham. I heard him fay the King's Proclamation was out, and he rejoyced with others.

Mr. *Soll. Gen*. Did he furrender himfelf to the Governour?

Bradinham. I cannot fay that. He went afhore.

Mr. *B. Hatfell*. Now fet up *Jofeph Palmer*.

Mr. *J. Turton*. Gentlemen, I would not have you under any Miftake; that furrendering himfelf comes not under your Confideration, it was after all the Facts were done that the Prifoner is charged with.

Mr. *Knapp*. Mr. *Palmer*, give my Lord and the Jury an Account of what you know concerning Captain *Kidd's* Voyage from *England* in the *Adventure*-Gally, when he went out of *England*, and his Proceedings afterwards.

Palmer. About the laſt of *April*, or beginning of *May*, he went from *Plymouth* to *New-York;* and in the way took a *French* Banker, and carried her to *New-York*, and condemend her there. And at *New-York* he ſet up Articles, to invite Men to come aboard his Ship; that if any would come aboard, they ſhould have a Share of ſuch Treaſure as he ſhould take: He was to have forty Shares himſelf, and every Man a half or whole Share. And about the firſt of *September* following, he went from *New-York* to *Maderas*, from thence to *Bonavis*, from thence to St. *Jauger*, then to *Madagaſcar*, then to *Malabar*, then to *Joanna*, then to *Mahala*, then to *Joanna* again, then to the *Red-Sea*.

Mr. *Knapp*. Pray give an Account of what was done there.

Palmer. There he watered, and took *Guiny* Corn to Victual his Ship. And then to *Babs*-Key, near the *Red-Sea*.

Mr. *Knapp*. Give an Account what he did there.

Palmer. He ſent out his Boat three times to diſcover the Fleet, and likewiſe ſome Spies on the High Land to look out on both Sides, to ſee that the Ships did not paſs by.

Mr. *Soll. Gen.* What Ships?

Palmer. Mooriſh Ships from *Moco.*

Mr. *Soll. Gen.* Whoſe Ships were thoſe *Mooriſh* Ships?

Palmer. They were *Turks* and *Moors* together.

Mr. *Knapp*. What did he do then?

Palmer. He called the Men by Lot to look out, and he ſent his Boat out twice, and they returned without bringing any Tidings. And he ſent the Boat the third time, with Orders to take a Priſoner, or to ſee what Ships lay there. And the third time word was brought, that there were about 14 or 15 Ships lay in the Road ready to ſail, with *Dutch, Engliſh* and *Mooriſh* Colours. And when this News came, Captain *Kidd* ordered the Men to go on the other ſide upon the high Lands, to ſee that the Ships did not paſs by in the Night. And in four or five Days the Ships came down in the Evening, and Capt. *Kidd* went after them. And ſome of the Men ſaid, we will go among them to Night. No, fays Capt. *Kidd*, we will go in the Morning, and then we will take our choice.

Kidd. Did you hear me fay fo?

Palmer. I heard you fay fo.

Kidd. I am fure you never heard me fay fuch a word to fuch a Logger-head as you.

Palmer. Thefe are the words I heard him fay. And the next Morning he fell in with this Fleet, and went through them; and there was a *Dutch* and *Englifh* Convoy; and they fired at one another.

Kidd. Hear me - - -

Mr. *Knapp*. You fhall ask him what Queftions you will prefently.

Mr. J. *Turton*. Who fired firft?

Palmer. The *Dutch* and *Englifh* fired firft. When we lay between the *Englifh* and *Dutch*, a *Moorifh* Ship came by, and he fired feveral Shot after her. And the *Englifh* Ship, flung a Shot almoft home, and then he made Sail, and went out of the Fleet. And from thence he went to *Carrawar*, and in the way met with a Ship, whereof *Parker* was Commander, and there was one *Antonio* a *Portugueze*.

Mr. *Soll. Gen.* Where was this done?

Palmer. About 50 Leagues from *Carrawar*.

Mr. *Soll. Gen.* What time of the Year was it?

Palmer. It was about *September*.

Mr. B. *Hatfell*. The Witnefs is now come to fpeak to the Ship, for which the Prifoners are Indicted.

Mr. *Soll. Gen.* Go on, What did they do with that Ship?

Palmer. He fought the Ship, and took her, and took out of her feveral Bails of Coffee, and he retained only one Bail, and fent the reft back again. And he took a Bail of Pepper, and fome Myrrh, to ufe inftead of Pitch.

Mr. *Soll. Gen.* What quantity of Pepper was there?

Palmer. About 60 pound weight.

Mr. *Soll. Gen.* What Myrrh?

Palmer. About 30 pound weight.

Mr. *Soll. Gen.* What Value was it of?

Palmer. I cannot tell that.

Mr. *Soll. Gen.* What *Arabian* Gold?

Palmer. I did not fee it. I did not fee any taken out then. But a pretty while afterwards, when Captain *Kidd* came to *Carrawar*, he gave every Mefs two Pieces of *Arabian* Gold?

Mr. *Knapp.* How long was this after the Ship was taken?

Palmer. Ten or Twelve Days.

Mr. *Soll. Gen.* How was the Pepper difpofed of?

Palmer. It was divided among the Meffes.

Mr. *Soll. Gen.* Had thefe Prifoners their part.

Palmer. Yes.

Mr. *Knapp.* How did they ufe the Men of this Ship?

Palmer. There were feveral hoifted up, and drubb'd with a naked Cutlace.

Kidd. Where was this done?

Palmer. In your Ship.

Kidd. What Ship?

Palmer. The *Adventure-Galley.*

Kidd. Did not a parcel of Rogues go aboard their Ship, and do it?

Mr. *Knapp.* For what purpofe was this done?

Palmer. Becaufe they thought they had more Money in the Ship.

Knapp. What Country-man was *Parker.*?

Palmer. An *Englifh-man*, born in the North of *England.* He faid fo.

Mr. J. *Turton.* Who elfe was detained, befides *Parker*?

Palmer. One *Antonio* a *Portigueze. Parker* was detained for a Pilot, and the other for a Linguifter.

Mr. J. *Turton.* What do you mean by a Linguifter?

Palmer. To fpeak *Moorifh* and *Portugueze.*

Mr. *Soll. Gen.* Where did they go then?

Palmer. From thence we went to *Carrawar*, and watered and wooded the Ship; and a great many of his Men left him there. And when he faw his Men leave him, he went to Sea, he would not truft any more to go afhore. And the next Evening he met a *Portugueze* Man of War, and fought her, but did not take her.

Mr. J. *Turton.* Did you know any that left him?

Palmer. Peter Lehair, and *Churchill*, and others. They went to the *Englifh* Factory, to know whether they would entertain them or no.

Mr. J. *Turton*. Who went?

Palmer. Mr. *Lehair, Nicholas Churchill*, and another, they went to know whether they fhould be entertained. And they told them, they were loth to entertain them, for fear Captain *Kidd* fhould know of it, and do them an injury.

Kidd. My Lord, a parcel of thefe Men went afhore to run away with this Ship.

Mr. J. *Turton*. Were there any more of thefe Prifoners at the Bar, that would have gone off, befides *Churchill*?

Palmer. No, but he would have gone off.

Mr. J. *Turton*. How do you know that?

Palmer. He told me fo.

Mr. B. *Gold*. Had they an opportunity to go off?

Palmer. Some more were taken going off afterwards, and had got a Boat for that purpofe; but they were taken, and Captain *Kidd* order'd them to be brought aboard, and whipt at the Gun.

Kidd. Certainly you have not the Impudence to fay that?

Palmer. I fay you order'd them to be whipt for attenptimg to go afhore.

Mr. *Soll. Gen*. Whither did you go then?

Palmer. That Evening we went and met with a *Portugueze* Man of War.

Mr. *Soll. Gen*. You may go on from that. Whither did you go then?

Palmer. To the *Malabar* Iflands.

Mr. *Soll. Gen*. What to do?

Palmer. To take in Water. His Cooper went afhore, and the Natives cut his Throat. And Capt. Kidd fent his Men afhore, and order'd them to divide themfelves into Squadrons, and to burn all the Hcufes they came near, except the Houfes that had white Flags upon them.

Mr. *Soll. Gen*. Why not them?

Palmer. Becaufe they helped us to water the Ship.

Mr. *Knapp*. And were there any Houfes burnt?

Palmer. Yes, a great many.

Mr. *Knapp.* What did he do more?

Palmer. I heard what he did, I did not fee it.

Mr. B. *Hatfell.* What do you know of any other Ship?

Palmer. About the 27th of *November*, he took the Ship *Maden* near *Callicut.* We spy'd a Ship in the Night, and chaced her all Night, and the next Morning he took her.

Mr. J. *Turton.* What Ship was that?

Palmer. Skipper *Mitchel* was Commander, it was a *Moorifh* Ship, fhe belong'd to *Suratt.* She was taken in *November*, and after that fhe was called, *The November.*

Mr. *Soll. Gen.* How was fhe taken?

Palmer. Capt. *Kidd* chaced her under *French* Colours, and this Ship had *French* Colours, and when he haled her, it was in *French.* And this Skipper *Mitchell* anfwered in *French.*

Mr. *Soll. Gen.* Had the Moorifh Ship *French* Colours before Capt. *Kidd* put up *French* Colours, or after?

Palmer. After.

Mr. *Soll. Gen.* What Colours had fhe, when fhe was chaced at firft?

Palmer. It was in the Night: In the Morning Capt. *Kidd* hoifted up French Colours, and then the *Moorifh* Ship likewife hoifted up *French* Colours.

Mr. *Soll. Gen.* What followed?

Kidd. Speak true.

Palmer. I will. He fired three or four Shot at the Ship, and commanded them aboard. And *Mitchel* did fo, and fome of his Men with him. And he ordered Monfieur *Leroy* to be as Captain. And he came from below Deck, and received him as Captain.

Kidd. Did you fee that?

Palmer. I did not fee that, but I know he was ordered to do fo, and he received him as Captain, I was not in the Cabin at that time. Monfieur *Leroy* received him as Captain, and carried him aft. They haled this Ship in *French*, and bid him come aboard in *French*, and this *Frenchman* received him as Captain. And I heard them fay, that he brought a *French* Pafs along with him.

Mr. *Soll. Gen.* Who did you hear fay fo?

Palmer. I heard People on board fay fo.

Kidd. Palmer, Did you not fee that Pafs?

Palmer. Indeed Captain I did not.

Mr. *Soll. Gen.* What did you do with the Ship?

Palmer. There were two Horfes on board, and ten or twelve Bails of Cotton, and fome Quilts, and Capt. *Kidd* fold them at *Malabar.*

Mr. *Soll. Gen.* What Goods were there?

Palmer. Two Horfes.

Mr. *Soll. Gen.* What befides?

Palmer. Ten or twelve Bails of Cotton, and fome Quilts.

Mr. J. *Turton.* What Countryman was Skipper *Mitchel* the Captain?

Palmer. A *Dutchman.*

Mr. *Soll. Gen.* What was the Ship worth?

Palmer. I cannot tell the Value of her.

Mr. *Soll. Gen.* What Burden was fhe?

Palmer. About 150 Tun.

Mr. *Soll. Gen.* What did they do with thofe Horfes, and the Cotton?

Palmer. They Sold them to the *Banians.*

Mr. *Soll. Gen.* What did they do with the Proceed of thofe Goods?

Palmer. Capt. *Kidd* kept it, till they had a pretty deal of Money together, and then they Shared it.

Mr. *Soll. Gen.* Had the Prifoners at the Bar any Shares of it?

Palmer. Yes.

Cl. of Arr. Had Captain *Kidd* himfelf any Share?

Palmer. Yes.

Cl. of Arr. Had *Nicholas Churchill* any Share?

Palmer. Yes, he had a whole Share.

Cl. of Arr. Had *James Howe* any Share?

Palmer. Yes, a whole Share.

Mr. J. *Turton.* Where did they Share it?

Palmer. On the Coaft of *Malabar.*

Cl. of Arr. Had *Robert Lamley* any?

A SCENE ON BROAD STREET ABOUT 1660
from a library reference clipping

Palmer. Yes, half a Share.

Cl. of Arr. Had *William Jenkins* any Share?

Palmer. He had half a Share.

Cl. of Arr. Had *Gabriel Loffe* any ?

Palmer. He had half a Share.

Cl. of Arr. Had *Hugh Parrot* any?

Palmer. He had a whole Share.

H. Parrot. Did you fee me have any Share? Can you fpeak that to my Face now? Did you fee any of us have any?

Palmer. When Capt. *Kidd* fhared this Money, I did not actually fee him pay their Shares; but he called every Man by the Lift, and they came with their Hats in their Hands, and he gave them their Money, and they fwept it up, and went away.

Mr. *Soll. Gen.* Were thefe Men called by the Lift?

Palmer. Yes.

Mr. *Soll. Gen.* And did they mifs none?

Palmer. Not that I know of.

Cl. of Arr. What fay you to *Richard Barlicorn*? had he any?

Palmer. He had half a Share; whether his Mafter had it or no afterwards, I know not.

Cl. of Arr. Had *Abel Owens* any Share?

Palmer. He had a whole Share.

Cl. of Arr. What had *Darby Mullins*?

Palmer. He had a half Share.

Mr. *Knapp.* I think you were fpeaking of *Arabian* Gold, that they had it in Mefles, had thefe Prifoners their Share of that?

Palmer. Yes, there was no difference, they had all their Shares.

Mr. *Knapp.* Now, if you will ask this Witnefs any Queftion, you may.

Kidd. What fignifies it to ask him any Queftions? We have no Witneffes, and what we fay fignifies nothing.

Cl. of Arr. *Nicholas Churchill*, Will you ask him any Queftions?

Churchill. No, I have acknowledged all thefe Crimes, and Surrender'd my felf, and rely on the King's Mercy.

Cl. of Arr. James Howe, Will you ask him any Thing?

Howe. No.

Cl. of Arr. Robert Lamley, Will you ask him any Thing?

Lamley. Mr. *Palmer,* How can you tell I had a half Share?

Palmer. There was a half Share directed for you.

Lamley. I had not a Farthing.

Mr. J. *Turton.* Was he an Apprentice?

Palmer. Yes, he was Servant to Mr. *Owen.*

Jenkins. Can you fay I had any Share?

Palmer. I know there was a Share half appointed for you, but I know not whether your Mafter had it.

Mr. J. *Turton.* Was his Mafter Aboard then?

Plamer. Yes, his Mafter was Aboard then.

Cl. of Arr. Gabriel Loffe, Have you any Queftions to ask him?

Loffe. Had I any Share?

Palmer. You had a half Share, I did not fee you take it, but you were in the Lift.

Cl. of Arr. Hugh Parrot, Have you any Queftions to ask him?

Jury-Man. Did you fee them come out with the Money in their Hats?

Palmer. Yes.

Mr. *Soll. Gen.* Did *Gabriel Loffe* come out as contented as the reft?

Palmer. No, becaufe he had but half a Share.

Loffe. Did you fee me come out with any Money?

Palmer. I faw you come out with Money in your Hat, and I heard you fay you had half a Share.

Loffe. As I live I had no Hat then.

Cl. of Arr. Have you any Queftions to ask him, *Hugh Parrot.*

Parrot. Did you fee me have any Share?

Palmer. I did not fee you receive any Share, but you was called amcng the reft.

Mr. J. *Turton.* He fays they were all called Man by Man to take their Shares.

Cl. of Arr. *Richard Barlicorn*, Have you any Thing to ask him?

Barlicorn. I defire of him, Whether he faw me have any Goods, or take any Share'?

Palmer. My Lord, when the Goods were fhared at *Madagafcar*, I was at *Bonavis;* I was not prefent, but I heard of it afterwards.

Barlicorn. I hope the Jury will take notice of this.

Mr. B. *Hatfell.* Mr. *Bradinham*, Did any of thefe Men complain that they had not their Share?

Bradinham. No, no, I heard nothing of that.

Mr. J. *Turton.* Were thefe Shares fuch as were agreed on in the Articles at *New York*?

Palmer. Yes. Capt. *Kidd* ordered the Goods to be hoifted out.

Kidd. Did I order the Goods to be hoifted out?

Palmer. Yes, you did.

Kidd. It was the Mutinous Men that did it.

Parrot. How do you know that I had any Share? you did not fee me in a year after.

Palmer. I do not fay I faw it given you.

Kidd. My Lord, there were 95 Men that deferted my Ship, and took away what they pleafed, we could not ftand in Defence of any Thing.

Barlicorn. Was not I an Apprentice to Captain *Kidd*, and waited on him continually in the Ship?

Palmer. Yes you were.

Mr. *Soll. Gen.* Had he a Share allotted him?

Palmer. Yes, but I am apt to think his Mafter had it.

Mr. J. *Turton.* Who was his Mafter?

Palmer. Captain *Kidd*.

Cl. of Arr. *Abel Owens*, have you any Thing to fay for your felf?

Owens. I refer my felf to the King's Proclamation.

Cl. of Arr. *Darby Mullins*, have you any Thing to fay for your felf?

Mullins. I came to Cape *May*, where I heard of the King's Proclamation. Did not you and I come afhore together?

Palmer. Yes we did, the fame Day.

Darby Mullins. Did not we come afhore on the King's Proclamation?

Palmer. We did hear of it.

Darby Mullins. Did not you hear that all the Men were glad at the News, when they heard of the Proclamation?

Dr. *Oxenden.* What did the Men fay then?

Jofeph Palmer. They all rejoiced to hear of fuch a Thing.

Darby Mullins. From the Time I came from *Madagafcar,* I was fick of the Bloody-Flux, I could not walk a Mile in a Day.

Jofeph Palmer. I know you was fick.

Darby Mullins. I have no more to fay: I ftand to your Lordfhip's Mercy, and the King's gracious Proclamation.

Mr. Juftice *Turton.* If you have any Witneffes to call for your felves, you may call them. Captain *Kidd,* what have you to fay for your felf? You may make your Defence firft for that Ship taken in *September,* then for that in *November.*

William Kidd. What is it the near for me to fpeak? I have no Witneffes for thefe Things.

Mr. Baron *Hatfell.* Yefterday you produced your Commiffions; if you will, they may be read now.

William Kidd. It availed nothing then. Here is all thefe Men faw the *French* Pafs.

Jofeph Palmer. Indeed, Captain, I never faw it.

William Kidd. You left my Ship, with 95 Men more, and you went a roguing afterwards.

Mr. *Soll. Gen.* Why did you go aboard that Pirate?

William Kidd. My Lord, I had a Defign to take that Frigate, and then I defigned to come for *England.* I would not go with fuch a Roguifh Crew as you were. Was not I threatened to be fhot in the Cabin by fuch Villains as you, if I would not go along with you? This was the Reafon I could not come home. Did not you, with others, fet fire to the Boat, to deftroy my Ship?

Palmer. I know nothing of that; but I am fure I faved your Life on the *Malabar* Ifland, when you burnt the Boat.

Kidd. My Lord, they took what they pleafed out of this

Ship, and I was forced to ſtay by my ſelf, and pick up here a Man, and there a Man, to carry her home.

Cl. of Arr. N. Churchill. what have you to ſay for your ſelf?

Churchill. My Lord, I plead guilty and rely on the King's proclamation.

Cl. of Arr. James Howe, have you any Thing to ſay for your ſelf?

Howe. I plead guilty, my Lord.

Kidd. Here are ſome Gentlemen here, I deſire they mey be heard as to my Reputation. Here is Coll. *Hewſon.*

Mr. J. *Turton.* What do you ask Coll. Hewſon?

Kidd. I ask him what he knows as to my Reputation in the *Weſt-Indies?*

Coll. *Hewſon.* My Lord, he was a mighty Man there. He ſerved under my Command. He was ſent to me by the order of Coll. *Codrington.*

Mr. *Soll. Gen.* How long was this ago?

Coll. *Hewſon.* About Nine Years ago. He was with me in two Engagements againſt the French, and fought as well as any Man I evei ſaw, according to the Proportion of his Men. We had ſix *Frenchmen* to deal with, and we had only mine and his Ship.

Kidd. Do you think I was a Pirate?

Coll. Hewſon. I know his Men would have gone a Pira-teering, and he refuſed it, and his Men ſeized upon his Ship. And when he went this Voyage, he conſulted me, and told me they had engaged him in ſuch an Expedition; and I told him he had enough already, and might be contented with what he had: And he ſaid it was his own Inclination; but my Lord *Bellamont* told him, if he did not go the Voyage, that there were Great Men, and they would ſtop his *Brigantine* in the River, if he did not go.

Mr. J. *Turton.* Who told you ſo, did he?

Coll. *Hewſon.* Yes, my Lord.

Mr. J. *Turton.* If he kept to the honeſt Deſign of that Ex-pedition, he had done very well. Did you apprehend that his Intention in that Undertaking was to be a Pirate?

Coll. *Hewfon.* No, my Lord. He told me his Bufinefs was to go a cruifing, and furprize Pirates.

Mr. *Soll. Gen.* Did he tell you he had no fuch Defign?

Coll. *Hewfon.* Yes, he faid he would be fhot to Death before he would do any fuch Thing. I know he was very ferviceable in the *Weft-Indies.*

Cl. of Arr. *Robert Lamley,* have you any Thing more to fay?

Lamley. I can fay nothing, for I have none of my Friends here.

William Kidd. Call *Thomas Cooper. (who appeared.)*

Mr. J. *Turton.* What Queftions do you ask him?

Kidd. Sir, pray tell my Lord what you knew of me in the *Indies.*

Thomas Cooper. I was aboard the *Lion,* and this Captain *Kidd* brought his Ship from a Place that belonged to the *Dutch,* and brought her into the King's Service at the Beginning of the War, about Ten Years ago. And he took Service under the Colonel; and we fought Monfieur *Du Cafs* a whole Day, and I thank God we got the better of it, and Captain *Kidd* behaved himfelf very well in the Face of his Enemies.

Juryman. How many Years ago was this?

Tho. Cooper. About Ten Years ago.

Cl. of Arr. *Robert Lamley,* have you any Thing more to fay?

Lamley. I have no Friends here, I am a Prentice, my Lord.

Cl. of Arr. *William Jenkins,* have you any more to fay?

William Jenkins. I was an Apprentice, my Lord.

Cl. of Arr. *Gabriel Loffe,* have you any Thing to fay for your felf?

Gabriel Loffe. My Lord, I was a Servant under Captain *Kidd,* and always obeyed his Commands, and had no Share. I came home with Captain *Kidd* to *Bofton,* and went to my Lord *Bellamont,* and the Men came and told us he had difcharged us, and I went about my Bufinefs. And fome Days after we were committed to Prifon, and I was fick, and my Lord let me be in the Keeper's House, and I was trufted by him four or five Months with the Keys to look after the

Prifoners. Mr. *Davis* can teftify this. If I had had a Mind to have done any ill Thing, I might have done it then. (*Then* Davis *appeared*) Pray, Mr. *Davis*, declare what you know of me when I came to *Bofton*, and how the Keeper intrufted me with the Prifoners.

Mr. *Davis*. I remember when he came there to the *Road-Ifland*, Captain Kidd fent him home. And when he came to Bofton, he was trufted with the Keys, and had Liberty to go where he pleafed not out of the Yard.

Mr. J. *Turton*. Was this after he was a Prifoner?

Mr. *Davis*. Yes, my Lord.

Gabriel Loffe. I hope the Jury will take notice of this.

Kidd. Mr. Davis, did you hear of any French Paffes that I had?

Mr. *Davis*. I heard of them, and I faw them.

Mr. *Soll. Gen*. How do you know they were *French* Paffes?

Mr. *Davis*. He told me they were *French* Paffes, I did not know it, I could not read them.

Mr. Juftice *Turton*. They shewed you the Papers, did you know what Ship they belonged to?

Mr. *Davis*. No, my Lord, not I.

William Kidd. I defire Captain *Hunt* may be called, to know what my Lord *Bellamont* faid of me.

Mr. Baron *Hatfell*. That will fignify nothing.

Cl. of Arr. *Hugh Parrot*, have you any Thing to fay for your felf?

Hugh Parrot. My Lord, I had no Share of the Goods.

William Kidd. My Lord, I defire this Commiffion may be read.

Mr. Baron *Hatfell*. It is under the Broad-Seal?

Mr. *Crawley*. It is a letter of Mart and Reprifal, my Lord.

(*Then the Commiffion was read, dated the 11th of* December, 1695.)

William Kidd. Now, my Lord, in purfuance of this Commiffion, I went and took thefe Ships, which had *French* Paffes on Board, and my Lord *Bellamont* took them by force from me.

Mr. J. *Turton*. You took one *French* Ship, and acted in a

regular manner to condemn her; but did you do fo with the reft?

Will. Kidd. I could not carry the Ships home, by reafon my Men left me.

Mr. Juftice *Turton.* Mr. *Bradinham.* with what Number of Men did you go out of *England?*

Robert Bradinham. With about Seventy Men.

Mr. Juftice *Turton.* What Number had you when you went from *New-York?*

Robert Bradinham. About 155.

Mr. Juftice *Turton.* So that your Number was increafed.

Robert Bradinham. Yes, my Lord.

Mr. Juftice *Turton.* Was there any other Ship condemned, befides the *French* Banker.

Robert Bradinham. No, my Lord.

William Kidd. Thefe Men were fome of them that left me, and took the Goods. What was left I carried with me.

Cl. of Arr. *Hugh Parrot,* have you any more to fay?

Hugh Parrot. The Evidence cannot prove that I had any Share. I came with my Commander from *Madagafcar,* and he paid me an hundred Pieces of Eight, and my Lord *Bellamont* feized all. And I had opportunity enough to have gone a pirateering with Captain *Culliford,* but I told them I would not. And I came to my Lord *Bellamont,* and furrendered my felf.

Cl. of Arr. *Robert Barlicorn,* have you any Thing to fay in your own Defence?

Robert Barlicorn. I defire Witnefs may be called, to know whether I was not a Servant aboard.

Mr. Juftice *Turton.* The King's Evidence fay you were.

Cl. of Arr. *Abel Owens,* what have you to fay?

Abel Owens. I own my felf guilty. I came in upon the King's Proclamation.

Cl. of Arr. *D. Mullins,* what have you to fay?

Darby Mullins. I did what I did under the King's Commiffion. I obeyed my Captain, and came home with him. I durft not for my Life do other wife. Examine the Witneffes, and they will not fay otherwife. Mr Bradinham did I do any Thing againft the Captain's Command?

Robert Bradinham. I cannot fay but he did always obey the Captain's Command.

Mr. *Soll. Gen.* Did he not go aboard Captain *Culliford* afterwards?

Robert Bradinham. Yes, my Lord.

Darby Mullins. I went for want.

Cl. of Arr. Have any of you any more to fay?

Hugh Parrot. My Lord, I did not go out of *England* with Captain *Kidd*, but I fhipt my felf on Board a Merchant-man bound for *Newfoundland*, and I was taken by a *French* Privateer. And afterwards coming to *Madagafcar*, Captain *Kidd* was there, and he took a Piftol to fhoot me, but I avoided it. But hearing afterwards that Captain *Kidd* had the King's Commiffion, I went aboard him.

Mr. Juftice *Turton.* Had he any Commiffion to take any Goods from the King's Subjects?

Mr. Baron *Hatfell.* Captain *Kidd* fays the Seamen forced him from the Ship, and you fhared the Goods your felves.

Hugh Parrot. He does not fay fo of us. My Lord, with fubmiffion, be pleafed to ask my Commander, whether I ever difobeyed his Commands, or was forward to attempt any ill Thing, or did any Thing of that which is alledged againft me.

William Kidd. Mr *Bradinham*, are not you promifed your Life, to take away mine?

Mr. Juftice *Turton.* He is not bound to anfwer that Queftion. He is very fit to be made an Evidence for the King, perhaps there can be no other in this Cafe, than fuch who are in his Circumftances.

Hugh Parrot. With Submiffion, I ask the Evidence, whether I ever difobeyed the Captain's Orders.

Mr. Juftice, Turton. The Captain's Orders will excufe you in honeft Things, but not in unlawful Actions.

Hugh Parrot. As for the Ships that were taken, I had no Hand in it.

Mr. *Knapp.* But you received your Share, and knew of the robbing of the Ships.

Mr. Juſtice *Turton*. Gentlemen of the Jury, here is *William Kidd, Nicholas Churchill, James Howe, Robert Lamley, William Jenkins, Gabriel Loffe, Hugh Parrot, Richard Barlicorn, Abel Owens*, and *Darby Mullins*, the Priſoners at the Bar; who are all indicted for Piracy, or Piratical and felonious taking a *Mooriſh* Ship on the High Seas, about fifty Leagues from *Carawar* in the *Eaſt-Indies*, and ſeizing the Goods that were in that Ship to a conſiderable Value. And they were alſo indicted for the piratical and felonious taking another Ship, which was likewiſe a Mooriſh Ship, with the Tackle and Apparel thereof, to the Value of a Hundred and Five Pounds, four Leagues from *Callicut* in the *Eaſt-Indies*. Now to theſe Indictments they have pleaded, not guilty. And whether they are guilty or no, you are to determine, on the Evidence you have heard.

I need not tell you the Heinouſneſs of this Offence wherewith they are charged, and of what ill Conſequence it is to all Trading Nations. Pirates are called *Hoſtes humani generis*, the Enemies of all Mankind, but they are eſpecially ſo to thoſe that depend upon Trade. And theſe Things that they ſtand charged with. are the moſt miſchievous and prejudical to Trade that can happen. But as it is not my Buſineſs to aggravate the Offence, ſo it is yours to conſider whether they or any of them are guilty or not.

Two Witneſſes have been produced for the King, and both of them were concerned in all the Tranſactions relating to the Priſoners. And by their Evidence it appears, that in the Year 1696, about the beginning of *May*, Captain *Kidd*, Who was Captain of the *Adventure Galley*, was fitted out on a very good Deſign, for he was to take Pirates, and to ſeize the Ships and Effects of the King's Enemies: That was the End of this Expedition. He went out from *Plyomuth* with about Seventy Men from *England;* then ſailed to *New-York*, and in their paſſage they ſeized a *French* Veſſel; and that Veſſel was condemned in a due manner, and that was purſuant to their Commiſſion.

When they came to *New-York*, there were other Things in Contemplation; then he made a Proclamation, to give notice, that if any would come aboard him, he propofed Terms for their Encouragement, that they fhould be Sharers in all they could acquire; he himfelf would have Forty Shares, becaufe the Ships, Arms, Ammunition and Provifions were his, and the reft fhould be divided proportionably to thofe that fhould be aboard him. And whereas they went out with Seventy Men, there their Number was encreafed to 155, for with that Number he failed from *New-York*.

Gentlemen, The Witneffes tell you whether they went afterwards; I will not mention all the particulars Place, but only fuch where any Thing remarkable was done. They fay they came to a Place called *Babs*-Key; and there it feems they had an Intention to obferve a Fleet called the *Moco* Fleet, there they ftayed about three Weeks, and in that Time Captain *Kidd* fent his Boat Three Times to *Moco*, where this Fleet was; the Two firft Times they brought no certain Account; but the laft Boat that was fent, brought Intelligence that there were Fourteen or Fifteen Ships lay in the River or Harbour there, and were ready to Sail, and that they had *Dutch* Colours, *Englifh* Colours, and *Moorifh* Colours. And Captain *Kidd* faid then, he expected to make a confiderable Advantage of them. And after this Advertifement, he fent fome Men to the *High Lands* to obferve the Motion of this Fleet, who after fome Time gave Notice that the Fleet was coming, and then he went out with his Veffel; and as they tell you, he went into this Fleet, and difcharged fome Guns at them. But they having a Convoy, he found he was not a Match for them, and that it would be in vain to attempt any Thing further on fo great a Difadvantage; and fo that Defign was fruftrated. But it must be obferved, that thefe Ships were all *Englifh*, *Dutch*, and *Moorifh*, and none of them *French*, which fhews Captain *Kidd's* Inclinations to take fuch Ships for which he had no Authority by any Commiffion.

But they tell you, after this, when he had met with this Difappointment, then he failed towards the Coaft of *Carawar;* and there they met with the firft *Moorish* Ship that he is now charged with. And this Ship they feized, and took one *Parker*, who was the Captain; they feized him, and alfo a *Portu-*

gueze, whom they made ufe of as an Interpreter, and fome
of the Men, whom they treated in a barbarous manner. They
tell you, that there happening to be an *Englifh* Factory underftanding that this *Parker* and the Portugufee were aboard
the Ship, they fent to demand them; and Captain *Kidd* denied them, and faid there were no fuch Men on board, and
yet he had hid them under the Deck. You are alfo told by
the Witneffes what they found and feized aboard this Ship,
viz. Pepper, Coffee, Myrrh, and fome Gold. They have told
you, the Gold was fhared amongft them, and in Specie, as I
remember, every Mefs had two Pieces, and the reft of the
Goods were divided amongft them in Proportion, according
to their Original Agreement, of they had their Shares of the
Money for which they were fold. This was the firft Ship that
he ftands charged with the Piratical taking of. and this Ship
was a *Moorifh* Ship, and did belong to the Natives of that
Place.

And then it appears they went to the Coaft of *Malabar,*
and there they took the other Ship that he is charged with
by the other Indictment; the firft was taken in *September,*
and this in *November.* There was on Board that Ship two
Horfes, and feveral Bails of Cotton, and fome other Goods;
and this alfo belonged to the *Moors,* and one Skipper *Mitchel,* a Dutchman, was Captain of her. When they had taken
this Ship, they went to *Madagafcar;* and there it is told you,
they funk this Veffel. And they having feveral other Goods
that they had taken out of another Veffel, the Goods were
fold, and divided between the Captain and the reft of the
Men, according to their feveral Proportions. And it is proved
to you, that every one of thefe Prifoners had fome Share of
the Product of thofe Goods. And now to fhow what Captain
Kidd was, and that he was a Favourer of thofe he ought to
have oppcfed, there was ancther Pirate there, one Captain
Culliford, who had a Veffel that he ufed to the fame Purpofe,
called the Great *Mahomet;* and he having heard of *Kidd's*
Commiffion, had a Jealoufie that Captain *Kidd* had a Defign
to take him and his Company: But he told them he had no
fuch Defign, he was fo far from that, that he affures them,

nay Swore he would be true to them, and there were great Appearances of Friendfhip between Captain *Kidd* and Captain *Culliford*, they made mutual Vifits to each other. And Captain *Kidd* did accommodate *Culliford* with fome Guns, and gave him liberty to take any Thing he had; and Captain *Culliford* likewife prefented him with *China* Silks. Now this alfo is given in Evidence, to fhow that Captain *Kidd* had a Piratical Defign in all this, and that he did affift thofe that were engaged in the like Defign with him, inftead of endeavouring to fupprefs them.

Now, Gentlemen, the firft Witnefs, *Robert Bradinham*, has declared all this to you, and likewife *Joseph Palmer* has fpoken to the fame purpofe, though fomething more than the other. And he tells you how they went afhore on one of the *Malabar* Iflands, and how they burnt fome Houfes, and did other very barbarous Things. But that concerns not this Matter for which they are now indicted. He tells you alfo, that when they took one of thefe Ships, whereof Captain *Parker* was Commander, they took two of the Men on board that Ship, and hoifted them up, and ufed them feverely, which they did to caufe them to difcover what Things of Value they had on Board; but it feems they had nothing of any confiderable Worth on Board. However this fhows that Captain *Kidd* had a Defign to act Piratically. The Witnefs gives you an Account of all the Tranfactions, in taking the two Ships, and difpofing of the Goods, and dividing the Money. Indeed he fays, when the Diftribution was made, he was not in the Cabin, but tells you he heard the Lift called over, and all the other Prifoners feverally went in, and brought out their Shares in their Hats, or otherwife, and did not hear any one complain that he had not his Share.

Gentlemen, There are three Perfons that were Servants, that is, *Robert Lamley*, he was Servant to *Owens* the Cook; William Jenkins, he was Servant to the Mate, and *Richard Barlicorn*, who was Servant to Captain *Kidd*. Now though thefe might have their Shares delivered them, yet it is to be prefumed that they were to be accountable to their Mafters;

And they being Servants, I fuppofe you will think fit to diftinguifh them from the reft.

Gentlemen, This is the Sum of the Evidence given for the
King. And indeed this feems to be as ftrong an Evidence
againft the Prifoners at the Bar as can be. They did endeavour to take the *Moco* Fleet, but they were too ftrong for them;
And they could have no fufpicion that they were *French*, for
they had *Englifh*, and *Dutch*, and *Moorifh* Colours; So that
Captain *Kidd* could have no pretence from his Commlffion,
to look after thefe Ships; There were no *French* among them,
and yet there he lay three Weeks waiting for them. But they
did actually take thefe two Ships mentioned in the Indictments, and difpofed of the Goods, and fhared the Product
among themfelves. Here is all the Evidence that can be given
of Piracy.

Now Captain *Kidd*, when he comes to make his Defence,
tells you, he had a Commiffion, and it was produced; (and
that is no more than what is common in time of War) whereby he is Authorized to take the Ships and Goods of any of the
Subjects of the *French* King. But it is Penned with great
caution, he is to take none but the Goods and Ships of the
French King, or his Subjects, and he is to keep an exact Account of all that he takes, and to procure them to be condemned in the Admiralty. Now if he had purfued this Commiffion, and gone no further, it had been well, he had done
juftly, and anfwered the end on which he was fent out. And it
does appear, that the firft Veffel that he took in his Paffage
to *New-York*, was thus condemned. But afterwards I do not
find that he had any regard to his Commiffion; but waited
for that great *Moco* Fleet a confiderable time, I think about
three Weeks; and being difappointed there, he afterwards did
take thefe two Ships mentioned in the Indictment; and it
does not appear that they were *French* Ships, neither were
there any *French* Paffes on board. One of the Witneffes indeed fays he heard of *French* Paffes, but neither he or any
other Perfon that hath been produced had feen one of them.
Now I do not obferve that his Commiffion does any manner
of way tend to excufe the Captain in taking both, or either of

thefe Ships. One of them was under an *Englifh* Commander, which was *Parker*, the other under a *Dutchman;* there were no *Frenchmen* aboard, only *Levy*, who was made a kind of a Mock Captain by *Kidd* to ferve a prefent Turn. But what Captain *Kidd* has faid from his Commiffion, is fo far from juftifying him, that it feems rather an aggravation of his Crime. For he that will go out with the King's Commiffion on a juft and laudable Defign to take the Ships and Effects of the *French* King in War, and alfo to deftroy Pirates (which were the principal Ends of his being fitted out to Sea) and inftead thereof will turn Pirate himfelf, make ufe of the Force with which he was entrufted for the promoting his Piratical Purpofes, and for the Felonious taking the Ships and Goods of thofe that were in Amity with the King of *England*, appears to guilty of a manifeft Breach and Violation of his Truft; attended with very aggravating Circumftances.

Now for thofe three that were Servants, I muft leave it to you, whether they did act other wife than they might do. A Servant is to obey his Mafter, but it muft be in Things lawful and honeft; If they did any thing elfe, you have heard the Evidence will confider of their Guilt, and whether their Cafes differ from the reft; but there is fome probability that their Shares might be accounted for to their refpective Mafters.

Now, as to the reft, there are fome of them that do pretend they did Surrender themfelves, one of them to Mr. *Riches*, a Juftice of Peace in *Surrey*, others to Colonel *Bafs*, that was a Commander in *Eaft-Jerfy;* and it does appear that they did Surrender themfelves accordingly. But that does not come under your Confideratuon, yoi are to confider only whether they are Guilty of the Facts they ftand charged with, or no. As to what effect their Surrendering themfelves may have with his Majefty, muft be left to the King's Royal Pleafure; but we are to confider the Evidence. Now they generally fay, they did obey the Captain, and that they underftocd he had the King's Commiffion; Truly, fo far as he purfued the King's Commiffion, they were to obey him; But when he acts contrary to the King's Commiffion, in acts of

Piracy upon the Ships, Goods and Effects of the King's Friends, and thofe in Amity with the Crown of *England*, they fhould have been fo far from obeying and affifting him, that they fhould have obftructed him, and feized him, that he might have been brought to Juftice, and that would have been a greater Vindication of their Innocencies. But, as the Matter now appears, I do not fee that any thing they have faid tends to their Defence, and therefore I muft leave it to your Confideration.

Indeed, there are fome Witneffes appear for Captain *Kidd*. Colonel *Hewfon* gives you this account of Captain Kidd, that he was under his Command in the beginning of the War, and that he Fought and behaved himfelf very well, and was ferviceable in the Weft-Indies; and he fays, he difcourfed him about his going out on the Expedition he was fent, and that *Kidd* faid he had no Inclination to go. And Mr Cooper likewife tells you, that about ten or twelve Years ago he knew him, and that he Fought the French, and behaved himfelf very well at that time; and that feveral of his Men ran away with his Ship when he was at *Antegoa*.

Then there is *Gabriel Loffe*, he has produced a Witnefs for himfelf, one *Davis*. And *Davis* tells you, he was a Prifoner in *New-York* by order from my Lord *Bellamont*; and at firft they were fome Days there before they were taken into Cuftody; and there was fo little Apprehenfion of his being a dangerous Man, that he had fome Favour allowed him, and had a great deal of Liberty. This is that he fays. I find not that any of the reft have produced any Evidence, only they fay they were under the Commander, and were to obferve him. But if that would excufe them, then all Pirates would be excufed. Now, as to Captain *Kidd*, it feems he has wofully tranfgreffed the Bufinefs of his Commiffion, and acted contrary to the End and Defign of his being fent out, in the Piratical taking the Ships and Goods mentioned in the Indictments, in which the other Prifoners at the Bar have joined with him; and they were fo far from being the Ship and Goods of the *French* King, or his Subjects, or Pirates, that they were the Ships and Goods of Perfons of other Nations in Amity with the King of *England*. Now if you believe thefe Witneffes, that Captain *Kidd* has taken thefe Ships in a Piratical manner, and that the other Perfons affifted him in it, and had their Shares of the Money and Goods, which is in evidence of their confenting to, and fpontaneous acting, I believe you will think fit to find them Guilty, but I leave it to you. And as to thefe three Perfons that were Servants, I muft leave their Cafes to your Confideration, whether you will think fit to diftinguish them from the reft, or not.

Then an Officer was fworn to keep the Jury.

And after about half an Hour the Jury return'd and brought in their Verdict.

Cl. of Arr. Gentlemen, Anfwer to your Names, *William Smith*,

William Smith. Here, &c.

Cl. of Ærr. Gentlemen, Are you all agreed of your Verdict?

Omnes. Yes.

Cl. of Arr. Who fhall fay for you?

Omnes. Foreman.

Cl. of Arr. William Kidd, Hold up thy Hand; (which he did) Look upon the Prifoner. How fay you? Is he Guilty of the Piracy and Robbery whereof he ftands Indicted by the firft Indictment, or not Guilty?

Foreman. Guilty.

Cl. of Arr. Is *Nicholas Churchill* Guilty, or not Guilty?

Foreman. Guilty.

Cl. of Arr. Is *James Howe* Guilty, or not Guilty?

Foreman. Guilty.

Cl. of Arr. Is *Robert Lamley* Guilty, ot nor Guilty?

Foreman. Not Guilty.

Cl. of Arr. Is *William Jenkins*, Guilty, or not Guilty?

Foreman. Not Guilty.

Cl. of Arr. Is *Gabriel Loffe* Guilty, or not Guilty?

Foreman. Guilty.

Cl. of Arr. Is *Hugh Parrot* Guilty, or not Guilty?

Foreman. Guilty.

Cl. of Arr. Is *Richard Barlicorn* Guilty, of not Guilty?

Foreman. Not Guilty.

Cl. of Arr. Is *Abel Owens* Guilty or not Guilty?
Foreman. Guilty.
Cl. of Arr. Is *Darby Mullins* Guilty, or not Guilty?
Foreman. Guilty.

> *In like Manner* Kidd, *and Six more, were found Guilty on the other Indictments, and the Three Servants Acquitted.*

The Tryal of *William Kidd*, and the other Nine Perfons upon Two more Indictments of Piracy:
One committed on a *Moorish* Ship Four Leagues from *Calicut*, the other on a *Portuguese* Ship, Twelve Leagues from *Calicut*.

The Prifoners being called to the Bar, and the Jury called; and Captain *Kidd* Challenging thofe that had Tryed him for the Murther, the Twelve that were Sworn are as followeth, *viz.*

JURY.

Jof. Watson,	*Tho. Plaifted,*
Jof. Villers,	*Sam. Rown,*
Geo. Afhby,	*Marm. Bludder,*
Ed. Fenwick,	*Jo. Scot,*
Gilbert Eaft,	*Jo. Reynolds,*
Tho. Humfrevil,	*Rich. Drew.*

Cl. of Arr. Cryer, Count thefe: *Jo. Watfon.*
Cryer. One, &c. Twelve Good Men and True, ftand together and hear your Evidence.
Mr. *J. Turton.* With what will you proceed on now?
Cl. of Arr. With the two other Ships.

> *Then the ufual Proclamation for Information was made, and the Prifoners being bid to hold up their Hands, the* Cl. of Arr. *charged the Jury with them thus.*

Cl. of Arr. You of the Jury, Look upon the Prifoners, and hearken to their Caufe. They ftand Indicted by the Names of *William Kidd*, late of *London*, Mariner, &c. (as before in the Indictment). Upon this Indictment they have been Arraigned, and thereunto have feverally pleaded Not Guilty, and for their Tryal have put themselves on God and their

Country, which Country You are. Your Charge is, to enquire whether they be Guilty of the Piracy and Robbery
whereof they ſtand Indicted, or not Guilty, &c.

Churchill. I plead Guilty, my Lord, I ſubmit my ſelf to the
King's Proclamation.

Cl. of Arr. James, Do you ſtand to your Plea?

Howe. Guilty, my Lord, I ſubmit to His Majeſty's Gracious Proclamation.

Cl. of Arr. Robert Lamley, What do you ſay?

Robert Lamley. No Guilty.

Mr. *J. Turton.* You may enter their retracting their Pleas
in Court.

Cl. of Arr. William Jenkins, What ſay you? Do you ſtand
to your Plea?

Jenkins. Not Guilty.

Cl. of Arr. Gabriel Loffe, What ſay you?

Loffe. Not Guilty.

Cl. of Arr. Hugh Parrot, What ſay you?

Parrot. Not Guilty.

Cl. of Arr. Richard Barlicorn, What ſay you?

Barlicorn. Not Guilty.

Cl. of Arr. Abel Owens, What ſay you?

Owens. Guilty. I came in upon the King's Proclamation.

Mr. *Knapp.* The Jury is not to be charged with them three
then.

Cl. of Arr. Here is a ſecond Indictment againſt them,
wherein they ſtand Indicted by the Name of *William Kidd,*
late of *London,* Mariner, &c. (as in the former Charge.) What
muſt I ſay now?

Mr. *J. Turton.* Ask them three, Whether they ſtand to
their Plea to this Indictment, or retract it?

Cl. of Arr. Nicholas Churchill, Do you confeſs this Indictment?

Churchill. Yes, my Lord.

Cl. of Arr. James Howe, What ſay you?

Howe. Guilty of that, and all the other.

Cl. of Arr. Abel Owens, What do you ſay?

Owens. Guilty of that, and all the other.

Cl. of Arr. Set them three by. Gentlemen of the Jury, Here is *William Kidd, Robert Lamley, William Jenkins, Gabriel Loffe, Hugh Parrot, Richard Barlicorn, and Darby Mullins,* have been Indicted upon two feveral Indictments that have been read; and for Trial have put themfelves on God and their Country, which Country you are.

Mr. *Knapp.* My Lord, and Gentlemen of the Jury, Thefe are two feveral Indictments of Piracy, againft *William Kidd,* and the fix other Prifoners at the Bar. The firft fets forth, That thefe Prifoners, the 28th of *December,* in the Eighth Year of his Majefty's Reign, about four Leagues from *Calicut,* did Piratically enter a certain Ship, called a *Moorifh* Ship; and that they took her, with the Apparel and Tackle and took out of her feveral Goods that have been read to you in this Indictment. To this Indictment they have pleaded, Not Guilty. If we prove them Guilty, you muft find them fo. The other Indictment fets forth, That on the 9th of *January, &c.* that they took another Ship, a *Portuguefe* Ship; and to this alfo they have pleaded, Not Guilty. If we prove them Guilty, you muft find accordingly. Call *Robert Bradinham,* and *Jofeph Palmer,* (who appeared, and were fworn.)

Mr. *Soll. Gen.* My Lord, and Gentlemen of the Jury, I am Council for the King againft the Prifoners at the Bar. They ftand Indicted for feveral Piracies committed on two Ships, and our Evidence againft them will be to this Purpofe; Captain *Kidd* had two Commiffions, one was to take Pirates, the other was to take *French* Ships. *William Kidd,* in his Ship the *Adventure Galley,* went out of *England* in the Year 1696. He afterwards went to *New-York,* and there he increafed the Number of his Men. And from thence went away with a Refolution to commit the Piracies, fome of which he has been Convicted of already. Then he went to *Babs-Key,* and laid in wait to interept the *Moco* Fleet; but was difappointed of that, they being well guarded. He went afterwards to other Places, and took two Ships; which were not the Ships here mentioned. After that he feized a Ship, called a *Moorifh* Ship, ten Leagues from *Calicut,* and there feizes one of the Ships for which he is now Indicted, a *Moorifh* Ship, and takes out of her Sugar-Candy, and other Goods, to the Value of about five and twenty Pounds. In *January* following, he meets another Ship, and feizes her too, and takes out of her to the Value of fixty Pounds. Thefe Goods he difpofes of, and divides the Proceed of it between himfelf and the Crew of the Ship. And this is the Piracy for which he is now Indicted. The Matter you are to inquire into, is, Whether they be Guilty of Piracy on thefe two Ships, or no. We will call our Witneffes, and, if we prove them Guilty, I doubt not but you will do right to your Country and them. Mr. *Bradinham*, Thefe Gentlemen have not been upon the Jury before, therefore you muft give an Account of the whole Matter from the beginning, from your going out of *Plymouth*.

Bradinham. In the Year 1696, the beginning of *May*, we went from *Plymouth* to *New-York*.

Mr. *Soll. Gen.* What Ship did you go in?

Bradinham. The *Adventure Galley.* And by the way he took a *French* Ship, which he condemned when he came to *New-York*. At *New-York* he put up his Articles, to get Men aboard his Ship, and they were to have a Share of what was taken. About the fixth of *September*, we failed.

Mr. *J. Gould.* What Number of Men had you when you went from *England*?

Bradinham. About feventy Men.

Mr. *J. Gould.* How many had you when you went from *New-York*?

Bradinham. About an hundred and fifty. The fixth of *September* we failed from *New-York*, and went to *Maderas*, then to *Bonavis*, then to *St. Jauger*, then to *Madagafcar*, then to *Joanna*, then to *Mahala*, then to *Joanna* again, then to *Meta* in the *Red-Sea*, and then to *Babs-Key?*

Mr. *Soll. Gen.* What did you do there?

Bradinham. He lay there about a Fortnight or three Weeks, to wait for the *Moco* Fleet, and fent out his Boat three times to make Difcovery; the two firft times they made no Difcovery, but the third time they brought Information that they were ready to Sail.

Mr. *B. Hatfell.* What was the *Moco* Fleet?

Bradinham. They were *Moorifh* Ships.

Mr. *B. Hatfell.* To what end did he wait for them?

Bradinham. He faid he would make a Voyage out of them.

Mr. *Soll. Gen.* What happened on that?

Bradinham. He ordered fome Men to look out for them on the *High Lands;* and when they faw them coming they were to give Notice, and he was to fetch them off in the Boat. This Fleet came, and he fell in with them, and fired at them; but they being under Convoy, he was forced to quit them. And then going to *Carrawar,* he met with one *Parker's* Ship; he took this *Parker's* Ship, and took him for a Pilot, and the *Portuguefe* for a Linguifter.

Mr. *Soll. Gen.* How did he ufe the Men there?

Bradinham. Two of them were brought on board the *Adventure-Galley* and they were hoifted up, and drubb'd with a named Cutlafs.

Mr. *Soll. Gen.* Why did he do that?

Bradinham. That they might make Difcovery of their Riches.

Mr. *Soll. Gen.* What did they take out of that Ship?

Bradinham. Some Coffee, Pepper, &c.

Mr. *Soll. Gen.* What did he do with the two Men?

Bradinham. He carried them with him to *Carrawar;* and when he came there they were demanded by the *Englifh* Factory there, and he denied them, and faid he had no fuch Men aboard.

Mr. *Soll. Gen.* Where had he put them?

Bradinham. He confined them aboard in the Hold.

Mr. *Soll. Gen.* Where did he go then?

Bradinham. He put to Sea, and the next Day he met with a *Portuguefe* Man of War, and fought her.

Kidd. He tells nothing but meer Lies.

Bradinham. Then he went to the *Malabar* Iflands, and Watered and Wooded, and caufed his Men to burn feveral Houfes, and plunder feveral boats, and afterwards burnt them.

Mr. *J. Turton.* Did you fee them burnt?

Bradinham. I was not afhore, but I faw the Smoke.

Kidd. It is a fine Trade, that you muſt take away ſo many of the King's Subject's Lives, and know nothing at all of the Matter.

Mr. *Soll. Gen.* What did you do with that Ship?

Bradinham. He took.her, and diſpoſed of the Goods, and carried her to *Madagaſcar*.

Mr. *Soll. Gen.* What did he do after that?

Bradinham. We went to the *Malabar* Iſlands ſome time in *December*, and he took a *Mooriſh* Ketch.

Kidd. How came you to keep this Account, when for five or ſix Months together you were under Deck?

Mr. *Soll. Gen.* Go on, Mr *Bradinham*, and give an Account of your further Proceedings.

Kidd. I hope the King's Council will not put him in the way. It is hard that a couple of Raſcals ſhould take away the King's Subject's Lives. They are a couple of Rogues and Raſcals.

Bradinham. This Ketch was taken by the Ship's Crew, about *December*, 1697. and one of the Boat's Crew was wounded at the taking of this Ketch.

Mr. *Soll. Gen.* What was there in this Ship?

Bradinham. Some Tubs of Sugar-Candy, Tobacco, &c.

Mr. *Soll. Gen.* What did he do with theſe Goods?

Bradinham. They were carried aboard, and ſhared into Meſſes, two Tubs and a half of Sugar-Candy to a Meſs.

Mr. *Soll. Gen.* Had the Priſoners at the Bar any Share?

Bradinham. Yes; and then he ſet the Ship on fire.

Cl. of Arr. Had Captain Kidd himſelf any Share?

Bradinham. Yes.

Cl. of Arr. How much had he?

Bradinham. He had 40 Shares.

Mr. *B. Hatfell.* You ſhould tell this Jury how many Shares the whole was divided into.

Bradinham. It was divided into 160 Shares, and Captain *Kidd* was to have 40 Shares, let them be as many as they would, and the reſt were to be divided among the Men.

Cl. of Arr. Had *Robert Lamley* and Share?

Bradinham. Yes.

Cl. of Arr. Had *William Jenkins* a Share?
Bradinham. Yes.
Cl. of Arr. Had *Gabriel Loffe* any Share?
Bradinham. Yes.
Cl. of Arr. Had *Hugh Parrot* any Share?
Bradinham. Yes.
Cl. of Arr. Had *Richard Barlicorn* any Share?
Bradinham. Yes.
Cl. of Arr. Had *Darby Mullins* any Share?
Bradinham. Yes.

Mr. *Soll. Gen.* What was done afterwards?
Bradinham. After they had done thefe things they burnt the Ketch.
Knapp. What did they do then?
Bradinham. The *Moors* were driven afhore by the Ship's Crew.
Kidd. How did you know they were *Moors*?
Bradinham. By information of the Ship's Crew.
Kidd. He was not within five Leagues of the Place.
Knapp. What did you meet with afterwards?
Bradinham. A *Portugueze* Ship. Some time in January, 1697/8, we met with a *Portugueze* Ship on the Coaft of *Malabar*, and he took her; and he took out of her fome Opium, fome *Eaft-India* Goods, fome Powder, and fifty or feventy Bags of Rice.

Mr. *Soll. Gen.* My Lord, this is the other Ship for which they are Indicted. What was the Value of thefe Goods?
Bradinham. There were fome *Eaft-India* Goods, Opium, Powder and Rice.
Kidd. Did you fee them brought aboard?
Bradinham. I am anfwering the Bench.
Mr. *Soll. Gen.* Were there any other Goods?
Bradinham. Yes, there was Bees-Wax and thirty Jarrs of Butter.
Mr. *Soll. Gen.* What was the Value of thefe Goods?
Bradinham. About four or five hundred Pounds.
Kidd. It is a fine Trade indeed, that he muft be inftructed what to fay.

Bradinham. After he had plunder'd this Ship, he was purfued by fome *Dutch* Ships; feveral Ships gave him chace, and
he was forced to leave this Ship.

Mr. *Soll. Gen.* What did they do with the Goods?

Bradinham. He fold the Opium on the Coaft, and the reft
he kept for Provifion.

Mr. *Soll. Gen.* What became of the Money?

Bradinham. Captain *Kidd* fhared it.

Mr. *Soll. Gen.* Who had their Shares? Give an account of
that.

Bradinham. The Prifoners at the Bar.

Cl. of Arr. Had Captain *Kidd* any Shares?

Bradinham. Yes.

Cl. of Arr. Had *Robert Lamley* any Share?

Bradinham. He had half a Share.

Cl. of Arr. Had *William Jenkins* any Share?

Bradinham. He had half a Share.

Cl. of Arr. Had *Gabriel Loffe* any Share?

Bradinham. He had half a Share.

Loffe. How do you know that? Did you fee me bring it out?

Bradinham. I did not fee you take it, but you brought it
out, and acknowledged it.

Kidd. Before you fwore, I paid them firft, and now you
fay they paid me firft.

Bradinham. They had all a Share as before.

Mr. *Knapp.* Now proceed in your Voyage, What did you
do after this?

Bradinham. After this we went a Cruizing on that Coaft,
and we met with the *Queda* Merchant, and took her: And
afterwards, about fifty Leagues from the Cape, we met with
a *Moorifh* Veffel; and Captain *Kidd* fent his Men aboard that
Veffel, and they took out of her ten Jarrs of Butter, and a
Main-fail; and he took out two of the Men (that he carried
to *Madagafcar*) becaufe he wanted Men.

Mr. *Knapp.* Can you tell of any thing elfe?

Bradinham. He took about a dozen *Malabar* Boats, and
plundered them, and then let them go.

Mr. *Knapp.* Go on.

Bradinham. Then we came to *Madagafcar.*

Mr. *Knapp.* What happened there?

Bradinham. There came a Canooe off, fome of the Men in this Canooe belonged to the *Moco* Frigate; they came on to Captain *Kidd,* and they told him, they heard he was come to take them, and hang them.

Mr. *Knapp.* What were thofe Men?

Bradinham. They were fuppofed to be Pirates.

Mr. *Knapp.* Who was the Commander of that Ship?

Bradinham. Captain *Culliford.*

Kidd. How came you to know this? He fays anything.

Mr. *Knapp.* Go on with this Story, and give an Account what paffed between them.

Bradinham. This Canooe came aboard Captain *Kidd,* and they told him, they heard he |was come to take them, and hang them; but he affured them it was no fuch thing; And he went aboard the Frigate, and fwore to be true to them, and that he would aid them in any thing he had; and Captain *Culliford* came aboard him, and they made Prefents to one another.

Mr. *Knapp.* What Prefents did Captain Kidd make *Culliford?*

Bradinham. He gave him fome fhirting ftuff.

Kidd. What! Did I give him fhirting-ftuff?

Bradinham. Yes; and he gave him two great Guns.

Kidd. Did I go aboard him, you Rafcal?

Mr. *Soll. Gen.* Mr *Kidd,* Ask him what Queftions you will.

Mr. *J. Turton.* Captain *Kidd,* Will you ask this Witnefs any Queftions?

Kidd. My Lord, What fignifies it? Were there not ninety of the Men that Mutinied? I faid, Let us take this Ship; and did they not all confult, and faid, Where there is one that will fire againft the Pirate, there are ten that will fire againft you; and fo they went, and took the Goods, and left me: I ask you whether this be not true?

Bradinham. My Lord, he never fpoke any thing like it, that he would take *Culliford,* but he fwore to be true to them.

Kidd. Did not I propofe to my Men to take Captain *Cul-iford*? Did you never hear any body fay fo?

Bradinham. No.

Kidd. Did you not fay yefterday that I was come to take them?

Bradinham. I faid, they came and told you they heard fo, and you affured them you intended no fuch thing.

Kidd. You fwore I gave him four Guns yefterday, and now you fay but two.

Mr. *Soll. Gen.* It was *Palmer* that faid four.

Bradinham. I faid but two, and no more.

Cl. of Arr. Captain *Kidd*, Have you any thing more to ask him?

Kidd. It fignifies nothing to ask him any thing.

Cl. of Arr. Robert Lamley, Will you ask this Witnefs any thing?

Lamley. I only ask whether I was not an Apprentice?

Mr. *J. Turton.* Anfwer that Queftion.

Bradinham. My Lord, he was a Servant.

Mr. *J. Turton.* To whom?

Bradinham. To Mr. *Owens.*

Mr. *J. Turton.* Was his Mafter aboard then?

Bradinham. Yes, my Lord.

Cl. of Arr. William Jenkins, Will you ask the Witnefs any thing?

Jenkins. I defire to fay whether I was a Servant, or not.

Bradinham. Yes, my Lord, he was Servant to the Mate.

Mr. *J. Turton.* Was his Mafter aboard then?

Bradinham. He was aboard then.

Cl. of Arr. Gabriel Loffe, Will you ask him any Queftions?

Loffe. No, Sir.

Cl. of Arr. Hugh Parrot, Will you ask him any Thing?

Parrot. No.

Cl. of Arr. R. Barlicorn, Will you ask this Witnefs any Thing?

Barlicorn. I have nothing to ask him, but to defire him to fpeak the Truth, whether I was not the Captain's Servant.

Bradinham. He was, my Lord.

Cl. of Arr. Darby Mullins, Will you ask him any Thing?

Mullins. I have nothing to fay but what I faid before. I fubmit my felf to the King's gracious Proclamation.

Kidd. He has Perjured himfelf in many Things.

Mr. *J. Turton.* In what? Give an inftance.

Kidd. In a great many Inftances: About the Guns, that is one thing; and then he fays the Ship went from *Plymouth* the beginning of *May,* and before he faid it was in *April,* that is another thing; and, my Lord, the Mariners came and took Anchors, and Cables, and what they would, and, he fays, I gave them to them, and this is falfe; and now he fays contrary to what he did before, for then he faid we went out in *April,* and now the beginning of *May.*

Mr. *J. Turton.* He did not confine himfelf to a Day, he faid about the beginning of *May.*

Mr. *Soll. Gen.* Call *Jofeph Palmer,* (who appeared). Mr. *Palmer,* pray give my Lord, and the Jury, an account of Captain *Kidd* and his Crew, where they went, and what they did.

Palmer. We went from *Plymouth* to *New-York,* in the Year 1696, and in the way took a *French* Ship, and carried her to *New-York,* and fold her; And there he put up Articles to invite Men aboard his Ship, and what they took was to be divided into many fo Shares, whereof Captain *Kidd* was to have forty, the reft to be divided among the Men; and in *September* following, we went from thence, and we had then about 160 Men: From thence we went to *Maderas,* from thence to *Bonavis,* then to St. *Jauger,* then to *Joanna,* then to *Mahala,* then to *Joanna* again, and then to *Meta* in the *Red-Sea,* where he watered and wooded his Ship, and then to *Babs-Key,* a fmall Ifland in the Red-Sea: And when he came there, he ordered his Men to look out on the *High-Lands* for the *Moco* Fleet, and expected the Fleet to came that way; and he fent fome Men in his Boat, with orders either to take a Prifoner, or to bring word what Ships were there; He fent his Boat twice and they made no Difcovery, but the third time they went they came within fight of the Ships, and brought word that there were 14 or 15 fail lying there, with *Dutch,* and *Englifh,* and *Moorifh* Colours, and a great Ship with red Colours ready to fail: And then Captain *Kidd* ordered his Men to look out on the other fide the High Lands, for fear that Ships fhould pafs him; and at laft the Ships came down.

Kidd. There is no great occafion for this.

Palmer. There were *Moors* and *Turks* belonging to thefe Ships: And about the 15th of *Auguft* the Fleet came down; and Captain *Kidd* fell in with them; his Quarter-mafter and fome of his Men were faying, Let us go aboard them to Night; No, fays he, we will take our choice of them in the Morning; and in the morning he went among them, and fired at them, but took none of them; he found they were too ftrong for him, and went away. And after this going to *Carrawar*, he took a Ship called the *Mayden;* it was between Carrawar and this place, they reckoned they were not far from the Ifland of St. *John:* He took this Ship, and took out of her fome Pepper, a Bail of Coffee, and fome more Bails of Coffee came on board, but he retained only one Bail and the Pepper, and faid he would not cumber his Ship with fuch Stuff; and *Parker*, and a *Portugueze* he took out, one for a Pilot, the other for a Linguifter: And two of the Men he ordered to be hoifted up, and whipt with a naked Cutlafs.

Kidd. I ask this one Thing, Did the *Moco* Fleet fire firft at me, or I at them?

Palmer. No, they fired firft.

Kidd. And juft now the other faid I fired firft; Is not be Perjured.

Mr. *J. Turton.* Mr. *Bradinham*, Did he fire firft, or no?

Bradinham. He fired at them. I only faid you fired at them, I did not fay firft or laft.

Palmer. After this he went to *Carrawar*, to an *Englifh* Factory, and Wooded and Watered his Ship; and one *Harvey* came and demanded thefe two Men; and Captain Kidd denied that he had any fuch Men on board, and kept them in the Hold.

Mr. *Soll. Gen.* Is that an *Englifh* Factory?

Palmer. Yes. Several of Captain *Kidd's* Men left him there, and feveral more would have left him, if they could have conveniently gone afhore: And the fame Evening he put to Sea, he met a *Portugueze* Ship, and fought her.

Kidd. Who fired there firft?

Palmer. The Portugueze fired firft.

Kidd. You do not tell that Story right.

Palmer. After he left this *Portugueze* Ship he went to the Ifland of *Malabar*, and robbed the Natives, and fet their Houfes on fire, and took one of the Natives, and bound him to a Tree, and shot him to Death.

Mr. *Soll. Gen.* Did you fee the Houfes on fire?

Palmer. Yes: And afterwards we went to *Calicut*, and met with a *Moorifh* Ship in *November*, *Schipper Mitchel* was Commander; and there were taken out of her two Horfes, and Cotton, and Quilts; and this Ship he carried to *Madagafcar:* Sometime in *December* following we came to the Coaft of *Malabar*.

Mr. *Knapp.* Can you tell what Year it was?

Palmer. It was in December, 1697.

Mr. *Knapp.* Where was this?

Palmer. About twelve Leagues from *Callicut*.

Mr. *Knapp.* What fort of Ship was it?

Palmer. A *Moorifh* Ketch.

Mr. *Knapp.* What Burden was fhe?

Palmer. About fifty Tun.

Mr. *Knapp.* What did you do there?

Palmer. Captain *Kidd* was lying at Anchor, and this Ketch came between him and the Shore, and he fent the Boat, and they brought the Ketch to the Ship, and took out of her thirty Bails of Sugar-Candy, Tobacco, Sugar and Myrrh.

Mr. *Knapp.* What did they do with thefe Goods?

Palmer. When they had taken them out, they were fhared between the Men in Meffes, feven Men to a Mefs, for their own fpending.

Mr. *Knapp.* Had the Prifoners at the Bar any Share?

Palmer. All the Men had.

Mr. *Knapp.* What Share had Captain *Kidd*?

Palmer. I cannot tell whether he had his 40 Shares of that, or no.

Mr. *Knapp*. What did they do with the Ship?

Palmer. They burnt her.

Mr. *Soll. Gen.* Pray now go on: What did they do next?

Palmer. Sometime in *January* they met with a *Portuguez* Ship.

Mr. *Soll. Gen.* Where?

Palmer. Off of *Anjingo*, an Englifh Factory: It was a pretty way off Shore.

Mr. *Soll. Gen.* What Ship was it?

Palmer. A *Portugueze* Ship.

Kidd. You faid it was juft by Callicut yefterday.

Mr. *Soll. Gen.* Whereabouts was it?

Palmer. On the Coaft of *Malabar;* it might be about ten or twelve Leagues from *Callicut*.

Mr. *Soll. Gen.* What Goods were in the Ship when fhe was taken?

Palmer. There were two Chefts of *Indian* Goods, two Chefts of Opium, fome Rice, Butter, Wax, and Iron.

Mr. *Soll. Gen.* What was the Value of thofe Goods?

Palmer. Truly I cannot tell the Value of them.

Mr. *Soll. Gen.* What did they do with thofe Goods?

Palmer. The Wax and Iron he put aboard the *November*, and fome aboard his own Ship.

Mr. *Soll. Gen.* Did he fell any of thefe Goods?

Palmer. No, but he fold the Opium on the Coaft.

Mr. *Soll. Gen.* Did he keep the Ship?

Palmer. No, but feven or eight Days, and then he quitted her; there were fome Dutchmen coming, and he funk that Ship: The Produce of the Ship was fhared.

Mr. *Soll. Gen.* Had the Prifoners at the Bar any Share?

Palmer. Yes.

Cl. of Arr. Had *William Kidd* any Share?

Palmer. Yes.

Cl. of Arr. Had *Robert Lamley* any Share?

Palmer. Yes.

Cl. of Arr. Had *William Jenkins* any Share?

Palmer. Yes.

Cl. of Arr. Had *Gabriel Loffe* any Share?

Palmer. Yes.

Cl. of Arr. Had *Hugh Parrot* any Share?

Palmer. Yes.

Cl. of Arr. Had *Richard Barlicorn* any Share?

Palmer. Yes.

Cl. of Arr. Had *Darby Mullins* any Share?

Palmer. Yes; thefe Goods were fhared, and we bought Provifion with them.

Kidd. You fay this Ship was taken off of *Anjingo*, and that it was twelve Leagues from *Calicut*, and this Anjingo is fifty Leagues from *Calicut*.

Palmer. It is all upon one Coaft.

Mr. *Soll. Gen.* Give an Account of your coming to *Madagafcar*, and what followed.

Palmer. They found a Ship called the Refolution, Captain *Culliford* was Commander; and feveral of the Men came off to Captain *Kidd*, that were formerly acquainted with him; and they faid, We hear you are come to hang us; fays he, It is no fuch Thing. And afterwards they went aboard each other, and Captain *Kidd* made Proteftations to be true to them. There were four Guns in the Ship, and he prefented thefe Guns to *Culiford*.

Kidd. Did I prefent him with my Guns? Becaufe I would not turn Pirate, you Rogues, you would make me one.

Mr. Baron *Hatfell*. What did Captain *Kidd* fay to *Culliford*, when they were drinking together.

Palmer. They made a Tub of Bomboo, as they call it (it is made of Water and Limes, and Sugar) and there they drank to one another; and fays Captain *Kidd*, before I would do you any Damage, I had rather my Soul fhould broil in Hell-fire.

Mr. *Soll. Gen.* Was you there then?

Palmer. This was on the Quarter-dedk of the *Moco* Frigate.

Mr. *Soll. Gen.* What were thofe Men in that Ship? What did you apprehend them to be?

Palmer. They were Pirates.

Mr. *Soll. Gen.* Did Captain *Kidd* or his Men offer to take them?

ST. PAUL'S

from a print in Walks in our Churchyards *by Felix Oldboy,* 1903

Palmer. He did never propofe any fuch Thing.

Mr. *Soll. Gen.* Now you may ask him what Queftions you will.

Kidd. There went twenty of them aboard, and left me.

Palmer. Captain *Kidd* and *Culliford* were as great Friends as could be.

Mr. *Soll. Gen.* Ask him what Queftions you pleafe.

Will. Kidd. If fiignifies nothing to ask any Queftions, a couple of Rogues will fwear any Thing.

Mr. *Soll. Gen.* Will ask you him any Queftions?

Kidd. No.

Cl. of Arr. *R. Lamley,* will you ask him any Queftions?

Robert Lamley. No.

Cl. of Arr. *William Jenkins,* will you ask him any Queftions?

William Jenkins. No; I have no more to fay, but what I faid before.

Cl. of Arr. *Gabriel Loffe,* have you any Thing to ask him?

Gabriel Loffe. No.

Cl. of Arr. *Hugh Parrot,* will you ask the Witnefs any Queftions?

Hugh Parrot. No.

Cl. of Arr. *Richard Barlicorn.* will you ask him any Thing?

Richard Barlicorn. No.

Cl. of Arr. *Darby Mullins,* will you ask him any Thing?

Darby Mullins. No; but only I fay I came home upon his Majefty's Proclamation; I came voluntarily, expecting to have the Benefit of it with the Evidence.

Mr. *J. Turton.* That does not fall under the Jury's Confideration.

Cl. of Arr. You, the Prifoners at the Bar, will you fay any Thing for your felves upon thefe two Indictments?

Cl. of Arr. You, the Prifoners at the Bar, will you fay any Thing for your felves upon thefe two Indictments?

Kidd. I will not trouble the Court any more, for it is a Folly.

Cl. of Arr. *Robert Lamley,* What have you to fay for your felf?

Robert Lamley. Nothing, but that I was a Servant.

Cl. of Arr. *W. Jenkins,* what have you to fay?

W. Jenkins. I was a Servant, my Lord.

Cl. of Arr. *Gabriel Loffe,* have you any Thing to fay?

G. Loffe. My Lord, I ask him whether I ever acted any Thing in taking thefe Ships, but only under my Captain's Command.

Palmer. He acted as other Men did.

Cl. of Arr. *Hugh Parrot,* have you any Thing to fay?

Hugh Parrot. I can fay no more than I have faid.

Cl. of Arr. *Richard Barlicorn,* have you any Thing to fay?

R. Barlicorn. My Lord, I am a Servant.

Cl. of Arr. *Darby Mullins,* what have you to fay?

Darby Mullins. Did not Captain *Kidd* often fay his Commiffion would bear him out in what he did?

Palmer. Yes, I have heard him often fay that.

Mr. *J. Turton.* But how came you to go aboard *Culliford?*

Darby Mullins. For What, my Lord.

Mr. *J. Turton.* Gentlemen of the Jury, Here are feveral Perfons, *viz. William Kidd, Rob. Lamley, Will. Jenkins, Gab. Loffe, Hugh Parrot, Richard Barlicorn,* and *Darby Mullins;* They all ftand Indicted for Piracy: Indeed there are three more Indicted with them, *viz. Nicholas Churchill, James Howe,* and *Abel Owens;* but they have confeffed themfelves guilty, and you are now eafed of any inquiry concerning them, and are only to confider of the other Seven, who are Indicted upon two feveral Indictments: One is, for the Piratical and Felonious taking away a *Moorifh* Ketch, to the Value of Fifty Pounds, and the Goods therein to the Value of one Hundred Pounds; this was in December, 1697. And the Other is, for Piratically feizing and taking away Goods to the Value of feventy Pounds from the *Portugal* Ship, twelve Leagues from *Calicut,* in the East-Indief. Now to thefe two Indictments thefe Prifoners at the Bar have pleaded, Not Guilty; and whether they are fo or no, you are to determine, upon the Evidence given you. There have been two Witneffes produced for the King, *Robert Bradinham,* and *Jofeph Palmer,* I will not trouble you with the Repetition of their diftinct

Evidence, becaufe they agree in all Things, and if I mention
what one has faid, it is in effect what the other faid alfo.

Gentlemen, It appears that Captain *Kidd*, with feventy
Perfons aboard his Ship called the *Adventure-Galley*, went
from *England* in the Year 1696, having a Commiffion of Mart
and Reprifal, to take the Veffels, Ships and Goods of the
French King, or any of his Subjects, he being then at War
with the King of *England*, and another Commiffion for feizing
Pirates. He has not indeed produced thefe Commiffions to
you now, though he did on another Trial. But he went out
on a very honeft Defign, and in purfuance of it he took a
French Ship in his Paffage to *New-York*, and brought her
thither, and had her legally condemned. But while he was
there, it appears that he had other Thoughts poffeffed him,
and wicked Intentions to turn Pirate, and not to take them
and that he might be well Manned he makes Proclamation
amongft theMariners there, that fuch of them as would come
aboard his Ship, and affift him in his Enterprifes, fhould have
their Shares of what Prizes or Booties could be taken; and
he propofed that he would have forty Shares for himfelf, and
the reft fhould be equally diftributed amongft the Mariners
according to agreement, the whole being divided into 160
Shares as I remember; by this means his Number was increafed from 70 to 150. They fet fail from *New-York*, and
(after many other Places mentioned by theWitneffes) they
came to a place called *Babs-Key*, which it feems is in the *Red-
Sea;* and there they ftayed a confiderable Time, I think about
three Weeks, and this was in expectation to meet with the
Moco Fleet, which he intended to make a Prize; and during
his Stay at *Babs-Key* he fent his Boat three feveral times to
get Intelligence of this Fleet; the two firft Times there was
no Account of any Thing, but the third Time there was notice brought that they were ready to fail, and what they had
Englifh, *Dutch*, and *Moorifh* Colours. And when he had this
Intelligence, to prevent their efcaping him, he fends Men
afhore, to go on the *High-Lands* to obfefve when they did
actually fail; and when he had notice that they were under
fail, he likewife failed, and went through the Fleet, and made

fome Shots at fome of the Ships; but it appearing that they had a Convoy, and that they were too ftrong for him, he quitted the Prize there, of which he had fo great Expectation. But afterwards he went on, and took his Courfe towards *Carawar*, and there he takes a *Moorifh* Ship; and *Parker* an Englifhman the Commander of her, and a Portuguefe alfo were taken out of her. From thence they went to *Malabar*, and there he fent fome Men afhore, and there they burnt fome Houfes; and after they took a *Moorifh* Ship for which they have been tried. Afterwards, in *December* 1697, (now I come to the Indictment) upon that very Coaft, fome Leagues from *Calicut*, they took a *Moorifh* Ketch, and this Ketch and the Goods aboard it, which were fome Quantities of Sugar-Candy Sugar, and Tobacco: It feems thefe Goods were fhared between them aboard the Ship; the Witnefs is not confident what Share the Captain then had, but what the Captain had not, was divided amongft them. The Witneffes fay they burnt this Ketch, becaufe fhe was not ufeful to them, and the Men that went on Board were put afhore. Now this is the Matter of the firft Indictment, the Piratically feizing and plundering this Ketch, and Taking the Goods out of her, and dividing them amongft the Prifoners: both the Witneffes prove there was a Diftribution of them.

They then come to the next Month, and that is *January;* and this is that Matter of the fecond Indictment, for piratically taking feveral Goods, to the Value of feventy Pounds, from the Mariners of the Ship called the *Portugal* Ship: And thefe Witneffes prove the taking of this Ship on the Coaft of *Calicut;* and there were aboard this Ship feveral forts of Goods, Opium, Rice, Beeswax, Butter, and other forts of Goods, which they judge might be worth four or five hundred Pounds. Now after this, there were fome *Dutch* Ships that gave chace to the Captain, and he was forced to leave the Ship; but he took fome of the Goods into his own Ship, and the reft were fold, and the Money divided among the Men: The Captain called them one by one into his Cabin, and fo they had their feveral Shares according to the Propofals at *New-York*. It is not poffible for them to fay they faw every

Man's Share paid, but they fay that they were all called by
Name to receive their Shares, and they went into the Cabin
for that Purpofe, and they believe they had all their Shares
according to Agreement, becaufe none complained that they
had it not.

Gentlemen, There is but one Thing more that I will men-
tion to you. When they came to *Madagafcar*, there was one
Culliford who was a Pirate; and he fent fome of his Crew
aboard, to know whether Captain *Kidd* was not come with a
Defign to feize them, and hang them; and he declared he had
no fuch Defign: And he and *Culliford* were extremely kind to
one another, and made Vifits and Prefents to each other:
And Captain *Kidd* gave two Guns to Culliford, as one of the
Witneffes fays; but the other Witnefs fays there were four
Guns that he gave to *Culliford*, who was engaged in the fame
Defign of Piracy, and *Culliford* prefented other Things to
Kidd.

But now, Gentlemen, the Bufinefs you are to inquire into
is, the Piratical taking of thefe Ships: and the Witneffes have
pofitively and directly proved not only the taking the Ships
but the feizing the Goods, and felling them, and fharing the
Money. And if thefe Witneffes fay true, as nothing appears
to the contrary, by the Prifoners crofs-examining them, or
otherwife; they are not at all contradicted, or their Credi-
bility made queftionable: And they are fuch as are moft likely
to know what was done, being with them in the whole Voyage, and engaged with them in thefe Enterprifes. And if you
can give entire Credit to the Witneffes, you will probably find
thefe Perfons guilty of the Piracy they are charged with:
which I leave to your Confideration.

Now indeed there are three of them that are Servants,
and perhaps you may think their Cafe is different from the
reft; *Robert Lamley*, who was a Servant to *Owens* the Cook;
William Jenkins, who was Servant to the Mate; and *R. Barlicorn*, who was Servant to Captain *Kidd*. And though the
Witneffes do prove that they had their Shares of the Goods
and Money; yet, not withftanding that, they being Servants,
their Mafters might be entitled to their Shares. So that if

you believe they were Servants, and commanded to ferve and
affift their Mafters in what they did, I muft leave it to you
whether you will think fit to diftinguifh their Cafe from the
reft. I do not find that the others fay any Thing material in
their own Defence, they have called on Witneffes at all. The
Captain lays the Blame on the Men, and the Men feem to
lay the Blame on him. He went out on a good Defign, to take
Pirates, had he purfued it; but inftead of that, it appears that
he turned Pirate himfelf, and took the Ships and Goods of
Friends inftead of Enemies, which was a notorious Breach of
Truft, as well as a manifeft Violation of Law. The Evidence
feems ftrong againft them, which I leave to you to confider of.

    *Then the Jury withdrew, and after a fhort Space brought
      in their Verdict.*

Cl. of Arr. Gentlemen, anfwer to your Names. *Jo. Watfon.*

J. Watfon. Here, &c.

Cl. of Arr. Are you all agreed of your Verdict.

Omnes. Yes.

Cl. of Arr. Who fhall fpeak for you?

Omnes. Foreman.

Cl. of Arr. *William Kidd,* hold up thy Hand, (*which he
did.*) Look upon the Prifoner. How fay you? Is *William Kidd*
guilty of the Piracy and Robbery whereof he ftand indicted
in the firft Indictment, or not guilty?

Foreman. Guilty.

Cl. of Arr. Is *Robert Lamley* guilty, or not guilty?

Foreman. Not guilty.

Cl. of Arr. Is *William Jenkins* guilty, or not guilty?

Foreman. Not guilty.

Cl. of Arr. Is *Gabriel Logge* guilty, or not guilty.?

Foreman. Guilty.

Cl. of Arr. Is *Hugh Parrot* guilty, or not guilty?

Foreman. Guilty.

Cl. of Arr. Is *Richard Barlicorn* guilty, or not guilty?

Foreman. Not guilty.

Cl. of Arr. Is *DarbyMullins* guilty, or not guilty?

Foreman. Guilty.

The same Verdict was given as to all the Prisoners upon the other Indictments.

Robert Culliford, Nicholas Churchill, Darby Mullins, and *John Eldrige,* were arraigned for taking the Ship called the *Great Mohamet,* and seizing the Goods to a confiderable Value, to which they pleaded not guilty.

Robert Culliford, Churchill, Howe, and *Mullins,* were again Indicted for another Ship taken piratically by them, to which they pleaded not guilty.

Robert Culliford, and *Robert Hickman* were again arraigned for piratically feizing another Ship called the *Satisfaction,* to which they pleaded not guilty.

Robert Culliford and *Rob. Hickman* were again indicted for Piracy committed on a *Moorish* Ship, to which they pleaded not guilty.

Then the Court proceeding to the Trials of the Perfons fore- mentioned, Rob. Culliford *retracted his Plea, and pleaded guilty, and argued his coming in upon his Majefty's Pro- clamation: and his Cafe being particular, was argued by his Council, for the Benefit of his Majefty's Pardon. And* Churchill, Howe, Mullins, *and* Hickman, *likewife plead- ing guilty;* John Eldrige *was tried by himfelf, and found guilty.*

After the Trials were over, Judgment againft Culliford *was refprited, and he fet afide; the other Prifoners were called to the Bar in order to receive their Sentence as follows:*

Cl. of Arr. *William Kidd,* Hold up thy Hand, (*which he did*) What canft thou fay for thy felf? Thou haft been in- dicted for feveral Piracies and Roberies, and Murder, and hereupon haft been convicted; What haft thou to fay for thy felf, why thou fhouldeft not die according to law?

Will. Kidd. I have nothing to fay, but that I have been fworn againft by perjured and wicked People.

Cl. of Arr. *Nich. Churchill,* hold up thy Hand, What haft thou to fay, &c?

N. Churchill. I came in upon his Majefty's Proclamation.

Cl. of Arr. *James Howe,* What haft thou to fay, &c?

J. Howe. I came in upon the King's gracious Proclamation, and hope I shall receive the Benefit thereof.

Cl. of Arr. *Gabriel Loffe*, What haſt thou to ſay, &c?

Cl. of Arr. *Hugh Parrot*, What haſt thou to ſay, &c?

Hugh Parrot. I came and ſurrendered my ſelf to my Lord *Bellamont.*

Cl. of Arr. *Gabriel Owens*, what haſt thou to ſay?

Gabriel Owens. I came in upon his Majeſty's Proclamation, and deſire the Benefit if ot.

Cl. of Arr. *Darby Mullins*, What haſt thou to ſay?

Darby Mullins. I came home upon the King's gracious Proclamation.

Cl. of Arr. *John Eldrige*, What haſt thou to ſay, &c?

J. Eldrige. I have but little to ſay, I am accuſed but for one Thing, and that is all, and I have been falſely accuſed; I caſt my ſelf on your Lordſhips and the Honourable Bench.

Cl. of Arr. *Robert Hickman*, What haſt thou to ſay, &c?

Robert Hickman. I came in according to the King's Proclamation, I came in within the Time limited.

Then Proclamation for Silence was made, while Sentence was pronouncing.

Dr. Oxenden. You the Priſoners at the Bar, *William Kidd, N. Churchill, J. Howe, Gabriel Loffe, Hugh Parrot, Abel Owens, Darby Mullins, Robert Hickman,* and *J. Eldrige;* you have been ſeverally indicted for ſeveral Piracies and Robberies, and you *William Kidd* of Murder. You have been tryed by the Law of the Land, and convicted; and nothing now remains, but that Sentence be paſſed according to the Law. And the Sentence of the Law is this.

You ſhall be taken from the Place where you are, and be carried to the Place from whence you came, and from thence to the Place of Execution, and there be ſeverally hanged by your Necks until you be dead. And the Lord have Mercy on your Souls.

William Kidd. My Lord, It is a very hard Sentence. For my Part, I am the innocenteſt Perſon of them all, only I have been ſworn againſt by Perjured Perſons.

YE LAMENTABLE BALLAD OF CAPTAIN KIDD.

You captains, brave and bold, hear our cries, hear our cries,
 You captains brave and bold, hear our cries,
You captains brave and bold, though you seem uncontroul'd,
 Don't for the sake of gold lose your souls, lose your souls,
 Don't for the sake of gold lose your souls.

My name was Robert Kidd (sic), when I sail'd, when I sail'd,
 My name was Robert Kidd, when I sail'd,
My name was Robert Kidd, God's laws I did forbid,
 And so wickedly I did, when I sail'd.

My parents taught me well, when I sail'd, when I sail'd,
 My parents taught me well, when I sail'd,
My parents taught me well to shun the gates of hell,
 But against them I did rebel, when I sail'd.

I curs'd my father dear, when I sail'd, when I sail'd,
 I curs'd my father dear, when I sail'd,
I curs'd my father dear, and her that did me bear,
 And so wickedly did sware, when I sail'd.

I made a solemn vow, when I sail'd, when I sail'd,
 I made a solemn vow, when I sail'd,
I made a solemn vow, to God I would not bow,
 Nor myself one prayer allow, when I sail'd.

I'd a bible in my hand, when I sail'd, when I sail'd,
 I'd a bible in my hand, when I sail'd,
I'd a bible in my hand, by my father's great command,
 But I sunk it in the sand, when I sail'd.

I murder'd William Moore, as I sail'd, as I sail'd,
 I murder'd William Moore, as I sail'd;
I murder'd William Moore, and I left him in his gore,
 Not many leagues from shore, as I sail'd.

And being cruel still, as I sail'd, as I sail'd,
    And being cruel still, as I sail'd,
And being cruel still, my gunner I did kill,
    And his precious blood did spill, as I sail'd.

My mate took sick and died, as I sail'd, as I sail'd,
    My mate took sick and died, as I sail'd;
My mate took sick and died, which me much terrified,
    When he called me to his bedside, as I sail'd.

And unto me did say, see me die, see me die,
    And unto me did say, see me die;
And unto me did say, take warning now I pray,
    There'll come a reckoning day, you must die.

You cannot then withstand, when you die, when you die;
    You cannot then withstand, when you die;
You cannot then withstand, the judgments of God's hand,
    But bound in iron hands, you must die.

I was sick and nigh to death, as I sail'd, as I sail'd,
    I was sick and nigh to death, as I sail'd;
I was sick and nigh to death, and vow'd at every breath,
    To walk in wisdom's ways, as I sail'd.

I thought I was undone, as I sail'd, as I sail'd,
    I thought I was undone, as I sail'd,
I thought I was undone, that my wicked glass was run,
    But my health did soon return, as I sail'd.

My repentance lasted not, as I sail'd, as I sail'd,
    My repentance lasted not, as I sail'd;
My repentance lasted not, my vows I soon forgot,
    Damnation's my just lot, as I sail'd.

I steer'd from sound to sound, as I sail'd, as I sail'd,
    I steer'd from sound to sound, as I sail'd;
I steer'd from sound to sound, and many ships I found,
    And most of them I burn'd, as I sail'd.

I spy'd three ships of France, as I sail'd, as I sail'd,
    I spy'd three ships of France, as I sail'd;
I spy'd three ships of France, to them I did advance,
    And took them all by chance, as I sail'd.

I spy'd three ships of Spain, as I sail'd, as I sail'd,
    I spy'd three ships of Spain, as I sail'd;
I spy'd three ships of Spain, I fir'd on them amain,
    Till most of them were slain, as I sail'd.

I'd ninety bars of gold, as I sail'd, as I sail'd,
    I'd ninety bars of gold, as I sail'd;
I'd ninety bars of gold, and dollars manifold,
    With riches uncontroul'd, as I sail'd.

Then fourteen ships I see, as I sail'd, as I sail'd,
    Then fourteen ships I see, as I sail'd;
Then fourteen ships I see, and all brave men they be,
    And they were too hard for me, as I sail'd.

Thus being o'ertaken at last, I must die, I must die,
    Thus being o'ertaken at last, I must die;
Thus being o'ertaken at last, and into prison cast,
    And sentence being past, I must die.

Farewell to the raging main, for I must die, for I must die,
    Farewell to the raging main, for I must die,
Farewell to the raging main, to Turkey, France and Spain,
    I shall ne'er see you again, for I must die.

To Newgate now I'm cast, and must die, and must die,
    To Newgate now I'm cast, and must die;
To Newgate now I'm cast, with sad and heavy heart,
    To receive my just desert, I must die.

To Execution Dock, I must go, I must go,
    To Execution Dock, I must go;
To Execution Dock, will many thousands flock,
    But I must bear my shock, and must die.

Come all ye young and old, see me die, see me die,
 Come all ye young and old, see me die, see me die;
Come all ye young and old, you're welcome to my gold,
 For by it I've lost my soul, and must die.

Take warning now by me, for I must die, for I must die,
 Take warning now by me, for I must die;
Take warning now by me, and shun bad company,
 Lest you come to hell with me, for I must die,
 Lest you come to hell with me, for I must die.

BIBLIOGRAPHY

An Account of the Proceedings of the Earl of Bellamont, Governor of New York, and an Extraordinary Council, held at that place, May 8, 1698, relative to Colonel Fletcher's giving commissions to Pyrates; with the Earl's speech to the Assembly. Folio, broadside. New York: Printed and sold by William Bradford, Printer to the King. 1698.

The Arraignment, Tryal, and Condemnation of Captain William Kidd, for Murther and Piracy, Upon Six several Indictments, At the Admiralty Sessions, held by His Majesty's Commission at the Old Baily, on Thursday the 8th and Friday the 9th of May, 1701. Who upon full Evidence was found Guilty, receiv'd Sentence, and was accordingly Executed at Execution Dock May the 23d. As also the Tryals of Nicholas Churchill, James Howe, Robert Lamley, William Jenkins, Gabriel Loff, Hugh Parrot, Richard Barlicorn, Abel Owens, and Darby Mullins, and the same Time and Place of Piracy. Perused by the Judges and Council. To which are added, Captain Kidd's Two Commissions: One under the Great Seal of England, and the Other under the Great Seal of the Court of Admiralty. Folio, 60 pp. London: Printed for J. Nutt, Near Stationers-Hall. 1701.

Reissue: Sm. 8vo, 27 pp. London: Jonathan Robinson. 1703.

Articles of Agreement, made the 10th Day of October, in the Year of Our Lord 1695, Between the Right Honorable Richard Earl of Bellomont of the one part, and Robert Levingston Esq.; and Captain William Kidd, of the other part. (Colophon) Licensed according to Order. Folio, 2 pp. London: Printed for J. R|chardson, near Ludgate, 1701.

Republished in fascimile from the copy in the New York Public Library, by the Grolic Club, New York, October 1915.

A full Account of the Proceedings In Relation to Capt. Kidd. In Two Letters. Written by a Person of Quality to a Kinsman of the Earl of Bellomont in Ireland. Sm. 4to, 51 pp. London, Printed and Sold by the Booksellers of London and Westminster. MDCCI.

"The Publisher to the Reader," five pages unnumbered.

A full Account of the Proceedings In Relation to Captain Kidd. In Two Letters. Written by a Person of Quality to a Kinsman of the Earl of Bellomont in Ireland. The Second Edition. 8vo, 41 pp. London, Printed and Sold by the Booksellers of London and Westminster. 1701.

Reissued, 1705.

A True Account of the Behaviour, Confession, and last Dying Speeches of . . . W.K., and the rest of the Pirates, that were Executed . . . 23rd of May, 1701. Folio, Broadside. London: E. Mallet at the Hat and Hawk in Bride Lane. 1701.

A Full Account of the Actions of the Late Famous Pyrate, Capt. Kidd. With the Proceedings against Hin, amd a Vindication of the Right Honorable Richard Earl of Bellomont, Lord Coloony, late Governor of New England, and other Honourable Persons, from the Unjust Reflections cast upon Tehm (Them). By a Person of Quality. Sm. 4to, 4-42 pp. Dublin: Re-printed for Matthew Gunn, Bookseller in Essex Street. 1701.

A Compleat History of Europe, or a View of the Affairs Thereof, Civil and Military for the Year 1701. Containing All the Publick and Secret Transactions therein; the Several Steps taken by France, for an Universal Monarchy and to Enslave her Neighbors; The War in Italy, Poland, Livonia, Moscovy, &c. Intermix'd with Great Variety of Original Papers, Letters, Memoirs, Treaties, &c. Several of which never before made Publick. With the Remarkables of the Year; the Present State of the Imperial, all the Royal Families and other the Princes and Potentates of Europe; Their Births, Marriages, Issues, Alliances &c. More Exact than any Extant. Also A Catalogue of tha Nobility, and Privy Councils of England, Scotland, &c. With a List of All Persons in Offices or Places of Trust in His Majesty's Government, Truer than any heretofore Done. To be Continued Annually. 8vo, 387-(6) pp. Printed and Sold by the Booksellers of London and Westminster. MDCCII.

First (and only) volume of what was announced to be an annual publication; contains a long account of the charges against the Earl of Orford and Lord Chancellor Somers growing out of their relations with Kidd.

Dialogue between the Ghost of Captain Kidd, and the Napper in the Strand, Napt. Folio, Broadside. London:1702.

A dialogue followed by a set of verses in which Kidd and the Napper answer each other in alternate three-line rhymed stanzas, each ending "Which nobody can deny."

An Exact Abridgement Of all the Tryals, Not omitting any Material Passage therein, relating to High Treasons, Piracies, &c. in the Reigns of the late King William the III of Glorious Memory and of our present Gracious Soveraign Queen Anne. Together with Their Dying Speeches, as also the Dying Speeches of several Persons in the Reigns of King Charles the IId and King James the IId. 8vo, 432 pp. London: Printed for Jonathan Robinson at the Golden Lyon, and John Wyat at the Rose in St. Paul's Church-Yard, MDCCIII.

Captain Kidd, pp. 264-287.

The Dying Words of Captain Robert Kidd, (sic) a Noted Pirate who was Hanged at Execution Dock in England. Folio, Broadside. N.P. N.D.

A Collection of State Tracts, Publish'd during the Reign of King William III. Vol. III and last, in which is Inserted (being now first printed from the Manuscript) A Vindication of the late Revolution, in Answer to two Memorials, and a Protestation against the Peace of Reswick, and to other Papers publish'd in K. James' Name. With a Table of the several Tracts in this Volume And an Alphabetical Index of Matters. Folio, (4)-774-(32) pp. London: Printed in the Year M.DCC.VII.

"An account of the Proceedings in Relation to Captain Kidd," pp. 230-256.

The History of the Most Remarkable Tryals in Great Britain and Ireland, in Capital Cases, viz, Heresy, Treason, Felony, Incest, Poisoning, Adultry, Rapes, Sodomy, Witchcraft, Pyracy, Murder, Robbery, &c. Both by the unusual Methods of Ordeal, Combat, and Attainder, and by the Eccleciastical, Civil and Common Laws of these Realms. Faithfully extracted from Records, and other Authentick Authorities, as well Manuscript as printed. Two vols. 8vo, (8)-452-(4); 536 pp. London: Printed for A. Bell, in Cornhill; J. Pemberton, in Fleet Street, and J. Brown, without Temple-Bar, 1715. (Price 6s)

Vol. II, contains the Trial of Capt. Kidd and incidential references, pages 515-536.

A Complete History Of the most Remarkable Transactions at Sea, from
the Earliest Accounts of Time To the Conclusion of the Last War with France.
Wherein is given an account of the most considerable Naval Expeditions, Sea-
Fights, Stratagems, Discoveries, and Other Maritime Occurances that have
happened among all Nations which have flourished at Sea: And in more par-
ticular manner of Great Britain, from the time of the Revolution in the Year
1688, to the aforesaid Period. Adorn'd with Sea-Charts adapted to the History.
With an exact Index of the Names of all the Places where any considerable
Battle has been fought in any Part of the World. In Five Books. By Josiah
Burchett, Esq., Secretary of the Admiralty. Hae Tibi erunt artes. Virg. Folio.
Fifty-two pages of dedication and introduction; 800 pages of text, 29 pages of
index and two of errata. London: Printed by W. B. for J. Walthoe in the Temple
Cloysters, and J. Walthoe, Junior against the Royal Exchange in Cornhill.
MDCCXX.

Captain Kidd, pages 576-580. Drake and the Adventurers, the Algerines
and other Pirates noted. Engraved portrait of author by Vertue.

Tryals for High-Treason, and other Crimes, with Proceedings on Bills of
Attainder, and Impeachments. For Three Hundred Years Past. To which are
prefix'd A Preface, giving an account of the Nature and Usefulness of the
Work. And An Alphabetical Table of the respective Persons Try'd, and the
Points of Law Debated and Adjudg'd. By the same Hand that prepared the
Folio Edition for the Press. 5 vols., 8vo. London: Printed for D. Browne, G.
Strahan, W. Mears, R. Gosling, and F. Clay. MDCCXX.

Part V, includes the Trials of Joseph Dawson and five others for Piracy
and the Trials of Captain William Kidd for murder and Piracy and that of
nine members of his crew.

The History of the Pyrates, Containing the Lives of Captain Mission.
Captain Bowen. Captain Kidd. Captain Tew. Captain Halsey. Captain White.
Captain Condert. Captain Bellamy. Captain Ely. Captain Howard. Captain
Lewis. Captain Cornelius. Captain Williamson. Captain Burgess. Captain
North. And their several Crews. Intermixed with a description of Magadoxa
in Ethiopia; the natural Hatred and Cruelty of the Inhabitants to all
Whites; their Laws, Manners, Customs, Government and Religion: With a
particular Account of the beautiful Tombs, and their Ceremony of guarding
them taken from Captain Beavis's Journal; and that of a Molatto, who belong'd to the said Captain, was taken by, and lived several Years with the
Magadoxians. To the whole is added an Appendix, which compleats the Lives
in the first Volume, corrects some Mistakes, and contains the Tryal and Execution of the Pyrates at Providence, under Governor Rogers; with some other
necessary Insertions, which did not come to hand till after the Publication
of the first volume, and which makes up what was defective. Collected from
Journals of Pyrates, brought away by a Person who was taken by, and forc'd
to live with them 12 Years; and from those of the Commanders, who had
fallen into their Hands, some of whom have permitted their Names to be made
use of, as a Proof of the Veracity of what we have published. The whole in-
structive and entertaining. Vol. II. By Capt. Charles Johnson, Author of
Vol. I. *Omne tulit punctum, qui miscuit utile du'ci.* Horace. 8vo., 12 pp. of contents and 413 pp. of text. London: Printed for, and Sold by T. Woodward,
at the Cross Keys over against St. Dunstan's Church, Fleet Street. 1724.

There is an error of sixteen pages between 144 and 272, which must be
added for correct notation. This is the first edition of the second volume, a
work complete in itself.

The Naval History of England, in all its Branches; from the Norman Conquest in 1066 to the Conclusion of 1734. Collected from the most approved Historians, English and Foreign, Authentick Records and Manuscripts, Scarce Tracts, Original Journals, &c. With many Facts and Observations never before made Publick. By Thomas Lediard, Gent., Late Secretary to His Majesty's Envoy Extraordinary in Lower Germany. In two volumes. Folio, IV-(24)-XII-394; 395 to 933 pp. London: Printed for John Wilcox, at Virgil's Head, opposite the New Church, and Olive Payne, at Horace's Head, in Round Court, both in the Strand. MDCCXXXV.

Captain Kidd, pages 727-728.

A Critical Review of the State Trials. Containing, I. The Substance of the Indictment, or Charge. II, The Evidence. III. The Prisoner's Defence. IV. The Points of Law arising. V. The Event of the Trial, or the Fate of the Prisoner. VI. Remarks on the Whole. By Mr. Salmon. Folio, iv-922-(8) pp. London: Printed for William Mears, at the Lamb on Ludgate-Hill; and J. Stone, against Bedford-Row; and Sold by Mess. J. J. and P. Knapton; Mess. Innys and Manby; Mr. Rivington; Mr. Austen; Mr. Midwinter; Mr. Parker; Mr. Davis; Mess. Batley and Wood; Mess. Bettersworth and Hitch; Mr. Osborn; Mess. J. and J. Pemberton; Mr. Isted; Mr. Corbet; Mr. Tonson; Mr. Millar; Mr. Strahan; Mr. Brotherton; Mr. Symon; Mess. Hatchet and Comins; Mr. Clarke; Mr. Hazard; Mr. Birt; Mr. Ware; Mess. Ward and Wicksted; Mr. Waller; Mr. Meighan; Mr. Williamson; Mr. Gyles; Mr. Bradley; Mr. Payne; Mr. Lewis; Mr. Lyon; Mr. Chrichley; Mr. Millan; Mr. Ryal; Mr. Penn; Mr. Fox; Mr. Jackson; Mr. Jolliffe; Mr. Brindly; Mr. Shropshire; Mr. Hodges; Mr. Nevil; Mr. Jefferies; Mr. Wilmot; Mr. Thurlborne; Mr. Creighton; Mr Leake; Mr. Carlos; Mr. Brysan; Mr. Dillon; and Mr. Millar. M.DCC.XXXV.

Trial of Captain Kidd for Murder and Piracy, pages 738-739.

The History of His Own Time. Compiled from the Original Manuscripts Of His Late Excellency Matthew Prior Esq. Revised and Signed by Himself; And Copied fair for the Press By Mr. Adrian Drift, His Executor.

"I had rather be thought a good Englishman, than the best Poet or greatest Scholar that ever wrote." Matt. Prior. 8vo. VIII-472 pp. and 8 of index. London: Printed for the Editor MDCCXL. Price Six Shillings.

Contains an early, if not the earliest historical account of the Transactions of Captain William Kidd in their relation to the charges against the Earl of Orford.

The History of Massachusetts, from the first settlement thereof in 1628, until the year 1750. By Thomas Hutchinson, Esq. Late Governor of Massachusetts. Historia, non ostentationi, sed fidei, vertiatique componitur. Plin. Epist. L. 7 E. 33. In two volumes. The third edition, with additional notes and corrections. 8vo. Vol. I, 8-478 (10); Vol. II, 8-452; Vol. III, 4-551 pp. Printed at Salem By Thomas C. Cushing, for Thomas and Andrews, No. 45, Newbury Street. Boston. 1795.

Kidd Reference; Kidd, the famous bucaneer, seized at Boston, Vol. II, pp. 110-113.

The Dying Words of Capt. Robert (Sic) Kidd, a Noted Pirate who was hanged at Execution Dock, (Woodcut vignette in corner) 8 mo. folio, N.P.N.D. (Ca 1805). A lyric poem of 25 stanzas of 4 lines each.

Fort Braddock Letters: or, a tale of the French and Indian Wars, in America, at the beginning of the Eighteenth Century. 16mo, 98 pp. Worcester: Published by Dow & Howland. 1827.

Kidd references, pages 58-78.

First published in the Connecticut Mirror, Hartford, Hale & Hosmer. Written by John G. C. Brainard. Jan. 10, 1809 to Dec. 1815.

Fugitive Tales, No. 1, Fort Braddock Letters; by J. G. C. Brainard. 12mo. 97 pp. Washington, D. C.; Printed and published by Charles Galpin. 1830.

Kidd references, pages 60-70.

The Fort Braddock Letters, a Tale of the Old French War; or the Adventures of Du Quesne, Dudley, and Van Tromp; with the Capture of Captain Kidd, 16mo, VI-128 pp. Peekskill: Huestis & Brewer, Printers. 1832.

Kidd references, pages 76-101.

Interesting Events in the History of the United States: Being a Selection of the Most Important and Interesting Events which have Transpired since the Discovery of this Country to the Present Time. Carefully selected from the most approved Authorities.

By J. W. Barber. 12mo, iv-220-xxiv pp. New-Haven:Published by J. W. Barber. L. K. Dow, Printer. 1828.

Capt. Kidd, the pirate: p. 48.

The History of the late Province of New York, from its discovery to the appointment of Governor Colden in 1762. By the Hon. William Smith, formlery of New York, and late Chief-Justice of Lower Canada. Vol. I, 8vp. XVI-320 pp. New York: Published under the direction of the New-York Historical Society. 1829.

Richard, Earl of Bellomont sent by the King to govern the provinces, said "that he thought him a man of resolution and integrity, and with these qualities more likely than any other he could think of to put a stop to the growth of piracy: pages, 125-137.

The Mariner's Chronicle: Containing Naratives of the most remarkable Disasters at Sea, such as Shipwrecks, Storms, Fires, and Famine: also, Naval Engagements, Piratical Adventures, Incidents of Discorvery, and other Extradorinary and Interesting Occurances. Stereotyped by A. Chandler. 8vo. XII-504 pages. New Haven. Published by Durrie and Peck. 1834.

Kidd's Money, pages 496-501.

The South West. By a Yankee (J. H. Ingraham).
　　Where on my way I went;:
　　—A Pilgrim from its North—
　　Now more and more attracted, as I drew
　　Nearer and nearer.　　*Roger's Italy.*

In two Volumes. 12vo, XI-276: XI-294 pages. New York: Harper & Brothers, Cliff St. 1835.

Captain Kidd, page 97, Vol. I.

Celebrated Trials of all Countries, and Remarkable Cases of Criminal Jurisprudence. Selected by a Member of the Philadelphia Bar.

"The Annals of Criminal Jurisprudence exhibit human nature in a variety of positions, at once the most striking, interesting and affecting. They present

Captain Kidd's Marriage License from the Records in the Surrogate's Office, New York. The New England Historical and Geneological Register, p. 63. Boston, January, 1852.

Captain Kidd. By Joseph B. Felt. The New England Historical and Geneological Register. Vol.VI. 8vo. VI-402 pp. Boston. 1852.

Pp. 77-84, issue of January 1852.

Atlantic and Transatlantic Sketches, Afloat and Ashore. By Captain Mac-Kinnon, R. N. Author of "Steam Warfare in the Panama." In two volumes 8vo. XVIII-288; IX-292 pp. London: Colburn and Co., Publishers, Great Marlborough Street. 1852.

Notice is hereby given that the Publishers of this work reserve to themselves the right of publishing a translation in France.

"Kidd, the Pirate," Chapter 2, Vol. II, pp. 11-33. Based upon a paper read by Judge William W. Campbell, before the New York Historical Society.

New York issue of the book 8vo, 324 pp. Harper & Bros. 1852.

An Historical Sketch of Robin Hood and Captain Kidd, by William W. Campbell. "The Duke of Marlborough, the Duke of Cumberland and the Marquis of Granby, have flourished upon sign posts and have faded there; so have their compeers Prince Eugene and Prince Ferdinand; Rodney and Nelson are fading, and the time is not far distant when Wellington also will have had his day. But while England shall be England, Robin Hood will be a popular name." Southey. "Out of monuments, names, words, proverbs, traditions, private records, and evidences, fragments of stories, passages of books, and the like, we do save and recover somewhat from the deluge of time." Lord Bacon on the Advancement of Learning. 8vo, VIII-263 pp. New York: Charles Scribner, 145 Nassau Street. 1853.

William Kidd, pp. 97-263. "Ye Lamentable ballad," Etc., pp. 240-244.

Documents relating to the Colonial History of the State of New York, procured in Holland, England and France, by John Romeyn Broadhead, Esq., agent. under and by virtue of an Act of the Legislature entitled, "An act to appoint an agent to procure and transcribe documents in Europe relative to the Colonial History of the State," passed May 2, 1839. Edited by E. B. O'Callaghan, M. D. Vol. IV. 4 to, XIX-1192 pp. Albany: Weed, Parsons and Company, Printers. 1854.

The Documents relating to the Colonial History of the State of New York appear in 15 volumes. Vols. 1, to 11 relate to its general history; vol. 12 to New Sweden and the Delaware; Vol. 13 to the Hudson River; vol. 14 to Long Island; vol. 15 (properly vol. 1 of the Archives) to the American Revolution. Vols. 12 to 15 were an afterthought, because voll. 11 is the index to vols. 1 to 10. Vol. 4, takes in the period of *Captain Kidd's* appearance in our Colonial History. The following extract from the index shows the quantity and importance of the material:

William Kidd, invited to take part in an election in the City of New York, pages 128, 129, 144; Answer of Governor Fletcher to the deposition of, 179; Captures a French Vessel, 199; Several Young Men of New Jersey accompany, 201; Commissioned to suppress piracy, 275; Description of his crew, ibid; Commits notorious acts of piracy, 454; Excepted from the King's pardon, ibid; The Earl of Bellomont concerned with, 470; Turns Pirate, 521; Lands Pirates

An Account of some of the Traditions and Experiments respecting Captain Kidd's Piratical Vessel. 12mo, 12 pp. New York: Herald Book and Job Prntg. Office, 97 Nassau Street, 1844.

A Wonderful Mesmeric Revelation, giving an account of the discovery and description of a sunken vessel, near Caldwell's Landing, supposed to be that of the Pirate Kidd; including an account of his character and death, at a distance of nearly three hundred miles from the place.

Captain Kidd before the Council, By Peter Force, The National Intelligences, Washington, Jany. 22, 1845.

Collections of the Massachusetts Historical Society. Vol. I of the third series. 8vo, IV-299 pp. Boston: Printed MDCCCXXV. Reprinted Charles C. Little and James Brown. MDCCCXLVI.

By the Gouvernor and Council, proposals to Captain Kidd and Capt. Walkington to suppress an enemy privateer "now upon this coast," pp. 122. Propositions of Capt. Kidd, p. 123.

Lives, Exploits and Cruelties of the most celebrated Pirates and Sea Robbers. Brought down to the Latest Period. 18mo. 320-30 pp. London: Milner and Company, Palernoster Row 2 I. Colored frontispiece.

The Piracy of Captain Kidd. By Henry C. Murphy. Hunt's Merchant's Magazine, Vol. 14, pages 39-51. New York: January. 1846.

Reprinted in Littell's *Living Age* Vol. 8, pp. 201-7, January 31, 1846.

The Newgate Calendar, containing the Lives and Characters of the Most Notorious Housebreakers, Highwaymen, Thieves, Robbers, Murderers, Pirates, etc., Who have been convicted and condemned to death in violating the Laws of the country, with their confessions and last exclamations. By an Old Bailey Barrister. 18mo. 356 pp. Derby: Thomas Richardson and Son, 172, Fleetshire, London; and 9, Capel Street, Dublin. 1847.

The Life, Trial & Execution, of the Famous Pirate Captain Robert Kidd' Being an accurate history of the early life and adventures of that desperate pirate. The King's Commission appointing him High Admiral of England. His daring and extensive robberies upon the Ocean,—The murder of William Moore, his Gunner.—His Arrest, Imprisonment, Trial, and Execution. A full Account of what has Never Before Been Published. Also, The Letters of Kidd's Wife to Lord Bellomont And the Famous Kidd Letter Recently found enclosed in a bottle, in a ledge of rocks, in the Town of Palmer, Mass. This Letter discloses the Spot where Kidd buried a large portion of his immense treasures, which has never been discovered.

(Cut of Ship.)

Kidd Cruising near the Coast of Malabar.

Copyright secured. 8vo, 24 pp. Palmer, Mass. Gardner Shaw, Publisher. 1850.

The Lives and Exploits of the Most Notorious Pirates and their crews. By a Sea Captain. 18mo. 324 pp. Halifax: Printed and Published by William Milner, Cheapadi. MDCCCL.

Lives and Exploits of the Most Celebrated Pirates and Sea Robbers. By T. Douglas. 18mo. VI-349 pp. Newcastle-Upon-Tyne: Published by W. & T. Fordyce. MDCCCXLI.

tragedies of real life, often heightened in their effect by a grossness of the injustice, and the malignity of the prejudices which accompanied them. At the same time real culprits, as original characters, stand forward on the canvas of humanity as prominent objects for our special study. I have often wondered that the English language contains no book like the Causes Celebres of the French, particularly as the openness of our proceedings renders the records more certain and accessible, while our public history and domestic conflicts have afforded so many splendid examples of the unfortunate and the guilty. Such a collection, drawn from our own national sources, and varied by references to cases of the continental nations, would exhibit man as he is in action and principal, and not as he is usually drawn by poets and speculative philosophers." Burke. 8vo, 596-3 pp. Philadelphia: E. L. Carey and A. Hart, and for sale by all Booksellers. 1835.

Includes Trials of John Gow and Captain Kidd. Reissued, Philadelphia: Published by L. A. Godey, No. 100 Walnut Street, Stereotyped by L. Johnson. 1836.

The Pirates own Book, or authentic Narratives of the Lives, Exploits, and Executions of the most celebrated Sea Robbers. With Historic Sketches of the Gossamer, Spanish Ladrone, West India, Malay, and Algerine Pirates. 8vo, Sm. 432 pp. Boston: Printed and Published by S. W. Dickinson, 52 Washington Street. 1837.

Collections of the Massachusetts Historical Society. Vol .VII, Of the third series. 8vo, 304 pp. Boston: Charles C. Little and James Brown. 1838.

Captain Kidd turned pirate, pp. 209, 210.

History of Long Island: Containing an account of the Discovery and Settlement; with other Important and Interesting matters to the present Time. By Benjamin F. Thompson, Counselor at Law. "History presents *complete* examples. Experience is doubly *defective*; we are born too late to see the beginning, and we die too soon to see the *end* of many things. History supplies both of these defects: modern history shows the *causes*, when experience presents the *effects* alone; and ancient history enables us to guess at the *effects*, when experience presents the *causes* alone." *Bolingbroke.* 8vo, X-536 pp. New York: Published by E. French, 146 Nassau Street. 1839.

Kidd references: Pages 130, 201, 203. Second, and rarest edition, two vols., 8vo, 1,064 pp. New York: Gould, Banks & Co. 1843.

Vol. II, No. I. The People's Almanac 1839. Of useful and Entertaining Knowledge Containing Four sets of calculations, embracing the whole United States. 12mo, 36 pp. Boston: Printed by S. N. Dickinson, and for sale by the Trade.

Capt. Kidd, pages 4 and 10. Issued also with title reading. "Printed and Published by S. N. Dickinson, and sold by Thos. Groom."

The History of the Navy of the United States of America. By J. Fenimore Cooper. In two volumes. Vol. I, 8vo, XXXVI-394 pp. Philadelphia: Lea & Blanchard, Successors to Carey and Co. 1839.

Captain Kidd, Chapter 2, pages 54-59.

Lives, Exploits and Cruelties, of the most celebrated Pirates and Sea Robbers. Brought down to the Latest Period. 18mo. 448 pp. Liverpool: Thomas Johnson, Dale Street. 1841.

at Long Island, 532; Arrives in Delaware Bay, 543; The Earl of Bellomont se-
cures, 551; Particulars furnished by, 552; His Career and arrest, 583; Two of
the men of, escape from Boston, 591; Thomas Clarke offers to give up all the
Treasure he received from, 595; His sloop at the east end of Long Island, ibid;
Offers to recover the Quidah mercahnt and concealed treasure, 602; Two of
his crew arrested, 623; Mentioned, 633; Sent to England, 665; Papers trans-
mitted to England, 698; The Earl of Bellomont's name brought up in the House
of Commons in connection with, 725; By whom introduced to the Earl of Bellomont, 760; Agreement between the Earl of Bellomont, Robert Livingston and,
762; Robert Livingston embezzles goods brought by, 772; Goods conveyed to
Stamford by his ship, 793; Governor Fletcher makes a bargain with, 815;
Further particulars respecting the Earl of Bellomont's connection with, ibid;
Robert Livingston's defence from the charge of embezzling effects of, 882;
Artorney General Broughton applies for a house in New York belonging to,
914; John Harrison said to have been brought up with, 335; In addition to the
above, there are 87 articles relating to Pirates, as shown by the index.

Records of the Colony of Rhode Island and Providence Plantations, in
New England. Printed by order of the Legislature Transcribed and Edited by
John Russell Bartlett, Secretary of State. 10 vols. 1636-1792. 12mo, Vol. 3,'
595 pp. Providence, R. I. A Crawford Greene and Brother, State Printers. 1856

Kidd reference: Extract from Lord Bellomont's Journal, page 393. Note b·.
R. Bartlett, p. 400.

The New England History, From the Discovery of the Continent by the
Northmen A. D. 986, to the Period when the Colonies Declared their Independence, A. D. 1776. By Charles W. Elliott, Member of the New York, Ohio,
and Connecticut Historical Societies. In Two Volumes. Vol. II. 8vo, 492 pp.
New York: Charles Scribner, 377 & 379 Broadway, London: Trubner & Company. 1857.

Captain Kidd, Vol. II, p. 57.

Spencer's Boston Theatre. No. LXI. Captain Kyd; Or The Wizard of the
Sea. A Drama. In Four Acts. Now First Published, with Original Casts, Costumes, and all the Stage Business. 16mo, 44 pp. Boston: William V. Spencer,
123 Washington Street, Corner of Water, N. D. (Ca. 1857).

A brief historical relation of State affairs from September 1678 to April 1714.
By Narcissus Luttrell. In six volumes. 8vo. Vol. I, 621; Vol. II, 625; Vol. III,
568; Vol. IV, 724; Vol. V, 629; Vol. VI, 848 pp. Oxford: At the University
Press. M.DCCC.LVII.

Kidd references: Vol. IV, pp. 454, 456, 543-545, 549, 551, 557, 563, 564,
578, 589, 624, 632, 634, 637, 638, 669; Vol. V, pp. 25, 32-34, 37, 47, 48, 53, 54,
57.

A History of the United States. For Families and Libraries. By Benson J.
Lossing, Author of "Pictorial Field-Book of the Revolution," "History of the
United States for Schools," "Lives of Eminent Americans," Ets. Illustrated
with nearly three hundred engravings. 4to, viii-672 pp. New York: Mason
Brothers, 108&110, Duane Street. 1857.

Captain Kidd, p. 149.

The New England History, from the discovery of the Continent by the
Northmen, A.D., 986, to the Period when the Colonies declared their independence, A. D. 1776. By Charles W. Elliott, Member of the New York Club

and Connecticut Historical Societies. In two volumes. 8vo, Vol. I, XIII-18-479; Vol. II, VIII-12-492 pp. New York: Charles Scribner 377, 379 Broadway; Boston: Sanborn, Carter, Bazin & Co.; London: Trubner & Company. 1857. Kidd, the Pirate, Vol. II, pp. 57-63.

The Chapter contains the ballad, "Captain Robert Kidd" and a list of the Bags of gold with the weight and contents of each found on Gardiner's Island by order of the Earl of Bellomont.

Relics of Captain Kidd in the East, By Captain Richard F. Burton, Blackwood's Edinburgh Magazine, p. 213. Edinburgh: February, 1858.

Captain Kidd. By J. G. The Historical Magazine and notes and Queries concerning the Antiquities, history and biography of America, p. 276, New York: September, 1859.

Digging for Captain Kidd's Treasure; a Startling Narrative, by one of the party. 8vo, 24 pp. New York: J. B. Conklin, 54 Great Jones Street. 1859. (Price 15 cents. Copyright secured).

Historical Collection of the Essex Institute. Vol. I, 8vo, 206 pp.; Vol. 4, 289 pp. Salem: Published for the Essex Institute, by Henry Whipple & Son. 1859.

Kidd reference Vol. I, p. 78. Some remarks on the commerce of Salem from 1626 to 1740. With a sketch of Philip English, a merchant in Salem from about 1670 to about 1733-4. By George F. Chever.

Lecture before the Essex Institute, by Joseph B. Felt, March 24, 1862, on Piracy particularly of William Kidd. Vol. 4 pp. 28-37.

Journal of the Legislative Council of the Colony of New York. Began the 9th day of April 1691, and ended the 27th day of September, 1743. Published by order of the Senate of the State of New York. Folio, XXX-814 pp. Albany: Weed, Parsons & Company, Printers. 1861.

Kidd reference under minutes of a council held at "Fort William Henry," April 18-22-24, 1691. Question of rewarding him for the services rendered by himself and his vessel. This before he turned pirate, pp. 3-4-5.

On the 14th of May following he was voted a benefaction of One Hundred and Fifty pounds.

Lecture on Piracy; Particularly of Captain Kidd. By Joeph B. Felt. Essex Institute, Historical Collections. Vol. IV, 8m 4to, 269 pp. Salem. 1862.

Celebrated Trials connected with the Army and Navy. No. 1, Captain Kidd. A Pirate with a Royal Commission. By Serjeant Burke. The British Army and Navy Review, pp. 307-322. London: October. 1864.

Celebrated Naval and Military Trials. By Peter Burke, Sergeant-at-Law, Author of "Celebrated Trials connected with the Aristocracy," and of "The Romance of the Forum." 8vo, 399 pp. London: Wm. H. Allen & Co. 1866.

Contains account of Capt. William Kidd, his Career, trial and execution.

History of the City of New York, from its earliest settlement to the present time. By Mary L. Booth, translator of "Martin's History of France," etc. Illustrated with ever one hundred engravings. 8vo, XIX-(1)-22-850 pp. New York: W. R. C. Clark, 484 Broadwy. 1866.

Captain William Kidd becomes a daring and successful pirate; his arrest and execution. pp. 253-256.

Calendar of historical manuscripts in the office of the Secretary of State, Albany, N. Y. Edited by E. B. O'Callaghan. Part II. English manuscripts. 1664-1776. Roy. 8vo, 14-893 pp. Albany: Weed, Parsons and Company, printers. 1866.

Kidd references: pp. 160, 202, 208, 252, 253, 273, 274, 281, 285, 292. In "N. Y. Colonial Manuscripts," Vol. 35, p. 80; 37p. 16, 126; 40pp. 180, 190; 43 pp. 88, 103; 44 pp. 66, 152; 45 p. 99.

The Pirate Queen; or, Captain Kidd and the Treasure. London: Richards & Co., 4 Agar Street, Strand. 1867.

The Historical Magazine and notes and queries, concerning the antiquities, history and biography of America. Vol. 3. 8vo, 445 pp. Morrisania, N. Y.: Henry B. Dawson. 1868.

Extracts from Luttrell's brief historical relation of state affairs from September 1678 to April 1714. Vols. 1 to 6, pp. 286-298.

Kidd reference, pp. 293-296.

Captain Kidd- Why he was hung. By B. F. DeCosta. The Galaxy, pp. 742-746. New York, May 1869.

Collections of the New York Historical Society for the year 1869.| Publication fund series. 8vo, 560 pp. New York: Printed for the Society. MDCCCLXX. The Clarenden Papers.

Description of the "Money Pond", "Montock, so called" from the report of the Pirate Wm. Kidd's having sunk two chests of money in it about 1699," p. 259; his transactions on Gardiner's Island, pp. 268-269.

New England Legends. By Harriet Prescott Spofford. With Illustrations. 8vo, 40 pp. Boston: James and R. Osgood and Company, (Late Ticknor & Fields, and Fields, Osgood, & Co.) 1871.

Sam Lawson's Oldtown Fireside Stories. By Harriet Beecher Stowe. With Illustrations. 12mo, 287 pp. Boston: James R. Osgood & Company. 1871.

Captain Kidd's money, pp. 103-121.

Calendar of Treasury Papers, 1697-1701-2, preserved in Her Majesty's Public Record office. Prepared by Joseph Redington, Esq., one of the assistant Keepers of the Public Records. Under the direction of the master of the Rolls and with the sanction of the Lords Commissioners of Her Majesty's Treasury. 8vo, XIV-643-29 pp. London: Longman & Co., and Trubner & Co., Paternoster Row; also by Parker & Co., Oxford.; and Macmillan & Co., Cambridge; A. & C. Black, Edinburgh; and A. Thom. Dublin, 1871.

Increase of Piracy, pp. 480. Pirates, pp.26, 49, 139, 364, 379, 480, 481, 546. Courts for trials of pirates, pp. 419. Squadron in the East Indies to reduce the pirates p. 210. Pirates, New York, pp. 164, 180, 210, 229, 326, 398, 456.

Capt. William Kidd, Commander of the Ship "Adventure." The King's grant of what should be captured by him, &c, p. 49. The King's grant of pirates' goods to Capt. Kidd, p. 350. Capt. Kidd, lately from Madagascar, pp. 362, 364. Commission to Kidd; his effects, pp. 350, 389, 484.

Zanzibar: City, Island, Coast. By Richard F. Burton in Two Volumes. Vol. II. 8vo. VI-519 pp. London: Tinsley Bros., 18 Catherine St., Strand. 1872. (All Rights reserved.)

Capt. Kidd p. 8.

Calendar of Treasury Papers, 1702-1707, preserved in Her Majesty's Public Record Office. Prepared by Joseph Redington, Esq., one of the assistant keepers of the Public Records. Published by the Authority of the Lords Commissioners of Her Majesty's Treasury, under the direction of the master of the Rolls. 8vo, xxxii-693-31 pp. London: Longman & Co., and Trubner & Co., Paternoster Row; also by Parker & Co., Oxford; and Macmillan & Co., Cambridge; A. & C. Black, Edinburgh, and A. Thom, Dublin. 1874.

Pirates and piracy, pp. 132, 294, 403, 345. Pirate treasure taken with Captain Kidd, pp. 91, 354.

American Pioneers and Patriots. Captain William Kidd, and others of the Pirates or Buccaneers who Ravaged the Seas, the Islands, and the Continents of America two hundred years ago. By John S. C. Abbott. Frontispiece. Illustrated. 12mo, 373 pp. New York: Dodd & Mead, No. 762 Broadway. 1874.

The Buccaneer Chiefs; or, Captain Kidd and the Pirates of America. By John S. C. Abbott, with numerous Illustrations. 12mo, 373 pp. London: Ward, Lock & Co., Warwick House, Salisbury Square, E. C. N. D.

A Cruise with Kidd. By T. Belgravia Magazine, pp. 473-479. London, August, 1874.

History of New England from the Revolution of the Seventeenth Century. By John Gorham Palfrey. *Moribus antiquis res stat Romana virisque. -Enrius, apud Cic. de Rep. V.* 1. Vol. 4, 24-604 pp. Boston: Little, Brown and Company. 1875.

Kidd references; pp. 180-185.

"Captain Kidd," in "The Boatswain's Locker." The Aquatic Monthly, pp. 313-319. Published by August Brentano, Vol. 5, No. 5, New York, August. 1875.

Written by Dr. B. F. DeCosta. Republished Boston Globe, Sunday, Nov· 28, 1915, p. 46.

William Kidd, the Pirate. By J. B. Felt. New England Historical and Geneological Register, Vol. 6, p. 77.

The New England Historical and Geneological Register. Published quarterly, under the direction of the New England Historic, Geneological Society. For the year 1877. Vol. 31. 8vo, 468 pp. Boston: Published at the Society's house, 18 Somerset Street. Printed by David Clapp & Son. 1877.

The story of the Kidd diamond, p. 332.

The Life and Administration of Richard, Earl of Bellomont, Governor of the Provinces of New York, Massachusetts and New Hampshire, from 1697 to 1701. An address delivered before the New York Historical Society, at the celebration of its Seventy-fifth Anniversary, Tuesday, November 18th, 1879, ·by Frederick de Peyster, LL.D., F.R.H.S. President of the Society. 8vo, (8)- 59-(1)-xvii pp. New York: Published for the Society. MDCCCLXXIX.

Collections of the Massachusetts Historical Society. Vol. VI. Fifth Series. 8vo, iii-462 pp. Boston: Published by the Society. M.DCCC.LXXIX.

Captain Kidd and his treasure, notes to Diary of Samuel Sewell, pp.3, 4, 6, 7.

Calendar of Treasury Papers, 1708-1714, Preserved in Her Majesty's Public Record office. Prepared by Joseph Redington, Esq., one of the assistant keepers of the Public Records, Published by the authority of the Lords Commissioners of Her Majesty's Treasury, under the direction of the Masters of the Rolls, 8vo, xxii-734-32-(2) pp. London: Longman & Co., Paternoster Row; Trubner & Co., Ludgate Hill, also by Parker & Co.; Oxford; and Macmillan & Co., Cambridge; A. & C. Black, and Douglas & Foulis, Edinburgh; and A. Thom, Dublin. 1879.

Suppression of Piracy by Col. J. Dudley, p. 102.

Captain Kidd, p. 269.

History of the City of New York. By Mary L. Booth, translator of Martin's History of France, Etc. Illustrated. 8vo, 920 pp. New York: E. P. Dutton & Company, 713 Broadway. 1880. Second edition.

Captain William Kidd becomes a daring and successful pirate; his arrest and execution, pp. 253-256.

The Memorial History of Boston, including Suffolk County, Massachusetts. 1630-1880. Edited by Justin Winsor, Librarian of Harvard University. In four Volumes, Vol. I. The early and colonial periods. Issued under the business superintendence of the projector, Clarence F. Jewett. 4to. Vol. I The Early and colonial periods, xxxii-596 pp. Vol. II. The provincial period, xiii-lviii-577 pp. Vol. III. The Revolutionary period, the last hundred years. Part 1. xiii-xii-691 pp. Vol. IV. The last hundred years. Part II. Special topics. x-713 pp. 1880-1881.

Chapter by E. C. Hale referring to Capt. Kidd in Vol. 2, pp. 41, 173, 160, 184.

Collections of the New York Historical Society for the year 1880. Publication fund series. 8vo, 489 pp. New York: Printed for the Society. MDCCC XXXI.

Revolutionary papers, Vol. III, p. 256. The New York Assembly makes a law "effectually to oblige a busy Scotchman" and partner with Kidd; p. 316, Kidd's crew "freely" walk the streets of New York.

Documents relating to the Colonial History of the State of New Jersey, Edited by William A. Whitehead. Corresponding Secretary of the New Jersey Historical Society, author of East Jersey under the Proprietary Governments; Contributors to the Early History of Perth Amboy and the surrounding county; Editor of the papers of Lewis Morris; and of an Analytical Index to the Colonial Documents of New Jersey, Etc., Etc. Volume II. 1687-1703. 8vo, XXI-559 pp. Newark; N. J.: Daily Advertiser Printing House. 1881.

Letter from Colonel Quary to the Lords of Trade, about Pirates in Pennsylvania and Elsewhere. Letter from Col. Quary to ye Board, abt the arrival of Kidd and other Pirates at Pennsylvania and other places. Philadelphia: June 6th, 1699, pp. 280-285.

A gallop among American Scenery; or, Sketches of American scenes and military adventure by Augustus E. Silliman. 8vo, vi-337 pp. New York: A. S. Barnes & Co., 111 & 113 William Street. 1881.

Captain William Kidd. By Charles Burr Todd. Lippincott's Magazine, pp. 380-389. Philadelphia, April, 1882.

Collections of the Massachusetts Historical Society. Vol. VIII. Fifth series. 8vo, XVIII-596 pp. Boston: Published by the Society. M.DCCC.LXXXII.

Letters concerning Captain Kidd by the Hon. Fitz-John Winthrop to Lord Bellomont and others; and by Wait Winthrop to Fitz-John Winthrop, pp. 363, 366, 370, 376, 526, 553, 557.

Letters chiefly written by Fitz-John Winthrop: Act concerning pirates, p. 347; Concerning the seizure of Josiah Raynor and Thomas Canclin, pirates, p. 348; Arrival of pirates at Black Island, pp. 357, 358. Pirates seized by Fitz-John Winthrop, pp. 358, 360, 362. Concerning pirates, pp. 361, 362, 365, 366, 367, 370, 371, 372, 373, 374, 375, 376, 494, 547, 549, 552, 561, 562, 563, 566. Proclamation against privateers, p. 353.

Digging for Capt. Kidd's treasure in Narraganset. By Joseph P. Hazard. The Narraganset Register, p. 297. April, 1883.

The American Cyclopaedia; a popular dictionary of general knowledge. Edited by George Ripley and Charles A. Dana. With supplement. Vol. IX, Royal 8vo, 870-(7) pp. New York: D. Appleton and Company, 1, 3 and 5 Bond Street. London: 16 Little Britain. 1883.

Capt. Kidd, pp. 825, Vol. 9; p. 160, Vol. 15.

An Honest Earl and a Pirate Captain, once near Wall Street. By Theodorous Bailey Myers. The American Antiquarian, Vol. 3, p. 241. New York: Burns & Son, March. 1885.

The Old Bailey Chronicle; Containing a Circumstantial Account of the Lives, Trials and Confessions of the most notorious Offenders who have suffered Death and other exemplary Punishments, in England, Scotland and Ireland from the commencement of the Year 1700, to the End of the Year 1786, for Bigamy, Burglary, Felony, Forgery, Footpad-Robbery, Highway-Robbery, High-Treason, Horse-Stealing, Murder, Petit-Treason, Perjury, Piracy, Rapes, Riots, Street-Robbery, and various other Offenses and Misdemeanors, to which is added the Ordinary of Newgate's Account of every Capita Malefactor executed this Century. Properly arranged from the Records of Court by James Mountague, Esq., of the Temple. 8vo. Four volumes. Vol. I, iv-398; Vol. II, 396 p. Vol. III, 400; Vol. IV, 487 p. London: Printed by Authority for R., Randall, No. 116 Shoe Lane, Fleet Street, and G. Allen, Long-Acre, near Long-Acre Chapel, and sold by the Booksellers and News-Carriers in Great Britain and Ireland. MDCCLXXXVI.

Vol. I, p. 26- Particulars of the Life, together with an Account of the Trials of John (sic) Kidd, executed for Piracy.

Note: Titles of volumes II, IIIand IV read:
     "Old Bailey Chronicle; or, The Malefactor's Register."

The Manor of Gardiner's Island. By MarthaJ. Lamb. Magazine of American History, pp. 1-30. New York: January. 1885.

Bellomont and Rasle in 1699. By Charles W. Parsons. Magazine of American History, pp. 346-352. New York: April. 1885.

Collections of the Massachusetts Historical Society. Vol. I, Sixth series. 8vo, XXXIV-421 pp. Boston: Published by the Society. M.DCCC.LXXXVI.

Captain William Kidd, the pirate.pp. 216, 220.

The Memorial History of Boston, including Suffolk County, Massachusetts, 1620-1880. Edited by Justin Winsor, Librarian of Harvard University. In Four Volumes. Vol. II. The Provincial Period. Issued under the business superintendence of the projector, Clarence F. Jewett. 4to, XIII-LVIII-577 pp. Boston: Ticknor and Compnay. 1886.

Captain Kidd, pp. 41. Chap. V in "Lord Bellomont and Captain Kidd" by E. E. Hale, pp. 173-184.

Captain Kidd. By the Rev. Edward E. Hale. Leaflet, 8vo, 8 pp. Excerpt from the Memorial History of Boston. Second volume, pp. 280-287. Published Dec. 31, 1881.

Collections of the New York Historical Society for the year 1885. Publication fund series. 8vo, 678 pp. New York: Printed for the Society. MDCCCLXXXVI.

Captain Kidd's Gold. The True Story of an Adventurous Sailor Boy. 12mo., 282 pp. By J. F. Fitts. New York: A. L. Burt Company, Publishers. 1888.

The Burghers of New Amsterdam and the Freemen of New York, 1675-1886, pp. 571-572. Elizabeth Morris "doth pride her selfe A Servant unto the said Capt. William Kidd" for four years in return for "her Passage on board the Barquentine Called the Antequa (Capt. William Kidd late Owner)."

Collections of the Massachusetts Historical Society. Sixth series. Vol. III. Published at the charge of the Appleton fund. 8vo, XX-579 pp. Boston: Published by the Society. M. DCCC. LXXXIX.

Captain Kidd, pp. 48, 49. Privateers, pp. 3-12, 460, 488.

Appleton's Cyclopaedia of American biography Edited by James Grant Wilson and John Fiske. As it is the commendaton of a good huntsman to find game in a wide wood, so it is no imputation if he had not caught all. Plato. Royal 8vo, (10)-752 pp. New York: D. Appleton and Company, 1, 3 and 5 Bond Street. 1892.

Captain Kidd, p. 531.

Collections of the Massachusetts Historical Society. Sixth series Vol. V-Published at the charge of the Appleton fund. 8vo, XX-529 pp. Boston: Pub lished by the Society. M. DCCC. XCII.

Disposal of Captain Kidd's treasure. His connection with Lord Bellomont, pp. 58, 60.

Pirates on the coast of Massachusetts, pp. 343, 345.

The Memorial History of the City of New York, from its first Settlement to the Year 1892. Edited by James Grant Wilson. Four vols. 8vo, 24-605; 21-633; 22-664; 23-650 pp. New York History Company, 11 Nassau Street, 1892.

Kidd references: Vol. I, pp. 512, 515, 516, 519, 520, 605; Vol. II, pp. 13, 30, 32, 33, 34, 133; Vol. IV, p. 502.

"Benjamin Fletcher and the Rise of Piracy." By Charless Burr Todd. Vol. I, pp. 489-522; "The Earl of Bellomont and the Suppression of Piracy," by the Rev. Asbel G. Vermilye, Vol. II, pp. 1-49.

Benjamin Fletcher and the rise of Piracy, 1692-1698. By Charles Burr Todd. The National Magazine, pp. 625-651. New York, October, 1892.

Excerp from "The Memorial History."

The Earl of Bellomont and the suppression of Piracy, 1698-1701. By Ashbel G. Vermilye, D.D. The National Magazine, pp. 1-34, New York, Novembe , 1892.

Excerpt from "The Memorial History."

Dictionary of National Biography. Edited by Sidney Lee. 63 vols, 8vo, Vol. 31. Kenneth Lambert. 448 p. New York: Macmillan and Co. London: Smith, Elder & Co. 1892.

"William Kidd," by Prof. Sir J. K. Laughton, pp. 93-95.

Harper's Popular Cyclopaedia of United States History. From the aboriginal Period. Containing Brief Sketches of important Events and conspicuous actors. By Benson J. Lossing, LL.D. Illustrated by over one thousand engravings. In two volumes. Revised and enlarged edition. Imp. 8vo, VIII-794-795 to 1631 pp. New York: Harper and Brothers, Publishers, Franklin Square 1893.

William Kidd, p. 740.

Collections of the New York Historical Society for they year 1892. Publicao tion fund series. 8vo, 520 pp. New York: Printed for the Society. MDCCCXCIII.

Abstracts of wills on file in the Surrogates office, City of New York. VI.. I, 1665-1707. P. 158: Bequest of William Cox, rich merchant to "my dear and loving wife Sarah, which house she pleases to have, to her and her heirs." (The house chosen is now No. 86 Wall Street. Sarah afterward married John Oort, and after his death she married Capt. William Kidd).

Marriage license granted Capt. Kidd and Sarah Oort, p. 180.

William Kidd and his wife Sarah give bonds in five hundred pounds "for their true adminstrations" of the estate of John Oort, p. 197.

Inventory of the "goods and chattells of John Oort" by William Kidd and Sarah, his wife, p. 204.

Account of Capt. William Kidd and Sarah his wife," administrators, pp. 206-207.

Will of Samuel Bradley, giving City property to his "loving brother-in-law," Capt. William Kidd, "for and in consideration of his great so love unto me, as well as in recompense of money advanced," pp. 366-367.

Marriage license granted to Christopher Rousby and Sarah Kidd, the widow of Capt. William Kidd, p. 380.

Sarah, and Christopher Rousby (her fourth husband) granted letters of adminstration upon the estate of her first husband, William Cox, in the stead of the original executors who died before fully administrating upon the estate,, p. 393.

The Sea Robbers of New York. By Thomas A. Janvier Harper's Magazine pp. 813-827. New York: November 1894.

Collections of the New York Historical Society for the year 1893. Publication fund series. 8vo, 525 pp. New York: Printed for the Society. MDCCCXCIV.

The Return of the Half Moon. By Diedrich Crayon, Jr. 12 mo. 47 pp. Broadway Publishing Company. New York and Baltimore: 1909.
By Kenneth Bruce.

Abstracts of Wills on file in the Surrogate's office, City of New York. Vol. II, 1708-1728.

Mention of Capt. William Kidd as having "come lately from London in the Adventure Galley," p. 156.

The will of Robert Livingston, approved and allowed, pp. 348-349. Part of Livingston Manor, the William Cox grants bequeathed to his wife Sarah and her brother Samuel Bradley, later sold by them and Capt. William Kidd to Robert Livingston.

A History of the United States Navy from 1775 to 1894. By Edgar Stanton Maclay, A.M. With technical Revision by Lieutenant Roy C. Smith, U.S.N. In two volumes. Illustrated. 8vo, XXXII-577; XIII-640 pp. New York: D. Appleton & Company. 1895.

Captain Kidd, Vol. I, p. 6.

Johnson's Universal Cyclopaedia. A new edition prepared by a corps of thirty-six Editors, assisted by eminent European and American Specialists, under the direction of Charles Kendal Adams, LL.D. President of the University of Wisconsin, Editor-in-chief. Illustrated with maps, plans and engravings. Complete in eight volumes. Vol. IV. Royal 8vo, 11-(5)-912 pp. New York: D. Appleton and Company. A. J. Johnson Company. 1895.

Captain Kidd, p. 900.

Collections of the New York Historical Society for the year 1895. Pubilcation fund series. 8vo, 559 pp. New York: Printed for the Society. MDCCC-XCVI. Abstracts of wills on file in the Surrogate's office, City of New York. Vol IV, 1744-1793. With letters of Adminstration granted 1745-1753.

Will of Sarah Rousby, widow of Willam Cox, John Oort, Captain William Kidd and Christopher Rousby, who died owner of "houses and lands," p. 15.

The Pursuit of the The House-Boat. Being some Further Account of the Divers Doings of the Associated Shades under the leadership of Sherlock Holmes, Esq. By John Kendrick Bangs. Illustrated by Peter Newell. 16mo. VIII-204 pp. New York and London: Harper & Brothers. Published. 1897.

Capt. Kidd is a principal character in this phantasy.

The National Cyclopaedia of American Biography, having the history of the United States as illustrated in the lives of the founders, builders, and defenders of the Republic, and of the men and women who are doing the work and moulding the thought of the present time. Edited by distinguished biographers, selected from each state. Revised and approved by the most eminent historians, scholars, and statesmen of the day. Vol. VII, Royal 8vo, 531 pp. New York: James T. White & Company. 1897.

Capt. Kidd referred to briefly under Richard Coote, Earl of Bellomont, p. 373.

The Royal Navy. A History From the Earliest Times to the Present. By Wm. Laird Clowes, Fellow of King's College, London: Gold Medallist, U. S. Naval Institute; Hon. Member of the R. U. S. Institution. Assisted by Sir

Clements Markham, K.C.B., P.R.G.S., Captain A. T. Mahan, U. S. N., H·
W. Wilson, Theodore Roosevelt, E. Fraser, Etc. Twenty-five Photogravures
and Hundreds of Full Page and other Illustrations, Maps, Charts, Etc. In
Five Volumes. Imp. 8vo. Vol. I, xxiv-698 p. Vol. II, xiv-593 p.; Vol. III, xix-
609 pp. Vol. IV, xiv-624 pp. Boston: Little, Brown and Company. London:
Sampson, Low, Marston and Company, Limited, St. Dunstan's House, Fetter
Lane, E. C. 1897.

Captain William Kidd: Vol. II, pp. 498, 499; Vol. III, pp. 258. 259.

Collections of the New York Historical Society for the year 1897. Publica-
tion fund series. 8vo, 517 p. New York: Printed for the Society MDCCCXC-
VIII. Abstracts of wills on file in the Suurrogate's office, City of New York
Vol. VI, 1760-1766. With letters of administration granted 1760-1766.

Will of Garret Van Horne, whose house and lot—now No. 92 Pearl Street—
descended to him from his mother, a daughter of Robert Livingston, who
bought this and the lot No. 90 from Captain William Kidd and his wife,
pp. 392-393.

State Trials of Mary, Queen of Scots, Sir Walter Raleigh and Capt. William
Kidd. The Nation, Vol. 69, p. 1779. New York: August 3, 1899.

Review of preceding item.

Adrian van der Donck, 1656.
For I must tell you, if we miscarry it will be our own fault; we have nobody
else to blame; for such is the happiness of our Constitution, that we cannot
well be destroyed but by ourselves.
                                        William Penn, 1679.

New York's Landholding Sea-Rover. Oblong 4to, 10 pp. Issued by the New
York Title and Guarantee Company. 1900.

Frontispiece Photogravure of Kidd's House, Pearl and Hanover Streets,
New York, from the Painting by E. L. Henry, A.N.A.

Early New York Houses. With Historical & Genealogical notes by William
S. Pelletreau, A. M. Photographs of Old Houses & Original Illustrations by
C. G. Moller, Jr. In ten parts. 4to, viii-243 pp. New York: Francis P. Harper,
Publisher. A.D. 1900.

Captain Kidd's house located.

An Old Story Revived. "Ye Lamentable Ballad, and Ye True Historie of
Captaine Robert Kidd, who was hanged in chains at Execution Dock, May
1701, for Piracy and Murder on ye High Seas." Pamphlet, 10 pp. Illustrated.
New York: The Broun Green Company. 1901.

A Landmark History of New York. Also the orgin of Street Names and a
Bibliography. By Albert Ulmann, Member of the American Historical Society.
Co. 8vo, viii-285 pp. New York: D. Appleton and Company. 1901.

Captain Kidd, pp. 61-62.

State Trials of Mary, Queen of Scots, Sir Walter Raleigh, and Captain
William Kidd. Condensed and copied from the State Trials of Francis Har-
grave, Esq., London, 1776, and of T. D. Howell, Esq., F.R.S., F.S.A., London,
1816, with explanatory notes. By Charles Edward Lloyd. Roy. 8vo, VIII-260
pp. Chicago: Callaghan and Company. 1899.

The Dutch and Quaker Colonies in America by John Fiske. Meuw Nederlant is een seer schoon aengenaen gesont en lustigh lantschap daer het voor alderly slagh van menschen beter en ruymer aen de kost of gemackelycker door de merelt te geraken is als in Nederlant ofite eenige andere quartieren des merelts mijn bekent. In two volumes. 8vo, (16)-294; (16)-400 pp. Boston and New York: Houghton, Mifflin and Company. The Riverside Press, Cambridge, 1899.

Naval Yarns. Letters and Anecdotes. Comprising Accounts of Sea Fights and Wrecks, Actions with Pirates and Privateers, Etc, from 1616 to 1831. Collected and Edited by W. H. Long. 8vo, 1-32 pp. London: Gibbings & Co., Limited. 1899.

Capt. Kidd, Vol. 2, pp. 226, 227, 231-235; Piracy Vol. II, pp. 222-226.

Reissued 1903: Two volumes, 8vo, 27-256; (26)-374 pp. Kidd references pp. 210-211; 215-218; 220. Piracy pp. 207-209.

The Story of the Nations. The Thirteen Colonies. By Helen Ainslie Smith, author of "One hundred famous Americans," "Stories of persons and places in America," "The Colonies," "Animals: wild and tame," Etc. In two parts. New Jersey, Delaware, Maryland, Pennsylvania, Connecticut, Rhode Island, North Carolina, South Carolina, Georgia. Part II. 8vo, (8)-510 pp. G. P. Putnam's Sons, New York and London, The Knickerbocker Press. 1901.

Kidd references: Vol. I, p. 401; Vol. II, Kidd and other pirates infested the coast, p. 132; Pirates infest Atlantic Coast. Vol. I, pp. 259, 401; Vol. II, pp. 320, 334, 407, 411, 413, 421, 422, Algerine pirates; Vol. II, p. 365.

Historic Long Island. By Rufus Rockwell Wilson, author of "Rambles in Colonial By-Ways," "Washington: The Capital City," and "New York, Old and New." Fully illustrated. 8vo, 364 pp. New York: The Berkeley Press. 1902.

Appendix B: "The True Story of Captain Kidd, told by George Parsons Lathrop," pp. 344-364.

New York: Old and New. Its Story, Streets, and land marks. By Rufus Rockwell Wilson, Author of "Washington: The Capital City," "Rambles in Colonial By-Ways," etc. With many illustrations from Prints and Photographs and with decorations by Edward Stratton Holloway, Vol. I. Cr-8vo. 402 pp. Philadelphia & London: J. F. Lippincot Company. 1902.

Captain Kidd pp. 139-148.

The Reign of Queen Anne. By Justin McCarthy, Author of "A History of our own Times," "A History of the Four Georges and William IV," Etc. In Two Volumes. 8vo, Vol. I, 386 pp. Vol. II, 370 pp. New York and London: Harper & Brothers, Publishers. 1902.

Captain William Kidd, Vol. I, p. 326.

The True Captain Kidd. By John D. Champlin, Jr. Illustrated in colors by Howard Pyle. Harper's Magazine. Vol. CVI, No. 631. 1902. Pages 25 to 35.

Condensed in Current Literature, pp. 481-3. New York, April, 1903.

Harper's Encyclopaedia of United States History. From 458 A.D. to 1902. Based upon the plan of Benson John Lossing, LL.D. Complete in ten volumes. 8vo. Harper & Brothers, Publishers. New York. 1902. London.

Capt. Kidd, Vol. V, p. 250.

William Kidd a Pirate? Mail and Express, New York, December 13, 1902.

The Encyclopaedia Americana. A general dictionary of the arts and sciences, literature, history, biography, geography, etc., of the world. Editor-in-Chief, Frederick Converse Beach; Editor of the Scientific American; Managing Editor George Edward Rines; Editor and translator Edward Thomas Roe; Author and Editor, Thomas Campbell Copeland, expert statistician. In sixteen volumes. Roy. 8vo. n.p.The American Company, New York, Chicago. N.D. (1903).

Capt. Kidd, Vol. 9.

House of the Pirate Kidd. The Sun, New York. Sunday, February 22, 1903.

Captain Kidd and other Charades. By Florence L. Sahler. Sm. 4to (4)-65 pp. Robert Grier Cooke, New York, N.D. (1904).

William Kidd, Pirate. Legend and Literature. By Margaret Scovile Dorman, Connecticut Magazine, Vol. 9, pp. 269-278, April, 1905.

Historical Manuscripts Commission. Report on the manuscripts of his Grace the Duke of Portland, K.G., preserved at Welbeck Abbey. Vol. VIII. Presented to both Houses of Parliament by Command of His Majesty. Roy. 8vo, 432-viii pp. Printed for His Majesty's Stationery office by Ben Johnson & Co., York. And to be purchased either directly or through any Bookseller, from Wyman and Sons, Ltd., Fetter Lane, E.C., and 32, Abingson Street, Westminster, S.W., or of Oliver & Boyd, Edinburgh; or E. Ponsonby, 116, Grafton Street, Dublin. 1907. (cd. 3475). Price 1s. 10d.

The Storm Ship. Legend of Hudson and Kidd. Poem. By Arthur Guiterman. New York Times. Sunday, September 8, 1907.

Captain Kidd's Treasure Once More. The Magazine of History, p. 117, New York, February, 1908.

Where Capt. Kidd really left his Treasure. By Winfield M. Thompson. Boston Sunday Globe, July 18, 1909.

In the Wake of Captain Kidd. By Winfield M. Thompson. The Rudder, New York, September, 1909.

Maine Pioneer, Settlements. Olde Pemaquid. By Herbert Milton Sylvester· Roy-8vo., 431pp. Boston. W. B. Clarke Co. 26-28 Tremont St. 1909.

Captain Kidd pp. 218-219.

Acts of the Privy Council of England. Colonial Series. Vol. II, A.D. 1680-1720. Edited through the direction of the Lord President of the Council, by W. L. Grant, M.A., Best Lecturer in Colonial History in the University of Oxford, and James Munro, M.A., University Assistant in History at the University of Edinburgh. Under the general supervision of Sir Almeric W. Fitzroy, K.C.V.O., Clerk of the Privy Council. Published by the authority of the Lords Commissioners of His Majesty's Treasury. 8vo, XLX-918 pp. Hereford: Printed for His Majesty's Stationery Office, by the Hereford Times Co., Ltd. and to be purchased either directly or through any bookseller, from Wyman & Sons, Ltd., Fetter Lane, E.C., or Oliver & Boyd, Tweeddale Court, Edinburgh; or, E. Ponsonby, 116 Grafton Street, Dublin, 1910. Price 10 shillings.

Captain William Kidd, pp. 347, 367, 379.

BIBLIOGRAPHY 251

See also, Vol. VI, p. 17. "Captain Kidd's Treasure. Full title under "Pirates."

Calendar of State Papers. Colonial Series, America and West Indies. 1700. Preserved in the Public Record Office. Edited by Cecil Headlam, M.A., Published by the Authority of the Lords Commissioners of His Majesty's Treasury under the Direction of the Master of the Rolls. 8vo, lxviii-851-39 pp. London: Printed for His Majesty's Stationery Office by the Hereford Times Co., Ltd., Maylord Street, Hereford, And to be purchased directly or through any Bookseller, from Wyman and Sons, Ltd., Fetter Lane, E.C., or Oliver & Boyd, Tweeddale Court, Edinburgh; or, E. Ponsonby, Ltd., 116 Grafton Street, Dublin. 1910.

Adventure, Kidd's Galley, pp. 164, 196, 198-200, 277, 608. Copy of the articles of agreement between "Captain William Kidd, Commander of the good Ship Adventure, and John Walker, Quartermaster," Sept. 10, 1696. Signed by Kidd and the ship's company, pp. 199, 200.

Names of the thirty-two pirates, including Captain Kidd, brought home in H.M.S. Advice from New England, p. 162.

Captain William Kidd, pp. 14, 18, 23, 24, 37, 38, 39, 43-45, 46, 47, 53, 60, 74, 83, 85-87, 103, 116, 119, 153, 156, 159, 163-166, 167, 169, 191, 201, 208-212, 245, 266-282, 321, 389, 441, 493, 582, 606-609, 627, 680, 717-721, 760, 772-774.

The Cradle of the Deep. An Account of a Voyage to the West Indies. By Sir Frederick Treves, Bart. G.C.V.O., C.B., LL.D. Sergeant, Surgeon to H.M. The King, Surgeon in Ordinary to H.M. Queen Alexandra, Author of—"The Other Side of the Lantern"—"The Tale of a Field Hospital." With 54 Illustrations from Photographs by the Author and 4 Maps. Popular Edition 8vo. xii-378 pp. New York. E. P. Dutton & Company, 31 W. Twenty-Third Street 1910.

Capt. Kidd, pp. 263-266.

The Encyclopaedia Britannica. A dictionary of Arts, Sciences, Literature and general information. Eleventh Edition. 29 volumes. 4to. Cambridge, England: At the University Press, New York, 35 West 32nd Street. 1911.

Capt. Kidd: Vol. 15, p. 783; Vol. 19, p. 621, Vol. 25, p. 385.

The Real Captain Kidd. A Vindication. Sir Cornelius Neale Dalton, K.C.M.G., C.B., D.C.L. 12 mo, 335 pp. New York: Duffield and Company. 1911.

The Book of Buried Treasure. Being a True Hisotry of the Gold, Jewels, and Plate of Pirates, Galleons, etc., which are sought for to this day. By Ralph D. Paine, Author of "The Ships and Sailors of Old Salem," etc. Illustrated. 8vo, 425 pp. New York: Sturgis & Walton Company. 1911. All rights reserved.

Captain William Kidd: Privateer turned Pirate, 1697. Reproduction of Tapestry in article "New York's Newest Hotel," p. 237, The Architectural Record, March, 1913.

History and Reminiscences of Lower Wall Street and Vicinity. By Abram Wakeman, for 40 years in the Coffee and Tea District of New York, and Member of the following Societies: Descendents of the Colonial Governors, Sons of the Revolution, New York State Historical Society, the American Scenic and Historic Preservation Society, Aaron Burr Legion, Etc.,Etc., Etc. 8vo, viii-216 pp. New York: The Spice Mill Publishing Co. 1914.

Captain Kidd, pp. 10-11-12.

A Frame-up with Captain Kidd. By Franklin Clarkin. Boston Evening Transcript, November 10, 1915.

Farewell Romance. New York Evening Sun, November 11, 1915.

Ships and Shipping of Old New York. A Brief account of the Interestin Phases of the Commerce of New York, from the Foundation of the City to th beginning of the Civil War. 8vo, 61-(1) pp. Printed for the Bank of Manhattan Company, New York City, N.D. (1915).

William Kidd, p. 26.

Cruising the Carribean in the wake of Pirates. 8vo, 32 pp. United Fruit Company Steamship Service. (New York 1915).

Capt. Kidd, pp. 13-14.

New York's Part in History. By Sherman Williams, Author of "Some Successful Americans, "and "Stories from Early New York History." Illustrated. 8vo. lx-391 pp. New York and London. D. Appleton and Company. 1915.

Capt. Kidd. pp. 163-165.

Captain Kidd a Victim of Politics. Boston Sunday Globe. November 28, 1915.

Last of the Manors— Gardiner's Island. The Evening Post Saturday Magazine, New York, April 24, 1915.

Shows spot where Kidd buried his Treasure.

The Nutmeg Coast. By Winfield M. Thompson. Pages 481-491. Harper's Magazine. New York, September, 1916.

Kidd reference p. 489.

Hunting in Pearl Street for relics of Captain Kidd, the industrious 18-karat Pirate. New York Sunday World, October 15, 1916.

Nelson's Encyclopaedia. Everybody's book of reference. In 12 volumes Profusely illustrated. Editor-in-chief Frank Moore Colley, M.A. New York; George Sanderman, M.A., Edinburgh. Vol. VII, 8vo, 623 pp. New York: Thomas Nelson & Sons. London: Edinburg: Dub.in. N.D.

Captain Kidd, p. 104.

The Book of New York. By Robert Shackleton. Author of "The Book of Boston," "Unviolated Places of Old Europe," etc. 8vo. (6)-377 pp. Drawings by R. L. Boyer.

The Penn Publishing Company, Philadelphia. 1917.

Capt. Kidd, p. 53.

The Danish West Indies Under Company Rule. (1671-1754). With a Supplementary Chapter, 1755-1917. By Waldemar Westergaard, Ph.D. Assistant Professor of History at Pomona College. With an introduction by H. Morse Stephens, M.A.Litt.D. (Harv.) Sather Professor of the University of California. Maps and Illustrations. 8vo, xxiv-359 pp. New York: The Macmillan Company. 1917. All rights reserved.

Capt. Kidd, pp. 113 to 118.

Captain Kidd's Home to be a Restaurant. New York Evening Post, Saturday, April 5, 1919.

Said Captain Kidd's Spook, "Here's my buried Loot;" Thereby hangs this Tale. By Fay Stevenson. New York Evening World, Monday, August 4, 1919.

Bill Graig's Treasure Island. By Arthur Wynne, New York Sunday World Magazine, Oct. 10, 1919.

Pastor Digs Farm for Pirate Hoard as Dream Directs. New York World; November 6, 1919.

Acquits Captain Kidd of Piracy Charge. New York Times, July 28, 1921.

Captain Kidd as Victim of a Royal Frame-up. By Martin Storm. The Evening Post, New York, Dec. 21, 1921.

Was Captain Kidd a Pirate? By Joseph B. Gilder. The Outlook, pp. 551-553. New York, April 5, 1922.

More or Less Abandoned Estates of Long Island. By Charles Phillips. New York Times Book Review and Magazine, Aug. 13, 1922.

Kidd:A Moral Opuscule. The Verse (sic) by Richard J. Walsh. Illustrations (sic) by George Illian. New York: William Edwin Rudge, 1922. 4to. 24 pp. Boards, uncut.

A humorous poem on the notorious pirate. The "Colophony Note" lists Bruce Rogers as L.O.M.—Lay-Out-Man.

Madagascar: Land of the Man-Eating Tree. (By) Chase Salmon Osborne, LL.D. Honorary Member Aacdemie Malegachi, Author of "The Iron Hunter," "The Andean Land," "The Law of Divine Concord," Etc. With Maps and With Illustrations. 8vo. xi-443 pp. New York: Republic Publishing Company. 1924.

Captain Kidd, pp. 92-105.

Again They Dig for Captain Kidd's Gold. New York Times, Sunday Magazine, p. 2, Dec. 21, 1924.

Captain Kidd's Treasure. New York Times. Dec. 28, 1924. (Letter).

Pirates, Highwaymen and Adventurers. Edited by Eric Pastridge. 8vo. 250 (1) pp. London The Scholaritics Press. 1927.

Captain Kidd, pp. 83-84.

The Book of Pirates. By Henry Gilbert, Author of "The Conquerors of Mexico," "The Conquerors of Peru," "The Story of the Indian Mutiny," etc. Illustrated by Gilbert Reid. 8vo 329 pp. George C. Harrah & Co., Ltd. London, Calcutta, Sidney. N.D. (1819).

The Story of Captain Kidd, pp. 287-297.

The Rogues Gallery. Under the Black Flag. By Don C. Seitz, Auhtor of "Paul Jones; His Exploits in English Seas," "The Buccaneers," "Jospeh Pulitzer; His Life and Letters," "Braxton Bragg, General of the Confederacy," etc. Royal 8vo, 341 pp. Lincoln Macveigh, The Dial Press, New York. MCXXV.

"Of William Kidd," pp. 76-79.

The Book of Buried Treasure. Being a True History of the Gold, Jewels, and Plate of Pirates, Galleons, Etc., which are sought for to this Day. By Ralph D. Paine, Author of "The Ships and Sailors of Old Salem," etc. Illustrated. 8vo, 425 pp. New York: Sturgis and Walton Company. 1911. All rights reserved.

"Captain Kidd in Fact and Fiction," pp. 36-60; "Captain Kidd, his Treasure," 61-96; "Captain Kidd, His Trial and Death," pp. 97-128.

Old Cape Cod. The Land; The Men. The Sea. By Mary Rogers Bangs. 8vo, 298 pp. Boston and New York: Houghton, Mifflin Company. The Riverside Press, Cambridge. 1920.

Captain Kidd, pp. 187-188.

The Pirates of the New England Coast. 1630-1703. By George Francis Dow Curator of the Society for the Preservation of new England Antiques and John Henry Edmonds Massachusetts State Archivist. Introduction by Capt. Ernest H. Pentecost, R.N.R. Folio, xxii-394 pp. The Marine Society. Salem, Massachusetts. 1923.

"Capt. William Kidd, Privateer man and Reputed Pirate," pp. 73-83.

The Encyclopaedia Brittanica Eleventh Edition. Vol. xv. Cambridge, England: At the University Press. New York. Folio: XII-960 pp.

William Kidd, pp. 783-784.

Nooks and Corners of the New England Coast. By Samuels Adam Drake. 8vo, 450 pp. New York:Harper & Brothers., Publishers. 1875.

Malefactor's Register. The Malefactor's Register; or, The Newgate and Tyburn Calendar. etc.. from the Year 1700 to Lady-Day, 1779. 8vo, Five Volumes. Illustrated. London: Printed by Authority for Alexander Hogg, at No. 16 Paternoster Row.

The History of the Pirates, containing the Lives of these Noted Pirates, Captains Misson, Bowman, Kidd, Tew, Halsey, White, Condent, Bellamy, Fly, Howard, Landis, Cornelius, Williams, Burgews, North and their Several Crews. Also an account of John Augur, William Cunningham, Dennis Mac-Karthy, William Dowling, William Lewis, Thomas Norris, George Bendall, and William Ling, who were Tried, Condemned and Executed at Nassau,- New Providence, on the Tenth of December, 1718. To which is added a Correct Account of the Late Piracies Committed in the West Indies, and the Expedition of Commodore Porter. Omne tulit punctuam, qui miscuit utile. 12 mo., 5-283; 1 to 24 (14) pp. Hartford: Published by Henry Benton. 1829.

The Pirates' Who's Who, Giving Particulars the Lives and Deaths of the Pirates and Buccaneers. 8vo, 844 pp. London: Dulau and Company, Ltd. 34, 35 and 36 Margaret Street.

The Man they Hanged. By Robert W. Chambers. 12mo, 416 pp. New York and London: D. Appleton & Company. 1926.

The Trial of Captain William Kidd for Murder and PiracyUpon Six Several Indictments, as also, The Trials of Nicholas Churchill, James Howe, Robert Lamley, William Jenkins, Gabriel Loff, Hugh Parrot, Richard Barlicorn, Abel Owens and Darby Mullins. at the Admiralty Sessions held at the Old Bailey, London, on the 8th and 9th of May, 1701. Editedwith a Biography and Bibliography by Don C. Seitz, Litt.D 8vo, 9-256 pp. New York: The Press of the Pioneers. 1935.

A CATALOG OF SELECTED DOVER BOOKS IN ALL FIELDS OF INTEREST

CONCERNING THE SPIRITUAL IN ART, Wassily Kandinsky. Pioneering work by father of abstract art. Thoughts on color theory, nature of art. Analysis of earlier masters. 12 illustrations. 80pp. of text. 5⅜ x 8½. 23411-8 Pa. $4.95

ANIMALS: 1,419 Copyright-Free Illustrations of Mammals, Birds, Fish, Insects, etc., Jim Harter (ed.). Clear wood engravings present, in extremely lifelike poses, over 1,000 species of animals. One of the most extensive pictorial sourcebooks of its kind. Captions. Index. 284pp. 9 x 12. 23766-4 Pa. $14.95

CELTIC ART: The Methods of Construction, George Bain. Simple geometric techniques for making Celtic interlacements, spirals, Kells-type initials, animals, humans, etc. Over 500 illustrations. 160pp. 9 x 12. (Available in U.S. only.) 22923-8 Pa. $9.95

AN ATLAS OF ANATOMY FOR ARTISTS, Fritz Schider. Most thorough reference work on art anatomy in the world. Hundreds of illustrations, including selections from works by Vesalius, Leonardo, Goya, Ingres, Michelangelo, others. 593 illustrations. 192pp. 7⅛ x 10¼. 20241-0 Pa. $9.95

CELTIC HAND STROKE-BY-STROKE (Irish Half-Uncial from "The Book of Kells"): An Arthur Baker Calligraphy Manual, Arthur Baker. Complete guide to creating each letter of the alphabet in distinctive Celtic manner. Covers hand position, strokes, pens, inks, paper, more. Illustrated. 48pp. 8¼ x 11. 24336-2 Pa. $3.95

EASY ORIGAMI, John Montroll. Charming collection of 32 projects (hat, cup, pelican, piano, swan, many more) specially designed for the novice origami hobbyist. Clearly illustrated easy-to-follow instructions insure that even beginning papercrafters will achieve successful results. 48pp. 8¼ x 11. 27298-2 Pa. $3.50

THE COMPLETE BOOK OF BIRDHOUSE CONSTRUCTION FOR WOODWORKERS, Scott D. Campbell. Detailed instructions, illustrations, tables. Also data on bird habitat and instinct patterns. Bibliography. 3 tables. 63 illustrations in 15 figures. 48pp. 5¼ x 8½. 24407-5 Pa. $2.50

BLOOMINGDALE'S ILLUSTRATED 1886 CATALOG: Fashions, Dry Goods and Housewares, Bloomingdale Brothers. Famed merchants' extremely rare catalog depicting about 1,700 products: clothing, housewares, firearms, dry goods, jewelry, more. Invaluable for dating, identifying vintage items. Also, copyright-free graphics for artists, designers. Co-published with Henry Ford Museum & Greenfield Village. 160pp. 8¼ x 11. 25780-0 Pa. $10.95

HISTORIC COSTUME IN PICTURES, Braun & Schneider. Over 1,450 costumed figures in clearly detailed engravings–from dawn of civilization to end of 19th century. Captions. Many folk costumes. 256pp. 8⅜ x 11¾. 23150-X Pa. $12.95

STICKLEY CRAFTSMAN FURNITURE CATALOGS, Gustav Stickley and L. & J. G. Stickley. Beautiful, functional furniture in two authentic catalogs from 1910. 594 illustrations, including 277 photos, show settles, rockers, armchairs, reclining chairs, bookcases, desks, tables. 183pp. 6½ x 9¼. 23838-5 Pa. $11.95

AMERICAN LOCOMOTIVES IN HISTORIC PHOTOGRAPHS: 1858 to 1949, Ron Ziel (ed.). A rare collection of 126 meticulously detailed official photographs, called "builder portraits," of American locomotives that majestically chronicle the rise of steam locomotive power in America. Introduction. Detailed captions. xi+ 129pp. 9 x 12. 27393-8 Pa. $13.95

AMERICA'S LIGHTHOUSES: An Illustrated History, Francis Ross Holland, Jr. Delightfully written, profusely illustrated fact-filled survey of over 200 American lighthouses since 1716. History, anecdotes, technological advances, more. 240pp. 8 x 10¾. 25576-X Pa. $12.95

TOWARDS A NEW ARCHITECTURE, Le Corbusier. Pioneering manifesto by founder of "International School." Technical and aesthetic theories, views of industry, economics, relation of form to function, "mass-production split" and much more. Profusely illustrated. 320pp. 6⅛ x 9¼. (Available in U.S. only.) 25023-7 Pa. $10.95

HOW THE OTHER HALF LIVES, Jacob Riis. Famous journalistic record, exposing poverty and degradation of New York slums around 1900, by major social reformer. 100 striking and influential photographs. 233pp. 10 x 7⅞. 22012-5 Pa. $11.95

FRUIT KEY AND TWIG KEY TO TREES AND SHRUBS, William M. Harlow. One of the handiest and most widely used identification aids. Fruit key covers 120 deciduous and evergreen species; twig key 160 deciduous species. Easily used. Over 300 photographs. 126pp. 5⅜ x 8½. 20511-8 Pa. $3.95

COMMON BIRD SONGS, Dr. Donald J. Borror. Songs of 60 most common U.S. birds: robins, sparrows, cardinals, bluejays, finches, more–arranged in order of increasing complexity. Up to 9 variations of songs of each species. Cassette and manual 99911-4 $8.95

ORCHIDS AS HOUSE PLANTS, Rebecca Tyson Northen. Grow cattleyas and many other kinds of orchids–in a window, in a case, or under artificial light. 63 illustrations. 148pp. 5⅜ x 8½. 23261-1 Pa. $7.95

MONSTER MAZES, Dave Phillips. Masterful mazes at four levels of difficulty. Avoid deadly perils and evil creatures to find magical treasures. Solutions for all 32 exciting illustrated puzzles. 48pp. 8¼ x 11. 26005-4 Pa. $2.95

MOZART'S DON GIOVANNI (DOVER OPERA LIBRETTO SERIES), Wolfgang Amadeus Mozart. Introduced and translated by Ellen H. Bleiler. Standard Italian libretto, with complete English translation. Convenient and thoroughly portable–an ideal companion for reading along with a recording or the performance itself. Introduction. List of characters. Plot summary. 121pp. 5¼ x 8½. 24944-1 Pa. $3.95

TECHNICAL MANUAL AND DICTIONARY OF CLASSICAL BALLET, Gail Grant. Defines, explains, comments on steps, movements, poses and concepts. 15-page pictorial section. Basic book for student, viewer. 127pp. 5⅜ x 8½. 21843-0 Pa. $4.95

THE CLARINET AND CLARINET PLAYING, David Pino. Lively, comprehensive work features suggestions about technique, musicianship, and musical interpretation, as well as guidelines for teaching, making your own reeds, and preparing for public performance. Includes an intriguing look at clarinet history. "A godsend," *The Clarinet,* Journal of the International Clarinet Society. Appendixes. 7 illus. 320pp. 5⅜ x 8½.   40270-3 Pa. $9.95

HOLLYWOOD GLAMOR PORTRAITS, John Kobal (ed.). 145 photos from 1926-49. Harlow, Gable, Bogart, Bacall; 94 stars in all. Full background on photographers, technical aspects. 160pp. 8⅜ x 11¼.   23352-9 Pa. $12.95

THE ANNOTATED CASEY AT THE BAT: A Collection of Ballads about the Mighty Casey/Third, Revised Edition, Martin Gardner (ed.). Amusing sequels and parodies of one of America's best-loved poems: Casey's Revenge, Why Casey Whiffed, Casey's Sister at the Bat, others. 256pp. 5⅜ x 8½.   28598-7 Pa. $8.95

THE RAVEN AND OTHER FAVORITE POEMS, Edgar Allan Poe. Over 40 of the author's most memorable poems: "The Bells," "Ulalume," "Israfel," "To Helen," "The Conqueror Worm," "Eldorado," "Annabel Lee," many more. Alphabetic lists of titles and first lines. 64pp. 5³⁄₁₆ x 8¼.   26685-0 Pa. $1.00

PERSONAL MEMOIRS OF U. S. GRANT, Ulysses Simpson Grant. Intelligent, deeply moving firsthand account of Civil War campaigns, considered by many the finest military memoirs ever written. Includes letters, historic photographs, maps and more. 528pp. 6⅛ x 9¼.   28587-1 Pa. $12.95

ANCIENT EGYPTIAN MATERIALS AND INDUSTRIES, A. Lucas and J. Harris. Fascinating, comprehensive, thoroughly documented text describes this ancient civilization's vast resources and the processes that incorporated them in daily life, including the use of animal products, building materials, cosmetics, perfumes and incense, fibers, glazed ware, glass and its manufacture, materials used in the mummification process, and much more. 544pp. 6⅛ x 9¼. (Available in U.S. only.)   40446-3 Pa. $16.95

RUSSIAN STORIES/PYCCKNE PACCKA3bl: A Dual-Language Book, edited by Gleb Struve. Twelve tales by such masters as Chekhov, Tolstoy, Dostoevsky, Pushkin, others. Excellent word-for-word English translations on facing pages, plus teaching and study aids, Russian/English vocabulary, biographical/critical introductions, more. 416pp. 5⅜ x 8½.   26244-8 Pa. $9.95

PHILADELPHIA THEN AND NOW: 60 Sites Photographed in the Past and Present, Kenneth Finkel and Susan Oyama. Rare photographs of City Hall, Logan Square, Independence Hall, Betsy Ross House, other landmarks juxtaposed with contemporary views. Captures changing face of historic city. Introduction. Captions. 128pp. 8¼ x 11.   25790-8 Pa. $9.95

AIA ARCHITECTURAL GUIDE TO NASSAU AND SUFFOLK COUNTIES, LONG ISLAND, The American Institute of Architects, Long Island Chapter, and the Society for the Preservation of Long Island Antiquities. Comprehensive, well-researched and generously illustrated volume brings to life over three centuries of Long Island's great architectural heritage. More than 240 photographs with authoritative, extensively detailed captions. 176pp. 8¼ x 11.   26946-9 Pa. $14.95

NORTH AMERICAN INDIAN LIFE: Customs and Traditions of 23 Tribes, Elsie Clews Parsons (ed.). 27 fictionalized essays by noted anthropologists examine religion, customs, government, additional facets of life among the Winnebago, Crow, Zuni, Eskimo, other tribes. 480pp. 6⅛ x 9¼.   27377-6 Pa. $10.95

FRANK LLOYD WRIGHT'S DANA HOUSE, Donald Hoffmann. Pictorial essay of residential masterpiece with over 160 interior and exterior photos, plans, elevations, sketches and studies. 128pp. 9¼ x 10¾. 29120-0 Pa. $14.95

THE MALE AND FEMALE FIGURE IN MOTION: 60 Classic Photographic Sequences, Eadweard Muybridge. 60 true-action photographs of men and women walking, running, climbing, bending, turning, etc., reproduced from rare 19th-century masterpiece. vi + 121pp. 9 x 12. 24745-7 Pa. $12.95

1001 QUESTIONS ANSWERED ABOUT THE SEASHORE, N. J. Berrill and Jacquelyn Berrill. Queries answered about dolphins, sea snails, sponges, starfish, fishes, shore birds, many others. Covers appearance, breeding, growth, feeding, much more. 305pp. 5¼ x 8¼. 23366-9 Pa. $9.95

ATTRACTING BIRDS TO YOUR YARD, William J. Weber. Easy-to-follow guide offers advice on how to attract the greatest diversity of birds: birdhouses, feeders, water and waterers, much more. 96pp. 5$^{3}/_{16}$ x 8¼. 28927-3 Pa. $2.50

MEDICINAL AND OTHER USES OF NORTH AMERICAN PLANTS: A Historical Survey with Special Reference to the Eastern Indian Tribes, Charlotte Erichsen-Brown. Chronological historical citations document 500 years of usage of plants, trees, shrubs native to eastern Canada, northeastern U.S. Also complete identifying information. 343 illustrations. 544pp. 6½ x 9¼. 25951-X Pa. $12.95

STORYBOOK MAZES, Dave Phillips. 23 stories and mazes on two-page spreads: Wizard of Oz, Treasure Island, Robin Hood, etc. Solutions. 64pp. 8¼ x 11. 23628-5 Pa. $2.95

AMERICAN NEGRO SONGS: 230 Folk Songs and Spirituals, Religious and Secular, John W. Work. This authoritative study traces the African influences of songs sung and played by black Americans at work, in church, and as entertainment. The author discusses the lyric significance of such songs as "Swing Low, Sweet Chariot," "John Henry," and others and offers the words and music for 230 songs. Bibliography. Index of Song Titles. 272pp. 6½ x 9¼. 40271-1 Pa. $9.95

MOVIE-STAR PORTRAITS OF THE FORTIES, John Kobal (ed.). 163 glamor, studio photos of 106 stars of the 1940s: Rita Hayworth, Ava Gardner, Marlon Brando, Clark Gable, many more. 176pp. 8⅜ x 11¼. 23546-7 Pa. $14.95

BENCHLEY LOST AND FOUND, Robert Benchley. Finest humor from early 30s, about pet peeves, child psychologists, post office and others. Mostly unavailable elsewhere. 73 illustrations by Peter Arno and others. 183pp. 5⅜ x 8½. 22410-4 Pa. $6.95

YEKL and THE IMPORTED BRIDEGROOM AND OTHER STORIES OF YIDDISH NEW YORK, Abraham Cahan. Film Hester Street based on *Yekl* (1896). Novel, other stories among first about Jewish immigrants on N.Y.'s East Side. 240pp. 5⅜ x 8½. 22427-9 Pa. $7.95

SELECTED POEMS, Walt Whitman. Generous sampling from *Leaves of Grass*. Twenty-four poems include "I Hear America Singing," "Song of the Open Road," "I Sing the Body Electric," "When Lilacs Last in the Dooryard Bloom'd," "O Captain! My Captain!"–all reprinted from an authoritative edition. Lists of titles and first lines. 128pp. 5$^{3}/_{16}$ x 8¼. 26878-0 Pa. $1.00

THE BEST TALES OF HOFFMANN, E. T. A. Hoffmann. 10 of Hoffmann's most important stories: "Nutcracker and the King of Mice," "The Golden Flowerpot," etc. 458pp. 5⅜ x 8½.   21793-0 Pa. $9.95

FROM FETISH TO GOD IN ANCIENT EGYPT, E. A. Wallis Budge. Rich detailed survey of Egyptian conception of "God" and gods, magic, cult of animals, Osiris, more. Also, superb English translations of hymns and legends. 240 illustrations. 545pp. 5⅜ x 8½.   25803-3 Pa. $13.95

FRENCH STORIES/CONTES FRANÇAIS: A Dual-Language Book, Wallace Fowlie. Ten stories by French masters, Voltaire to Camus: "Micromegas" by Voltaire; "The Atheist's Mass" by Balzac; "Minuet" by de Maupassant; "The Guest" by Camus, six more. Excellent English translations on facing pages. Also French-English vocabulary list, exercises, more. 352pp. 5⅜ x 8½.   26443-2 Pa. $9.95

CHICAGO AT THE TURN OF THE CENTURY IN PHOTOGRAPHS: 122 Historic Views from the Collections of the Chicago Historical Society, Larry A. Viskochil. Rare large-format prints offer detailed views of City Hall, State Street, the Loop, Hull House, Union Station, many other landmarks, circa 1904-1913. Introduction. Captions. Maps. 144pp. 9⅜ x 12¼.   24656-6 Pa. $12.95

OLD BROOKLYN IN EARLY PHOTOGRAPHS, 1865-1929, William Lee Younger. Luna Park, Gravesend race track, construction of Grand Army Plaza, moving of Hotel Brighton, etc. 157 previously unpublished photographs. 165pp. 8⅞ x 11¾.
23587-4 Pa. $13.95

THE MYTHS OF THE NORTH AMERICAN INDIANS, Lewis Spence. Rich anthology of the myths and legends of the Algonquins, Iroquois, Pawnees and Sioux, prefaced by an extensive historical and ethnological commentary. 36 illustrations. 480pp. 5⅜ x 8½.   25967-6 Pa. $10.95

AN ENCYCLOPEDIA OF BATTLES: Accounts of Over 1,560 Battles from 1479 B.C. to the Present, David Eggenberger. Essential details of every major battle in recorded history from the first battle of Megiddo in 1479 B.C. to Grenada in 1984. List of Battle Maps. New Appendix covering the years 1967-1984. Index. 99 illustrations. 544pp. 6½ x 9¼.   24913-1 Pa. $16.95

SAILING ALONE AROUND THE WORLD, Captain Joshua Slocum. First man to sail around the world, alone, in small boat. One of great feats of seamanship told in delightful manner. 67 illustrations. 294pp. 5⅜ x 8½.   20326-3 Pa. $6.95

ANARCHISM AND OTHER ESSAYS, Emma Goldman. Powerful, penetrating, prophetic essays on direct action, role of minorities, prison reform, puritan hypocrisy, violence, etc. 271pp. 5⅜ x 8½.   22484-8 Pa. $8.95

MYTHS OF THE HINDUS AND BUDDHISTS, Ananda K. Coomaraswamy and Sister Nivedita. Great stories of the epics; deeds of Krishna, Shiva, taken from puranas, Vedas, folk tales; etc. 32 illustrations. 400pp. 5⅜ x 8½.   21759-0 Pa. $12.95

THE TRAUMA OF BIRTH, Otto Rank. Rank's controversial thesis that anxiety neurosis is caused by profound psychological trauma which occurs at birth. 256pp. 5⅜ x 8½.   27974-X Pa. $7.95

A THEOLOGICO-POLITICAL TREATISE, Benedict Spinoza. Also contains unfinished Political Treatise. Great classic on religious liberty, theory of government on common consent. R. Elwes translation. Total of 421pp. 5⅜ x 8½.   20249-6 Pa. $10.95

MY BONDAGE AND MY FREEDOM, Frederick Douglass. Born a slave, Douglass became outspoken force in antislavery movement. The best of Douglass' autobiographies. Graphic description of slave life. 464pp. 5⅜ x 8½. 22457-0 Pa. $8.95

FOLLOWING THE EQUATOR: A Journey Around the World, Mark Twain. Fascinating humorous account of 1897 voyage to Hawaii, Australia, India, New Zealand, etc. Ironic, bemused reports on peoples, customs, climate, flora and fauna, politics, much more. 197 illustrations. 720pp. 5⅜ x 8½. 26113-1 Pa. $15.95

THE PEOPLE CALLED SHAKERS, Edward D. Andrews. Definitive study of Shakers: origins, beliefs, practices, dances, social organization, furniture and crafts, etc. 33 illustrations. 351pp. 5⅜ x 8½. 21081-2 Pa. $12.95

THE MYTHS OF GREECE AND ROME, H. A. Guerber. A classic of mythology, generously illustrated, long prized for its simple, graphic, accurate retelling of the principal myths of Greece and Rome, and for its commentary on their origins and significance. With 64 illustrations by Michelangelo, Raphael, Titian, Rubens, Canova, Bernini and others. 480pp. 5⅜ x 8½. 27584-1 Pa. $10.95

PSYCHOLOGY OF MUSIC, Carl E. Seashore. Classic work discusses music as a medium from psychological viewpoint. Clear treatment of physical acoustics, auditory apparatus, sound perception, development of musical skills, nature of musical feeling, host of other topics. 88 figures. 408pp. 5⅜ x 8½. 21851-1 Pa. $11.95

THE PHILOSOPHY OF HISTORY, Georg W. Hegel. Great classic of Western thought develops concept that history is not chance but rational process, the evolution of freedom. 457pp. 5⅜ x 8½. 20112-0 Pa. $9.95

THE BOOK OF TEA, Kakuzo Okakura. Minor classic of the Orient: entertaining, charming explanation, interpretation of traditional Japanese culture in terms of tea ceremony. 94pp. 5⅜ x 8½. 20070-1 Pa. $3.95

LIFE IN ANCIENT EGYPT, Adolf Erman. Fullest, most thorough, detailed older account with much not in more recent books, domestic life, religion, magic, medicine, commerce, much more. Many illustrations reproduce tomb paintings, carvings, hieroglyphs, etc. 597pp. 5⅜ x 8½. 22632-8 Pa. $12.95

SUNDIALS, Their Theory and Construction, Albert Waugh. Far and away the best, most thorough coverage of ideas, mathematics concerned, types, construction, adjusting anywhere. Simple, nontechnical treatment allows even children to build several of these dials. Over 100 illustrations. 230pp. 5⅜ x 8½. 22947-5 Pa. $8.95

THEORETICAL HYDRODYNAMICS, L. M. Milne-Thomson. Classic exposition of the mathematical theory of fluid motion, applicable to both hydrodynamics and aerodynamics. Over 600 exercises. 768pp. 6⅛ x 9¼. 68970-0 Pa. $20.95

SONGS OF EXPERIENCE: Facsimile Reproduction with 26 Plates in Full Color, William Blake. 26 full-color plates from a rare 1826 edition. Includes "The Tyger," "London," "Holy Thursday," and other poems. Printed text of poems. 48pp. 5¼ x 7. 24636-1 Pa. $4.95

OLD-TIME VIGNETTES IN FULL COLOR, Carol Belanger Grafton (ed.). Over 390 charming, often sentimental illustrations, selected from archives of Victorian graphics—pretty women posing, children playing, food, flowers, kittens and puppies, smiling cherubs, birds and butterflies, much more. All copyright-free. 48pp. 9¼ x 12¼. 27269-9 Pa. $7.95

PERSPECTIVE FOR ARTISTS, Rex Vicat Cole. Depth, perspective of sky and sea, shadows, much more, not usually covered. 391 diagrams, 81 reproductions of drawings and paintings. 279pp. 5⅜ x 8½. 22487-2 Pa. $9.95

DRAWING THE LIVING FIGURE, Joseph Sheppard. Innovative approach to artistic anatomy focuses on specifics of surface anatomy, rather than muscles and bones. Over 170 drawings of live models in front, back and side views, and in widely varying poses. Accompanying diagrams. 177 illustrations. Introduction. Index. 144pp. 8⅜ x11¼. 26723-7 Pa. $9.95

GOTHIC AND OLD ENGLISH ALPHABETS: 100 Complete Fonts, Dan X. Solo. Add power, elegance to posters, signs, other graphics with 100 stunning copyright-free alphabets: Blackstone, Dolbey, Germania, 97 more–including many lower-case, numerals, punctuation marks. 104pp. 8⅛ x 11. 24695-7 Pa. $9.95

HOW TO DO BEADWORK, Mary White. Fundamental book on craft from simple projects to five-bead chains and woven works. 106 illustrations. 142pp. 5⅜ x 8. 20697-1 Pa. $5.95

THE BOOK OF WOOD CARVING, Charles Marshall Sayers. Finest book for beginners discusses fundamentals and offers 34 designs. "Absolutely first rate . . . well thought out and well executed."–E. J. Tangerman. 118pp. 7¾ x 10⅝. 23654-4 Pa. $7.95

ILLUSTRATED CATALOG OF CIVIL WAR MILITARY GOODS: Union Army Weapons, Insignia, Uniform Accessories, and Other Equipment, Schuyler, Hartley, and Graham. Rare, profusely illustrated 1846 catalog includes Union Army uniform and dress regulations, arms and ammunition, coats, insignia, flags, swords, rifles, etc. 226 illustrations. 160pp. 9 x 12. 24939-5 Pa. $12.95

WOMEN'S FASHIONS OF THE EARLY 1900s: An Unabridged Republication of "New York Fashions, 1909," National Cloak & Suit Co. Rare catalog of mail-order fashions documents women's and children's clothing styles shortly after the turn of the century. Captions offer full descriptions, prices. Invaluable resource for fashion, costume historians. Approximately 725 illustrations. 128pp. 8⅜ x 11¼. 27276-1 Pa. $12.95

THE 1912 AND 1915 GUSTAV STICKLEY FURNITURE CATALOGS, Gustav Stickley. With over 200 detailed illustrations and descriptions, these two catalogs are essential reading and reference materials and identification guides for Stickley furniture. Captions cite materials, dimensions and prices. 112pp. 6½ x 9¼. 26676-1 Pa. $9.95

EARLY AMERICAN LOCOMOTIVES, John H. White, Jr. Finest locomotive engravings from early 19th century: historical (1804–74), main-line (after 1870), special, foreign, etc. 147 plates. 142pp. 11⅜ x 8¼. 22772-3 Pa. $12.95

THE TALL SHIPS OF TODAY IN PHOTOGRAPHS, Frank O. Braynard. Lavishly illustrated tribute to nearly 100 majestic contemporary sailing vessels: Amerigo Vespucci, Clearwater, Constitution, Eagle, Mayflower, Sea Cloud, Victory, many more. Authoritative captions provide statistics, background on each ship. 190 black-and-white photographs and illustrations. Introduction. 128pp. 8⅞ x 11¾. 27163-3 Pa. $14.95

LITTLE BOOK OF EARLY AMERICAN CRAFTS AND TRADES, Peter Stockham (ed.). 1807 children's book explains crafts and trades: baker, hatter, cooper, potter, and many others. 23 copperplate illustrations. 140pp. 4⅝ x 6.
23336-7 Pa. $4.95

VICTORIAN FASHIONS AND COSTUMES FROM HARPER'S BAZAR, 1867–1898, Stella Blum (ed.). Day costumes, evening wear, sports clothes, shoes, hats, other accessories in over 1,000 detailed engravings. 320pp. 9⅜ x 12¼.
22990-4 Pa. $16.95

GUSTAV STICKLEY, THE CRAFTSMAN, Mary Ann Smith. Superb study surveys broad scope of Stickley's achievement, especially in architecture. Design philosophy, rise and fall of the Craftsman empire, descriptions and floor plans for many Craftsman houses, more. 86 black-and-white halftones. 31 line illustrations. Introduction 208pp. 6½ x 9¼.
27210-9 Pa. $9.95

THE LONG ISLAND RAIL ROAD IN EARLY PHOTOGRAPHS, Ron Ziel. Over 220 rare photos, informative text document origin (1844) and development of rail service on Long Island. Vintage views of early trains, locomotives, stations, passengers, crews, much more. Captions. 8⅞ x 11¾.
26301-0 Pa. $14.95

VOYAGE OF THE LIBERDADE, Joshua Slocum. Great 19th-century mariner's thrilling, first-hand account of the wreck of his ship off South America, the 35-foot boat he built from the wreckage, and its remarkable voyage home. 128pp. 5⅜ x 8½.
40022-0 Pa. $5.95

TEN BOOKS ON ARCHITECTURE, Vitruvius. The most important book ever written on architecture. Early Roman aesthetics, technology, classical orders, site selection, all other aspects. Morgan translation. 331pp. 5⅜ x 8½. 20645-9 Pa. $9.95

THE HUMAN FIGURE IN MOTION, Eadweard Muybridge. More than 4,500 stopped-action photos, in action series, showing undraped men, women, children jumping, lying down, throwing, sitting, wrestling, carrying, etc. 390pp. 7⅞ x 10⅝.
20204-6 Clothbd. $29.95

TREES OF THE EASTERN AND CENTRAL UNITED STATES AND CANADA, William M. Harlow. Best one-volume guide to 140 trees. Full descriptions, woodlore, range, etc. Over 600 illustrations. Handy size. 288pp. 4½ x 6⅜.
20395-6 Pa. $6.95

SONGS OF WESTERN BIRDS, Dr. Donald J. Borror. Complete song and call repertoire of 60 western species, including flycatchers, juncoes, cactus wrens, many more—includes fully illustrated booklet.   Cassette and manual 99913-0 $8.95

GROWING AND USING HERBS AND SPICES, Milo Miloradovich. Versatile handbook provides all the information needed for cultivation and use of all the herbs and spices available in North America. 4 illustrations. Index. Glossary. 236pp. 5⅜ x 8½.
25058-X Pa. $7.95

BIG BOOK OF MAZES AND LABYRINTHS, Walter Shepherd. 50 mazes and labyrinths in all—classical, solid, ripple, and more—in one great volume. Perfect inexpensive puzzler for clever youngsters. Full solutions. 112pp. 8⅛ x 11.
22951-3 Pa. $5.95

PIANO TUNING, J. Cree Fischer. Clearest, best book for beginner, amateur. Simple repairs, raising dropped notes, tuning by easy method of flattened fifths. No previous skills needed. 4 illustrations. 201pp. 5⅜ x 8½. 23267-0 Pa. $6.95

HINTS TO SINGERS, Lillian Nordica. Selecting the right teacher, developing confidence, overcoming stage fright, and many other important skills receive thoughtful discussion in this indispensible guide, written by a world-famous diva of four decades' experience. 96pp. 5⅜ x 8½. 40094-8 Pa. $4.95

THE COMPLETE NONSENSE OF EDWARD LEAR, Edward Lear. All nonsense limericks, zany alphabets, Owl and Pussycat, songs, nonsense botany, etc., illustrated by Lear. Total of 320pp. 5⅜ x 8½. (Available in U.S. only.) 20167-8 Pa. $7.95

VICTORIAN PARLOUR POETRY: An Annotated Anthology, Michael R. Turner. 117 gems by Longfellow, Tennyson, Browning, many lesser-known poets. "The Village Blacksmith," "Curfew Must Not Ring Tonight," "Only a Baby Small," dozens more, often difficult to find elsewhere. Index of poets, titles, first lines. xxiii + 325pp. 5⅝ x 8¼. 27044-0 Pa. $12.95

DUBLINERS, James Joyce. Fifteen stories offer vivid, tightly focused observations of the lives of Dublin's poorer classes. At least one, "The Dead," is considered a masterpiece. Reprinted complete and unabridged from standard edition. 160pp. 5³⁄₁₆ x 8¼. 26870-5 Pa. $1.50

GREAT WEIRD TALES: 14 Stories by Lovecraft, Blackwood, Machen and Others, S. T. Joshi (ed.). 14 spellbinding tales, including "The Sin Eater," by Fiona McLeod, "The Eye Above the Mantel," by Frank Belknap Long, as well as renowned works by R. H. Barlow, Lord Dunsany, Arthur Machen, W. C. Morrow and eight other masters of the genre. 256pp. 5⅜ x 8½. (Available in U.S. only.) 40436-6 Pa. $8.95

THE BOOK OF THE SACRED MAGIC OF ABRAMELIN THE MAGE, translated by S. MacGregor Mathers. Medieval manuscript of ceremonial magic. Basic document in Aleister Crowley, Golden Dawn groups. 268pp. 5⅜ x 8½. 23211-5 Pa. $9.95

NEW RUSSIAN-ENGLISH AND ENGLISH-RUSSIAN DICTIONARY, M. A. O'Brien. This is a remarkably handy Russian dictionary, containing a surprising amount of information, including over 70,000 entries. 366pp. 4½ x 6⅛. 20208-9 Pa. $10.95

HISTORIC HOMES OF THE AMERICAN PRESIDENTS, Second, Revised Edition, Irvin Haas. A traveler's guide to American Presidential homes, most open to the public, depicting and describing homes occupied by every American President from George Washington to George Bush. With visiting hours, admission charges, travel routes. 175 photographs. Index. 160pp. 8¼ x 11. 26751-2 Pa. $13.95

NEW YORK IN THE FORTIES, Andreas Feininger. 162 brilliant photographs by the well-known photographer, formerly with *Life* magazine. Commuters, shoppers, Times Square at night, much else from city at its peak. Captions by John von Hartz. 181pp. 9¼ x 10¾. 23585-8 Pa. $13.95

INDIAN SIGN LANGUAGE, William Tomkins. Over 525 signs developed by Sioux and other tribes. Written instructions and diagrams. Also 290 pictographs. 111pp. 6⅛ x 9¼. 22029-X Pa. $3.95

ANATOMY: A Complete Guide for Artists, Joseph Sheppard. A master of figure drawing shows artists how to render human anatomy convincingly. Over 460 illustrations. 224pp. 8⅜ x 11¼. 27279-6 Pa. $11.95

MEDIEVAL CALLIGRAPHY: Its History and Technique, Marc Drogin. Spirited history, comprehensive instruction manual covers 13 styles (ca. 4th century through 15th). Excellent photographs; directions for duplicating medieval techniques with modern tools. 224pp. 8⅜ x 11¼. 26142-5 Pa. $12.95

DRIED FLOWERS: How to Prepare Them, Sarah Whitlock and Martha Rankin. Complete instructions on how to use silica gel, meal and borax, perlite aggregate, sand and borax, glycerine and water to create attractive permanent flower arrangements. 12 illustrations. 32pp. 5⅜ x 8½. 21802-3 Pa. $1.00

EASY-TO-MAKE BIRD FEEDERS FOR WOODWORKERS, Scott D. Campbell. Detailed, simple-to-use guide for designing, constructing, caring for and using feeders. Text, illustrations for 12 classic and contemporary designs. 96pp. 5⅜ x 8½. 25847-5 Pa. $3.95

SCOTTISH WONDER TALES FROM MYTH AND LEGEND, Donald A. Mackenzie. 16 lively tales tell of giants rumbling down mountainsides, of a magic wand that turns stone pillars into warriors, of gods and goddesses, evil hags, powerful forces and more. 240pp. 5⅜ x 8½. 29677-6 Pa. $6.95

THE HISTORY OF UNDERCLOTHES, C. Willett Cunnington and Phyllis Cunnington. Fascinating, well-documented survey covering six centuries of English undergarments, enhanced with over 100 illustrations: 12th-century laced-up bodice, footed long drawers (1795), 19th-century bustles, 19th-century corsets for men, Victorian "bust improvers," much more. 272pp. 5⅝ x 8¼. 27124-2 Pa. $9.95

ARTS AND CRAFTS FURNITURE: The Complete Brooks Catalog of 1912, Brooks Manufacturing Co. Photos and detailed descriptions of more than 150 now very collectible furniture designs from the Arts and Crafts movement depict davenports, settees, buffets, desks, tables, chairs, bedsteads, dressers and more, all built of solid, quarter-sawed oak. Invaluable for students and enthusiasts of antiques, Americana and the decorative arts. 80pp. 6½ x 9¼. 27471-3 Pa. $8.95

WILBUR AND ORVILLE: A Biography of the Wright Brothers, Fred Howard. Definitive, crisply written study tells the full story of the brothers' lives and work. A vividly written biography, unparalleled in scope and color, that also captures the spirit of an extraordinary era. 560pp. 6⅛ x 9¼. 40297-5 Pa. $17.95

THE ARTS OF THE SAILOR: Knotting, Splicing and Ropework, Hervey Garrett Smith. Indispensable shipboard reference covers tools, basic knots and useful hitches; handsewing and canvas work, more. Over 100 illustrations. Delightful reading for sea lovers. 256pp. 5⅜ x 8½. 26440-8 Pa. $8.95

FRANK LLOYD WRIGHT'S FALLINGWATER: The House and Its History, Second, Revised Edition, Donald Hoffmann. A total revision–both in text and illustrations–of the standard document on Fallingwater, the boldest, most personal architectural statement of Wright's mature years, updated with valuable new material from the recently opened Frank Lloyd Wright Archives. "Fascinating"–*The New York Times*. 116 illustrations. 128pp. 9¼ x 10¾. 27430-6 Pa. $12.95

PHOTOGRAPHIC SKETCHBOOK OF THE CIVIL WAR, Alexander Gardner. 100 photos taken on field during the Civil War. Famous shots of Manassas Harper's Ferry, Lincoln, Richmond, slave pens, etc. 244pp. 10⅝ x 8¼. 22731-6 Pa. $10.95

FIVE ACRES AND INDEPENDENCE, Maurice G. Kains. Great back-to-the-land classic explains basics of self-sufficient farming. The one book to get. 95 illustrations. 397pp. 5⅜ x 8½. 20974-1 Pa. $7.95

SONGS OF EASTERN BIRDS, Dr. Donald J. Borror. Songs and calls of 60 species most common to eastern U.S.: warblers, woodpeckers, flycatchers, thrushes, larks, many more in high-quality recording. Cassette and manual 99912-2 $9.95

A MODERN HERBAL, Margaret Grieve. Much the fullest, most exact, most useful compilation of herbal material. Gigantic alphabetical encyclopedia, from aconite to zedoary, gives botanical information, medical properties, folklore, economic uses, much else. Indispensable to serious reader. 161 illustrations. 888pp. 6½ x 9¼. 2-vol. set. (Available in U.S. only.) Vol. I: 22798-7 Pa. $10.95
Vol. II: 22799-5 Pa. $10.95

HIDDEN TREASURE MAZE BOOK, Dave Phillips. Solve 34 challenging mazes accompanied by heroic tales of adventure. Evil dragons, people-eating plants, blood-thirsty giants, many more dangerous adversaries lurk at every twist and turn. 34 mazes, stories, solutions. 48pp. 8¼ x 11. 24566-7 Pa. $2.95

LETTERS OF W. A. MOZART, Wolfgang A. Mozart. Remarkable letters show bawdy wit, humor, imagination, musical insights, contemporary musical world; includes some letters from Leopold Mozart. 276pp. 5⅜ x 8½. 22859-2 Pa. $9.95

BASIC PRINCIPLES OF CLASSICAL BALLET, Agrippina Vaganova. Great Russian theoretician, teacher explains methods for teaching classical ballet. 118 illustrations. 175pp. 5⅜ x 8½. 22036-2 Pa. $6.95

THE JUMPING FROG, Mark Twain. Revenge edition. The original story of The Celebrated Jumping Frog of Calaveras County, a hapless French translation, and Twain's hilarious "retranslation" from the French. 12 illustrations. 66pp. 5⅜ x 8½. 22686-7 Pa. $4.95

BEST REMEMBERED POEMS, Martin Gardner (ed.). The 126 poems in this superb collection of 19th- and 20th-century British and American verse range from Shelley's "To a Skylark" to the impassioned "Renascence" of Edna St. Vincent Millay and to Edward Lear's whimsical "The Owl and the Pussycat." 224pp. 5⅜ x 8½. 27165-X Pa. $5.95

COMPLETE SONNETS, William Shakespeare. Over 150 exquisite poems deal with love, friendship, the tyranny of time, beauty's evanescence, death and other themes in language of remarkable power, precision and beauty. Glossary of archaic terms. 80pp. $5\frac{3}{16}$ x 8¼. 26686-9 Pa. $1.00

THE BATTLES THAT CHANGED HISTORY, Fletcher Pratt. Eminent historian profiles 16 crucial conflicts, ancient to modern, that changed the course of civilization. 352pp. 5⅜ x 8½. 41129-X Pa. $9.95

THE WIT AND HUMOR OF OSCAR WILDE, Alvin Redman (ed.). More than 1,000 ripostes, paradoxes, wisecracks: Work is the curse of the drinking classes; I can resist everything except temptation; etc. 258pp. 5⅜ x 8½. 20602-5 Pa. $6.95

SHAKESPEARE LEXICON AND QUOTATION DICTIONARY, Alexander Schmidt. Full definitions, locations, shades of meaning in every word in plays and poems. More than 50,000 exact quotations. 1,485pp. 6½ x 9¼. 2-vol. set.
Vol. 1: 22726-X Pa. $17.95
Vol. 2: 22727-8 Pa. $17.95

SELECTED POEMS, Emily Dickinson. Over 100 best-known, best-loved poems by one of America's foremost poets, reprinted from authoritative early editions. No comparable edition at this price. Index of first lines. 64pp. 5³⁄₁₆ x 8¼.
26466-1 Pa. $1.00

THE INSIDIOUS DR. FU-MANCHU, Sax Rohmer. The first of the popular mystery series introduces a pair of English detectives to their archnemesis, the diabolical Dr. Fu-Manchu. Flavorful atmosphere, fast-paced action, and colorful characters enliven this classic of the genre. 208pp. 5³⁄₁₆ x 8¼. 29898-1 Pa. $2.00

THE MALLEUS MALEFICARUM OF KRAMER AND SPRENGER, translated by Montague Summers. Full text of most important witchhunter's "bible," used by both Catholics and Protestants. 278pp. 6⅝ x 10. 22802-9 Pa. $12.95

SPANISH STORIES/CUENTOS ESPAÑOLES: A Dual-Language Book, Angel Flores (ed.). Unique format offers 13 great stories in Spanish by Cervantes, Borges, others. Faithful English translations on facing pages. 352pp. 5⅜ x 8½.
25399-6 Pa. $8.95

GARDEN CITY, LONG ISLAND, IN EARLY PHOTOGRAPHS, 1869–1919, Mildred H. Smith. Handsome treasury of 118 vintage pictures, accompanied by carefully researched captions, document the Garden City Hotel fire (1899), the Vanderbilt Cup Race (1908), the first airmail flight departing from the Nassau Boulevard Aerodrome (1911), and much more. 96pp. 8⅞ x 11¾. 40669-5 Pa. $12.95

OLD QUEENS, N.Y., IN EARLY PHOTOGRAPHS, Vincent F. Seyfried and William Asadorian. Over 160 rare photographs of Maspeth, Jamaica, Jackson Heights, and other areas. Vintage views of DeWitt Clinton mansion, 1939 World's Fair and more. Captions. 192pp. 8⅞ x 11. 26358-4 Pa. $14.95

CAPTURED BY THE INDIANS: 15 Firsthand Accounts, 1750-1870, Frederick Drimmer. Astounding true historical accounts of grisly torture, bloody conflicts, relentless pursuits, miraculous escapes and more, by people who lived to tell the tale. 384pp. 5⅜ x 8½. 24901-8 Pa. $9.95

THE WORLD'S GREAT SPEECHES (Fourth Enlarged Edition), Lewis Copeland, Lawrence W. Lamm, and Stephen J. McKenna. Nearly 300 speeches provide public speakers with a wealth of updated quotes and inspiration–from Pericles' funeral oration and William Jennings Bryan's "Cross of Gold Speech" to Malcolm X's powerful words on the Black Revolution and Earl of Spenser's tribute to his sister, Diana, Princess of Wales. 944pp. 5⅜ x 8⅜. 40903-1 Pa. $15.95

THE BOOK OF THE SWORD, Sir Richard F. Burton. Great Victorian scholar/adventurer's eloquent, erudite history of the "queen of weapons"–from prehistory to early Roman Empire. Evolution and development of early swords, variations (sabre, broadsword, cutlass, scimitar, etc.), much more. 336pp. 6⅛ x 9¼.
25434-8 Pa. $9.95

AUTOBIOGRAPHY: The Story of My Experiments with Truth, Mohandas K. Gandhi. Boyhood, legal studies, purification, the growth of the Satyagraha (nonviolent protest) movement. Critical, inspiring work of the man responsible for the freedom of India. 480pp. 5⅜ x 8½. (Available in U.S. only.) 24593-4 Pa. $9.95

CELTIC MYTHS AND LEGENDS, T. W. Rolleston. Masterful retelling of Irish and Welsh stories and tales. Cuchulain, King Arthur, Deirdre, the Grail, many more. First paperback edition. 58 full-page illustrations. 512pp. 5⅜ x 8½. 26507-2 Pa. $9.95

THE PRINCIPLES OF PSYCHOLOGY, William James. Famous long course complete, unabridged. Stream of thought, time perception, memory, experimental methods; great work decades ahead of its time. 94 figures. 1,391pp. 5⅜ x 8½. 2-vol. set.
Vol. I: 20381-6 Pa. $14.95
Vol. II: 20382-4 Pa. $14.95

THE WORLD AS WILL AND REPRESENTATION, Arthur Schopenhauer. Definitive English translation of Schopenhauer's life work, correcting more than 1,000 errors, omissions in earlier translations. Translated by E. F. J. Payne. Total of 1,269pp. 5⅜ x 8½. 2-vol. set.
Vol. 1: 21761-2 Pa. $12.95
Vol. 2: 21762-0 Pa. $12.95

MAGIC AND MYSTERY IN TIBET, Madame Alexandra David-Neel. Experiences among lamas, magicians, sages, sorcerers, Bonpa wizards. A true psychic discovery. 32 illustrations. 321pp. 5⅜ x 8½. (Available in U.S. only.) 22682-4 Pa. $9.95

THE EGYPTIAN BOOK OF THE DEAD, E. A. Wallis Budge. Complete reproduction of Ani's papyrus, finest ever found. Full hieroglyphic text, interlinear transliteration, word-for-word translation, smooth translation. 533pp. 6½ x 9¼.
21866-X Pa. $12.95

MATHEMATICS FOR THE NONMATHEMATICIAN, Morris Kline. Detailed, college-level treatment of mathematics in cultural and historical context, with numerous exercises. Recommended Reading Lists. Tables. Numerous figures. 641pp. 5⅜ x 8½.
24823-2 Pa. $11.95

PROBABILISTIC METHODS IN THE THEORY OF STRUCTURES, Isaac Elishakoff. Well-written introduction covers the elements of the theory of probability from two or more random variables, the reliability of such multivariable structures, the theory of random function, Monte Carlo methods of treating problems incapable of exact solution, and more. Examples. 502pp. 5³/₈ x 8¹/₂. 40691-1 Pa. $16.95

THE RIME OF THE ANCIENT MARINER, Gustave Doré, S. T. Coleridge. Doré's finest work; 34 plates capture moods, subtleties of poem. Flawless full-size reproductions printed on facing pages with authoritative text of poem. "Beautiful. Simply beautiful."–*Publisher's Weekly*. 77pp. 9¼ x 12. 22305-1 Pa. $7.95

NORTH AMERICAN INDIAN DESIGNS FOR ARTISTS AND CRAFTSPEOPLE, Eva Wilson. Over 360 authentic copyright-free designs adapted from Navajo blankets, Hopi pottery, Sioux buffalo hides, more. Geometrics, symbolic figures, plant and animal motifs, etc. 128pp. 8⅜ x 11. (Not for sale in the United Kingdom.) 25341-4 Pa. $9.95

SCULPTURE: Principles and Practice, Louis Slobodkin. Step-by-step approach to clay, plaster, metals, stone; classical and modern. 253 drawings, photos. 255pp. 8⅛ x 11.
22960-2 Pa. $11.95

THE INFLUENCE OF SEA POWER UPON HISTORY, 1660–1783, A. T. Mahan. Influential classic of naval history and tactics still used as text in war colleges. First paperback edition. 4 maps. 24 battle plans. 640pp. 5⅜ x 8½.   25509-3 Pa. $14.95

THE STORY OF THE TITANIC AS TOLD BY ITS SURVIVORS, Jack Winocour (ed.). What it was really like. Panic, despair, shocking inefficiency, and a little heroism. More thrilling than any fictional account. 26 illustrations. 320pp. 5⅜ x 8½.   20610-6 Pa. $8.95

FAIRY AND FOLK TALES OF THE IRISH PEASANTRY, William Butler Yeats (ed.). Treasury of 64 tales from the twilight world of Celtic myth and legend: "The Soul Cages," "The Kildare Pooka," "King O'Toole and his Goose," many more. Introduction and Notes by W. B. Yeats. 352pp. 5⅜ x 8½.   26941-8 Pa. $8.95

BUDDHIST MAHAYANA TEXTS, E. B. Cowell and others (eds.). Superb, accurate translations of basic documents in Mahayana Buddhism, highly important in history of religions. The Buddha-karita of Asvaghosha, Larger Sukhavativyuha, more. 448pp. 5⅜ x 8½.   25552-2 Pa. $12.95

ONE TWO THREE . . . INFINITY: Facts and Speculations of Science, George Gamow. Great physicist's fascinating, readable overview of contemporary science: number theory, relativity, fourth dimension, entropy, genes, atomic structure, much more. 128 illustrations. Index. 352pp. 5⅜ x 8½.   25664-2 Pa. $9.95

EXPERIMENTATION AND MEASUREMENT, W. J. Youden. Introductory manual explains laws of measurement in simple terms and offers tips for achieving accuracy and minimizing errors. Mathematics of measurement, use of instruments, experimenting with machines. 1994 edition. Foreword. Preface. Introduction. Epilogue. Selected Readings. Glossary. Index. Tables and figures. 128pp. 5³/₈ x 8¹/₂.   40451-X Pa. $6.95

DALÍ ON MODERN ART: The Cuckolds of Antiquated Modern Art, Salvador Dalí. Influential painter skewers modern art and its practitioners. Outrageous evaluations of Picasso, Cézanne, Turner, more. 15 renderings of paintings discussed. 44 calligraphic decorations by Dalí. 96pp. 5⅜ x 8½. (Available in U.S. only.)   29220-7 Pa. $5.95

ANTIQUE PLAYING CARDS: A Pictorial History, Henry René D'Allemagne. Over 900 elaborate, decorative images from rare playing cards (14th–20th centuries): Bacchus, death, dancing dogs, hunting scenes, royal coats of arms, players cheating, much more. 96pp. 9¼ x 12¼.   29265-7 Pa. $12.95

MAKING FURNITURE MASTERPIECES: 30 Projects with Measured Drawings, Franklin H. Gottshall. Step-by-step instructions, illustrations for constructing handsome, useful pieces, among them a Sheraton desk, Chippendale chair, Spanish desk, Queen Anne table and a William and Mary dressing mirror. 224pp. 8⅛ x 11¼.   29338-6 Pa. $13.95

THE FOSSIL BOOK: A Record of Prehistoric Life, Patricia V. Rich et al. Profusely illustrated definitive guide covers everything from single-celled organisms and dinosaurs to birds and mammals and the interplay between climate and man. Over 1,500 illustrations. 760pp. 7½ x 10⅛.   29371-8 Pa. $29.95

Prices subject to change without notice.

Available at your book dealer or write for free catalog to Dept. GI, Dover Publications, Inc., 31 East 2nd St., Mineola, N.Y. 11501. Dover publishes more than 500 books each year on science, elementary and advanced mathematics, biology, music, art, literary history, social sciences and other areas.